POSTCARD HISTORY SERIES

Latrobe and the Ligonier Valley

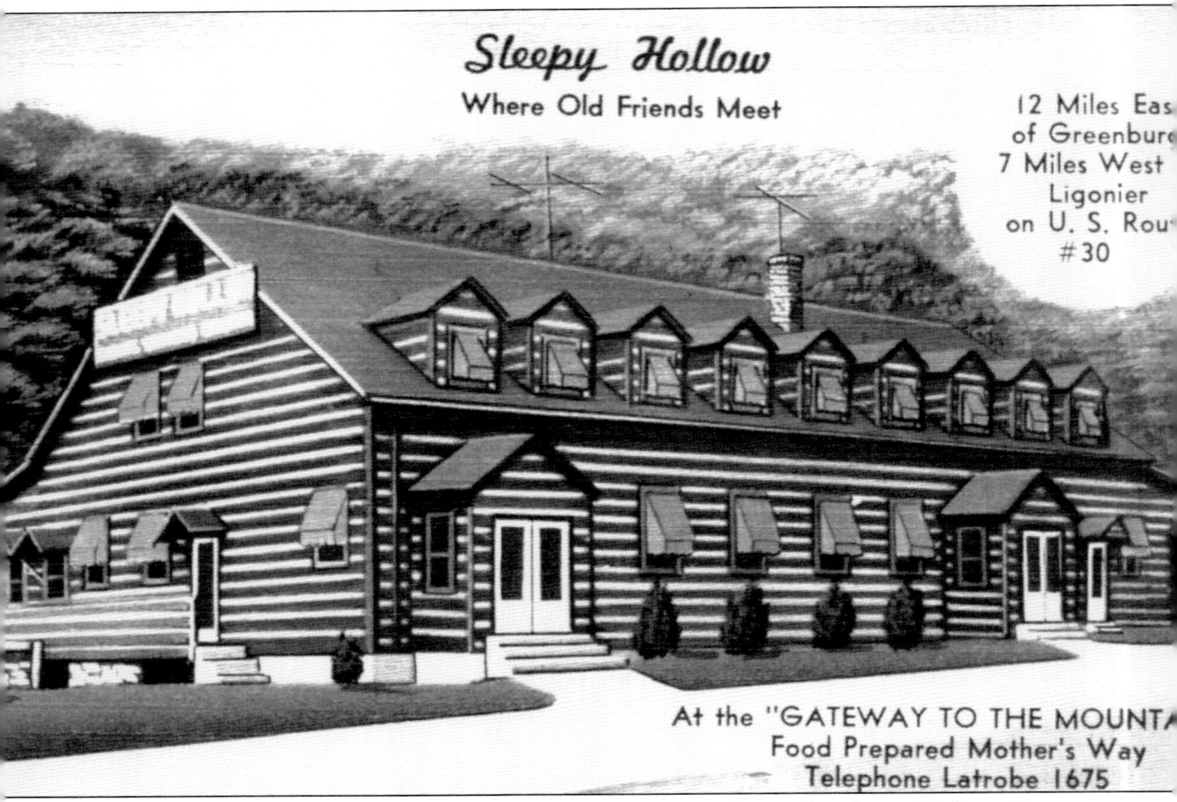

Located on the Lincoln Highway, 12 miles east of Greensburg, the Sleepy Hollow Tavern was known for its steak, seafood, and chicken prepared "mother's way." The tavern has changed owners several times over the past years but still remains open under the name the Hollow Tavern.

On the front cover: Please see page 11. (Author's collection.)
On the back cover: Please see page 33. (Author's collection.)

POSTCARD HISTORY SERIES

Latrobe and the Ligonier Valley

Rachel E. Smith

ARCADIA PUBLISHING

ISBN 978-0-7385-5729-8

Published by Arcadia Publishing
Charleston, South Carolina

Printed in the United States of America

Library of Congress Catalog Card Number: 2007937031

For all general information contact Arcadia Publishing at:
Telephone 843-853-2070
Fax 843-853-0044
E-mail sales@arcadiapublishing.com
For customer service and orders:
Toll-Free 1-888-313-2665

Visit us on the Internet at www.arcadiapublishing.com

*Dedicated to all those committed to preserving history
today, tomorrow, and forever*

Contents

Acknowledgments

As with each book, there are so many people to thank I do not know where to begin. First of all, so much love goes to my family who has supported me through writing both this book and the last one. They have done so much both in helping me find information for the books and also helping to promote it.

So many thanks go to Arthur Humphrey, who, once again, without his help this book would never have been possible. The images he has collected through the years are one of a kind, and his willingness to share them has been priceless. I look forward to having the chance to work with him again in the future.

Also, the individuals at the Latrobe Historical Society provided me with so much historical information; I do not know how I could have identified everything without them. Special thanks goes to Mary Lou Townsend, who spent a good part of an afternoon looking through the Latrobe postcards with me and recounting the history of Latrobe for me.

INTRODUCTION

Every town has a story to tell. Some towns were settled as part of the ever-expanding railroads. Some were founded along the National Road. Others were founded as the country began to push westward. In the case of Latrobe and Ligonier, each of these towns has its own interesting story to tell. From stories of the "Fort that Never Surrendered" to the birthplace of great television personalities and professional golfers, both Latrobe and Ligonier each have their stories to tell.

The town was named for Benjamin H. Latrobe, who was friends with Oliver W. Barnes, one of the town's founders. Latrobe never even visited the town that was named after him.

After being incorporated as a borough in 1854, Latrobe has developed a name for itself, being the birthplace of Rolling Rock Beer, the banana split, children's television personality Fred Rogers, and professional golf legend Arnold Palmer. St. Vincent College, the largest Benedictine College, is also home to five-time Super Bowl champion Pittsburgh Steelers training camp each year.

Fort Ligonier, located in Ligonier Borough, is often referred to as the "Fort that Never Surrendered" due to its service in the French and Indian War.

This postcard history is a journey through time, reliving some of these stories and remembering some of the buildings and landmarks that time has since forgotten and giving them new life.

Both longtime residents of Latrobe and Ligonier and those who may be new to the area will enjoy this book as it takes them on a postcard tour from when the area was just a few buildings 150 years ago to the city it is today.

So, please, relax and enjoy this story through time, told in vintage postcards.

One

LATROBE

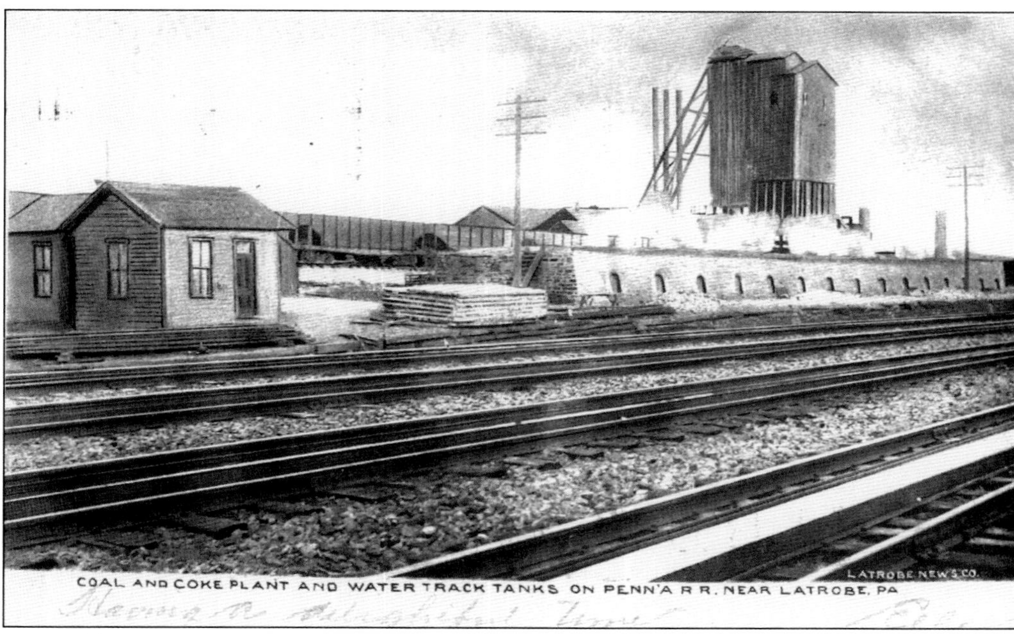

One of the major resources of Latrobe was the coal and coke industry. The Ligonier Valley Railroad hauled the coal and coke from the mines to the main line, producing the main source of freight revenue.

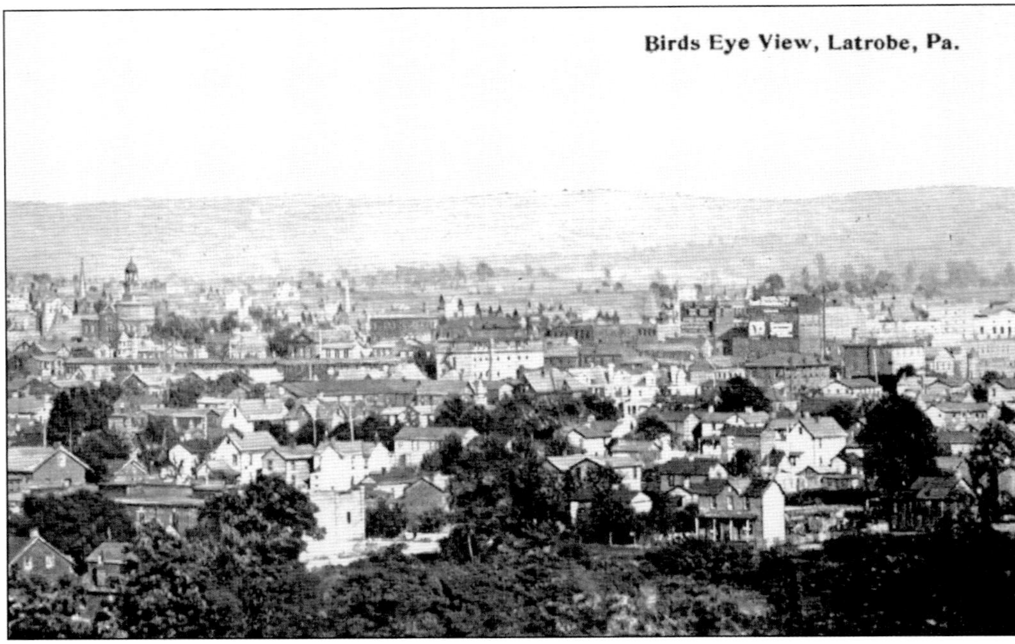

This postcard shows a bird's-eye view of Latrobe. By 1910, the city's population had nearly doubled to 8,770 citizens.

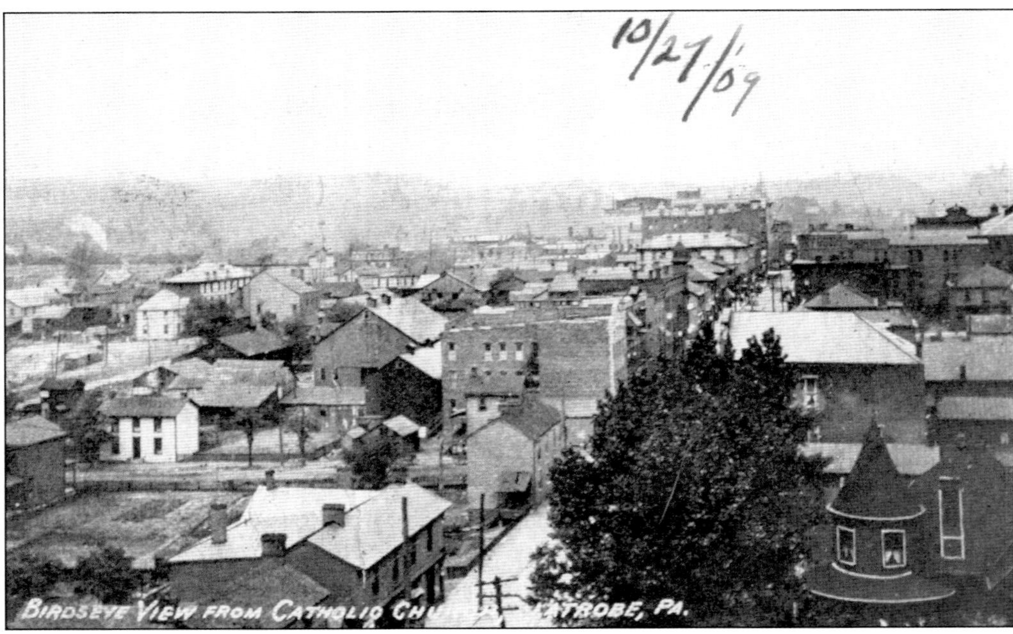

Prominent in the lower right-hand corner of the postcard is the American Legion Home. Formerly owned by the Anderson-Keener family and donated to the American Legion, the house was torn down in the 1950s.

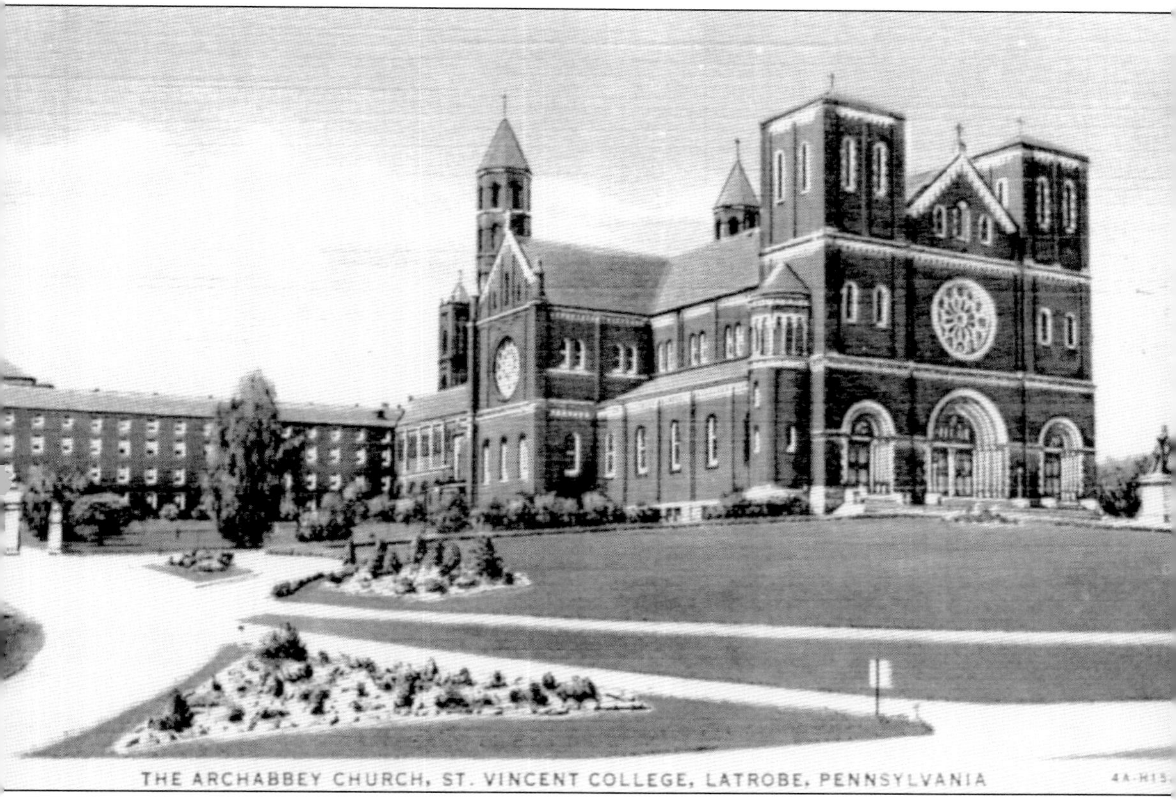

The cornerstone to the St. Vincent Archabbey Church was laid in 1892, and it took 13 years to construct the church. To the right is a statue of Archabbot Boniface Wimmer, the founder of St. Vincent.

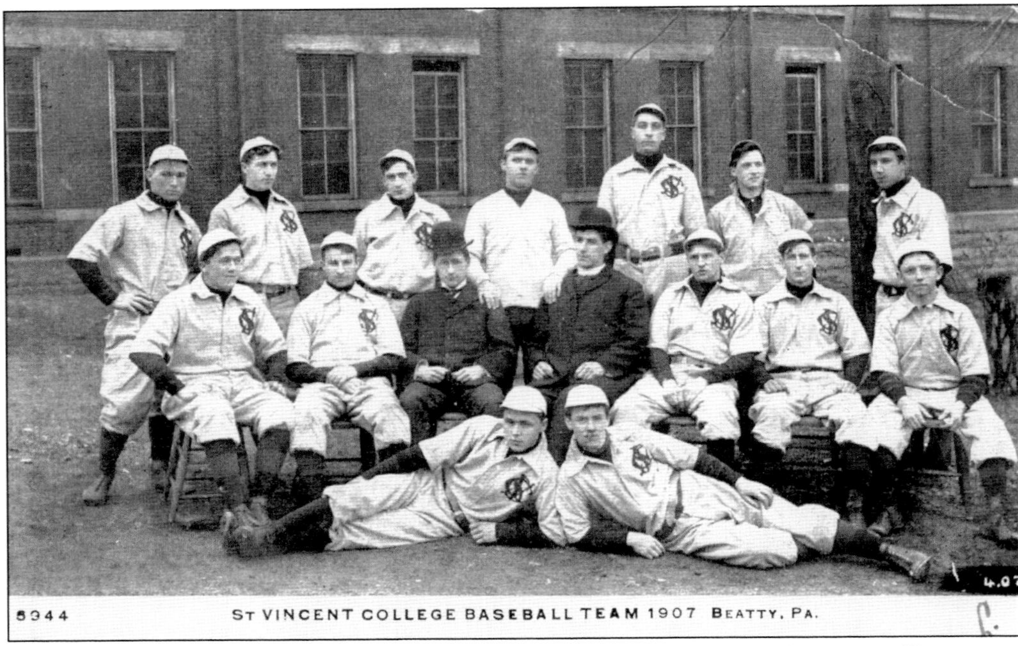

After the introduction of baseball to Westmoreland County in the mid-1860s, college teams began introducing their own varsity ball clubs. Baseball was as much a social event as it was an athletic contest. This 1907 postcard of the St. Vincent College baseball team shows a very professional-looking team.

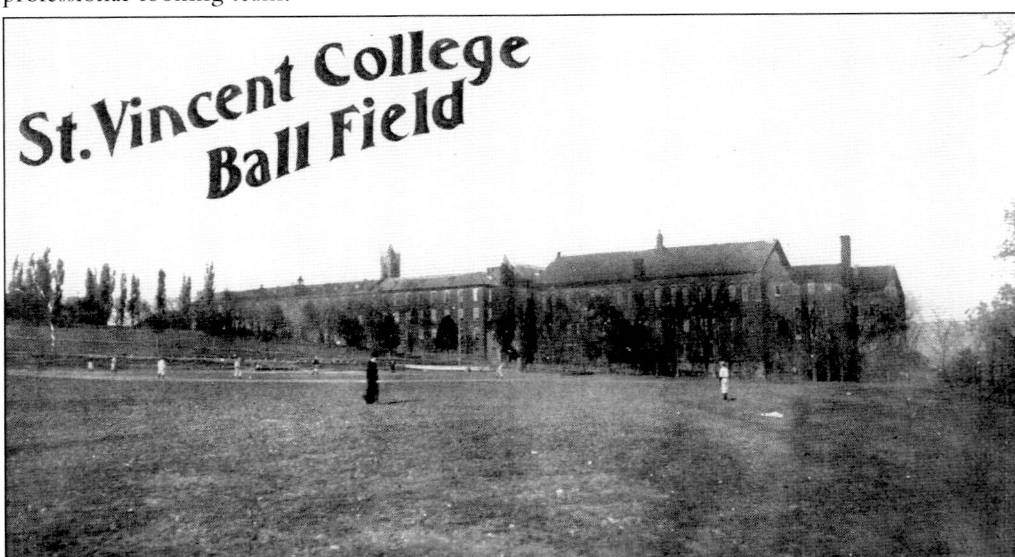

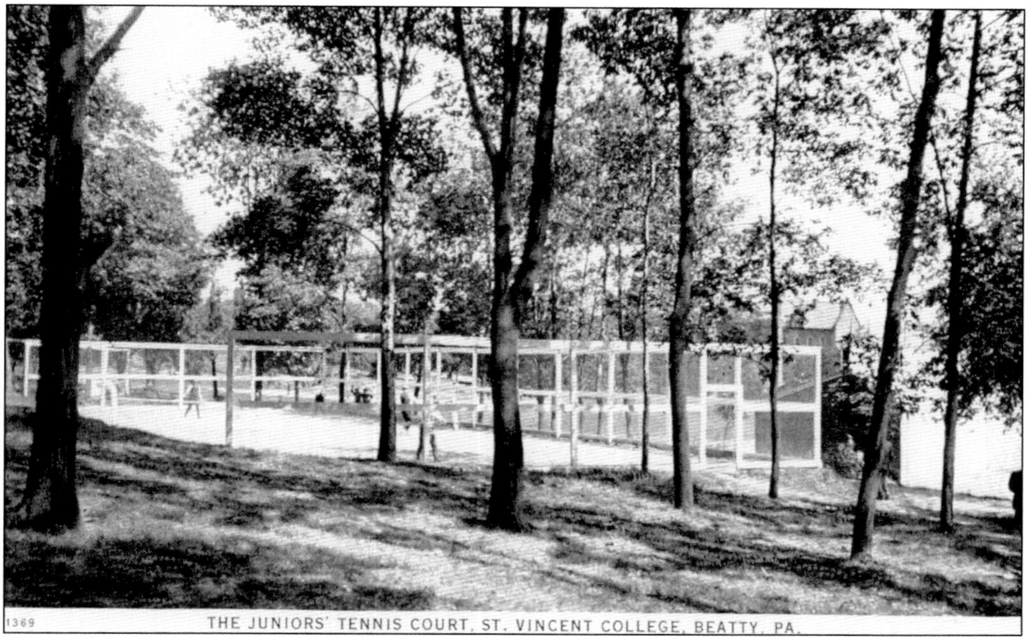

Students attending St. Vincent had the opportunity to participate in both individual and team sports. This postcard features the state-of-the-art tennis courts, which were located on campus.

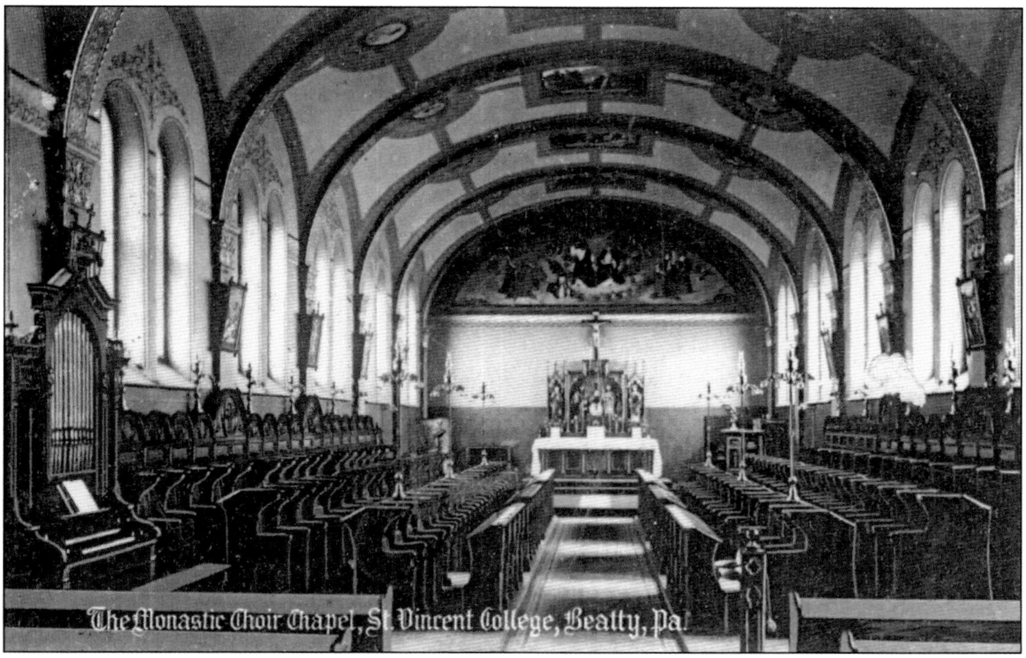

In addition to being an institution of higher learning, St. Vincent still embraces its Benedictine heritage. Each incoming student receives a copy of *The Rule*, St. Benedict's guidebook to Benedictine monastic life. A message inside the book says to students, "Welcome to Saint Vincent: A School for the Lord's Service. May you grow in knowledge and wisdom. The divine presence is everywhere. Wishing you every success at our Catholic, Benedictine, Liberal Arts School."

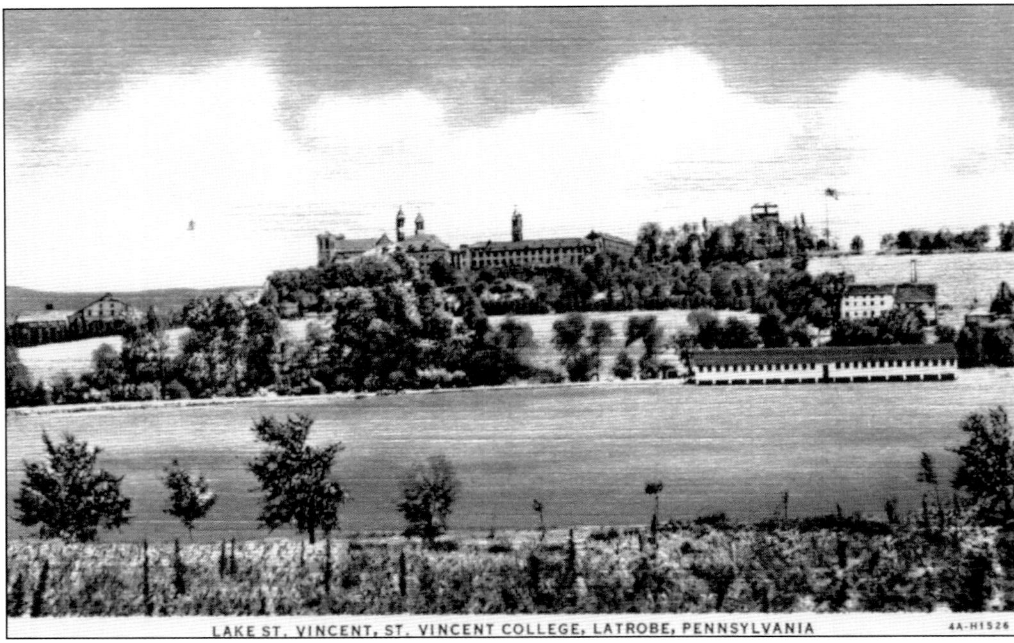

On January 28, 1963, a devastating fire burned almost half of the St. Vincent College campus. This included the complete destruction of the old Prep Student Chapel, the biology laboratory, and the bell tower. The top of what it is now referred to as "old Benedict Hall," which housed dormitory space for the prep, was burned out, and much of its second floor was damaged. Despite the devastation, no one died and classes resumed the next week.

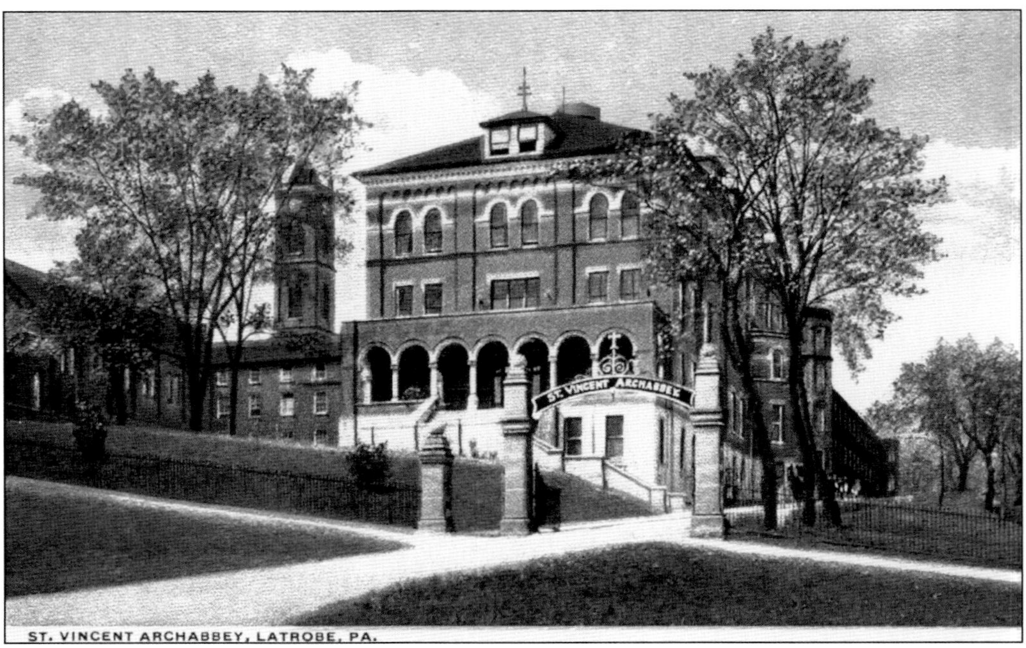

This postcard shows another view of the arch abbey. These steps lead up to the main church.

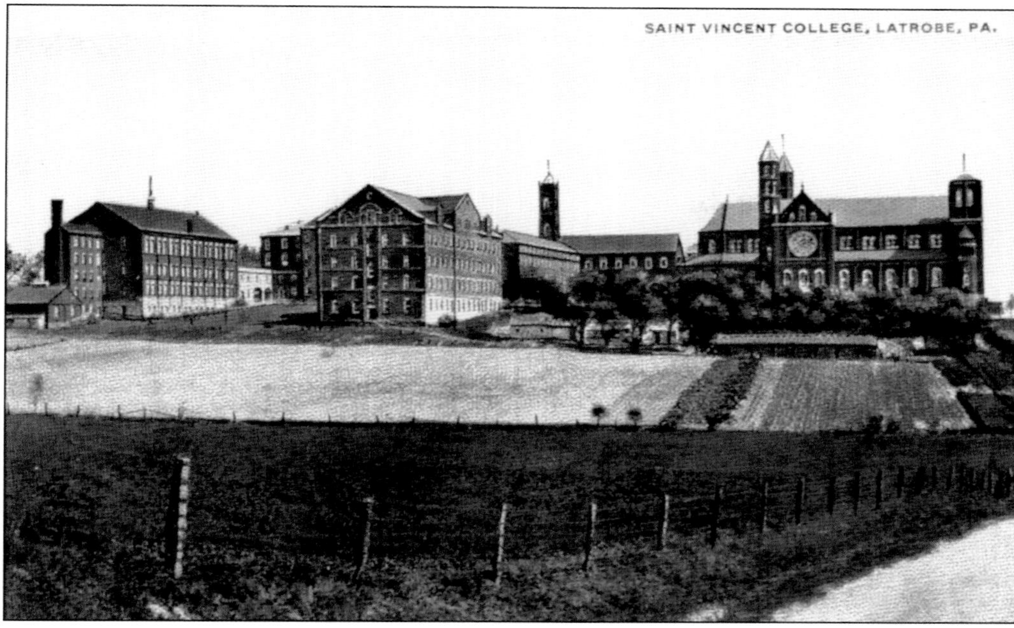

Today St. Vincent offers a modern liberal arts curriculum, focusing on all the major disciplines, natural and social sciences, humanities, arts, business, and foreign language. During World War II, however, pilot training was also part of the college curriculum. This was done in cooperation with the U.S. Army Air Forces Training Program to provide ground school training for the prospective pilots.

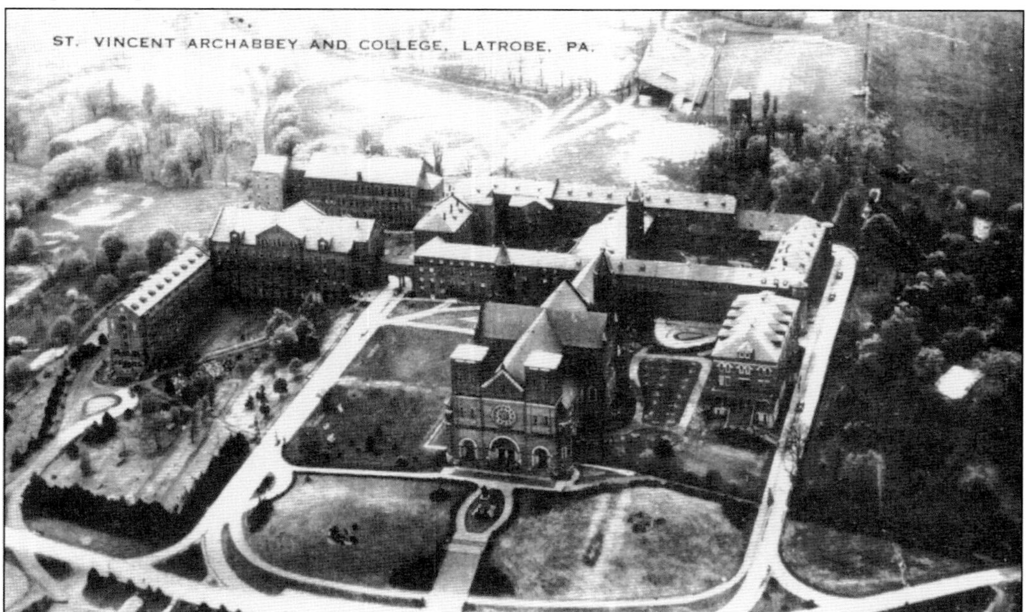

Prominent in this aerial postcard of St. Vincent is the old Bearcat Stadium in the top right-hand corner of the card. This stadium served the St. Vincent football team from 1936 to the 1960s. The college discontinued its varsity football program after the 1962 season, and eventually the stadium gave way to a new science center.

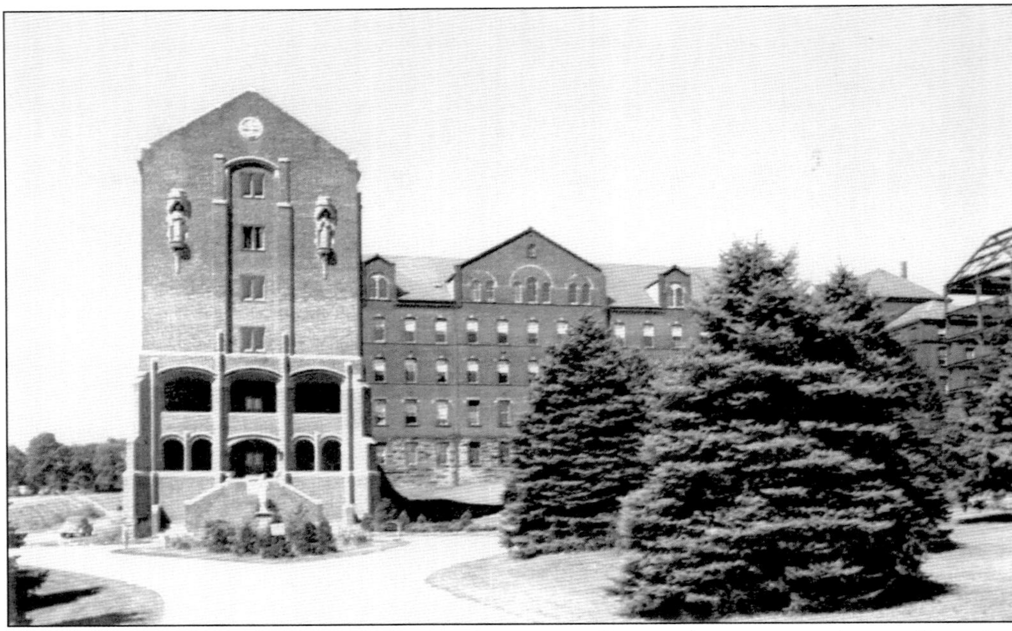

Built in 1921 in an effort to satisfy an increase in enrollment, the monastic chapter formed an agreement with the Diocese of Pittsburgh to construct Aurelius Hall. The building is now used for student housing.

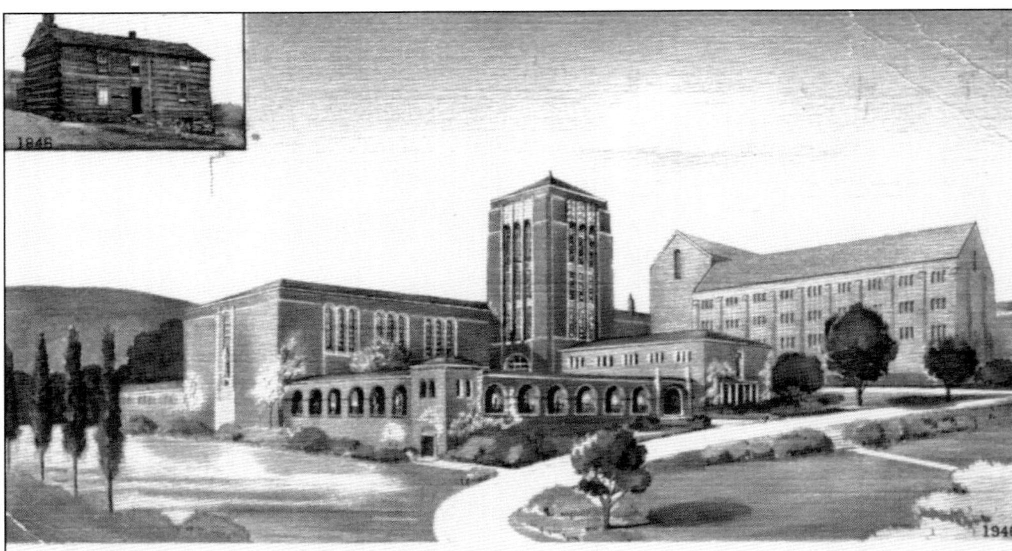

Designed with the spirit of the original sportsman's hall, the first building on the St. Vincent College campus, in mind, the new sportsman's hall was a student center. The building, which was opened in 1954, was originally known as Kennedy Hall, but in 2004, it was expanded and rededicated as the Robert S. Carey Student Center.

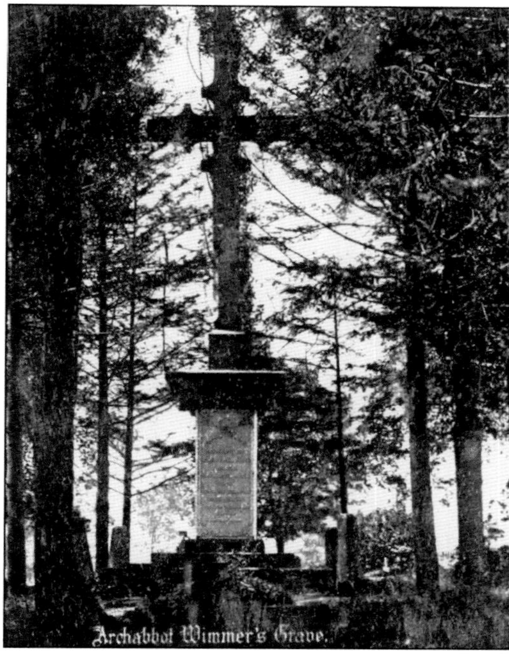

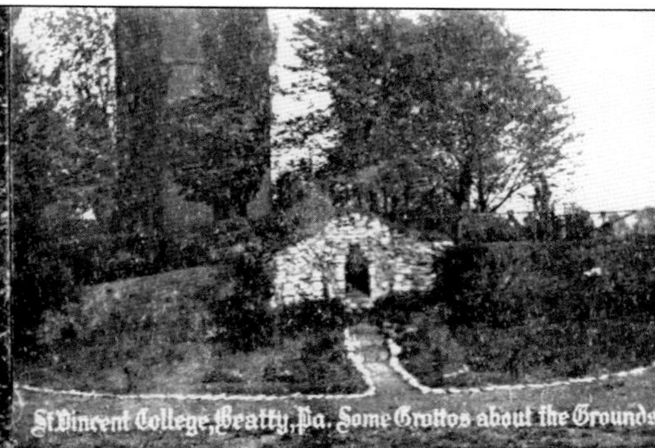

Sebastian Wimmer was born in Thalmassing, Bavaria, on January 14, 1809. In 1846, he and 18 companions immigrated to Beatty and laid the foundation for the first of many Benedictine schools and monasteries in the United States. Wimmer was named archabbot of St. Vincent in 1883. He died four years later in 1887.

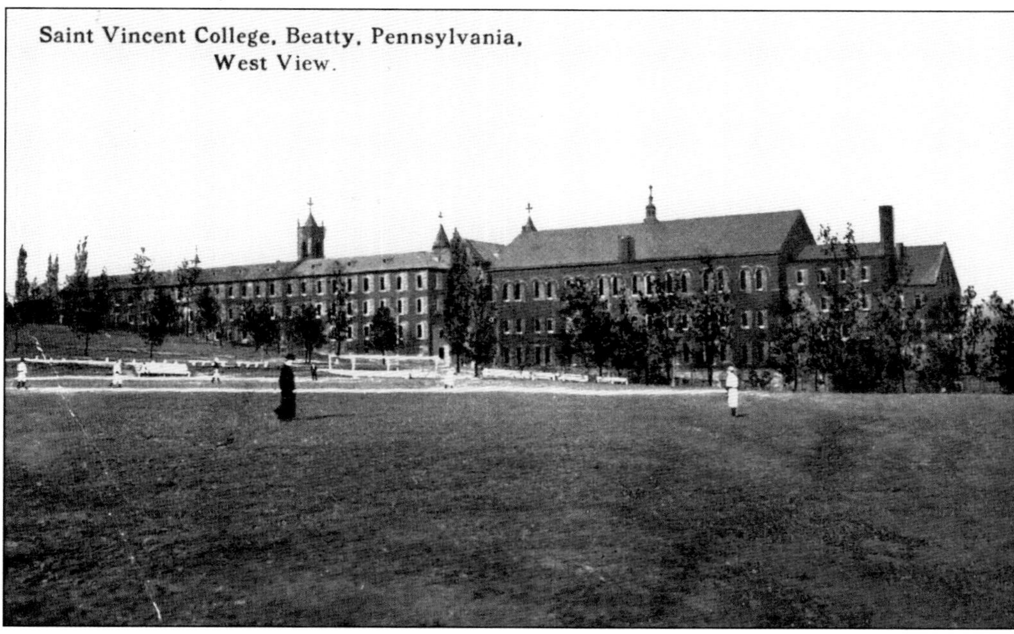

During the 1900s, every student at St. Vincent participated in at least one team sport. The college catalogue offered extracurricular activities such as baseball, football, basketball, gymnastics, hockey, tennis, and bowling. This postcard shows some students participating in one of the many team activities.

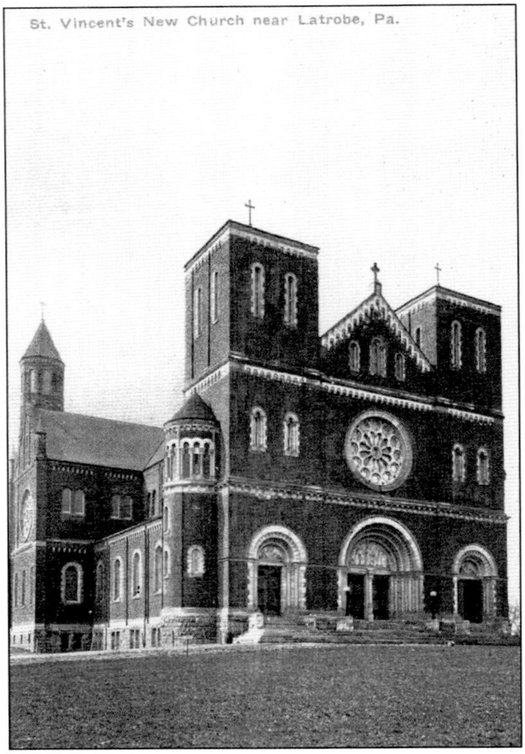

With the addition of the front towers, the church is one of the finest examples of Romanesque architecture in the country.

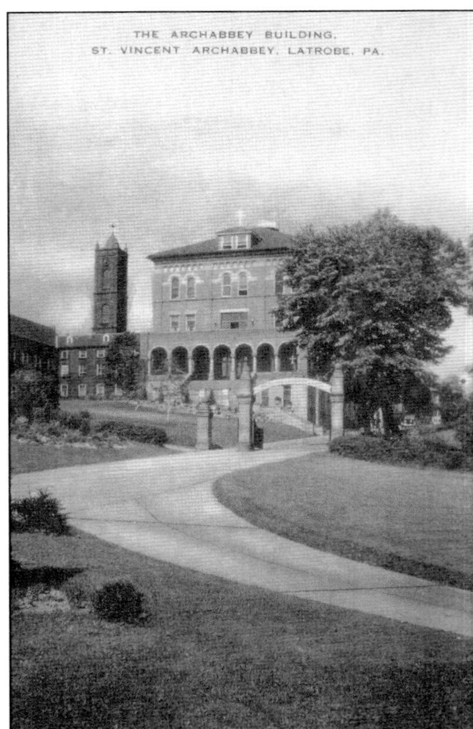

In addition to secular education, St. Vincent College also offered monastic education, training the area's young men to become Roman Catholic priests.

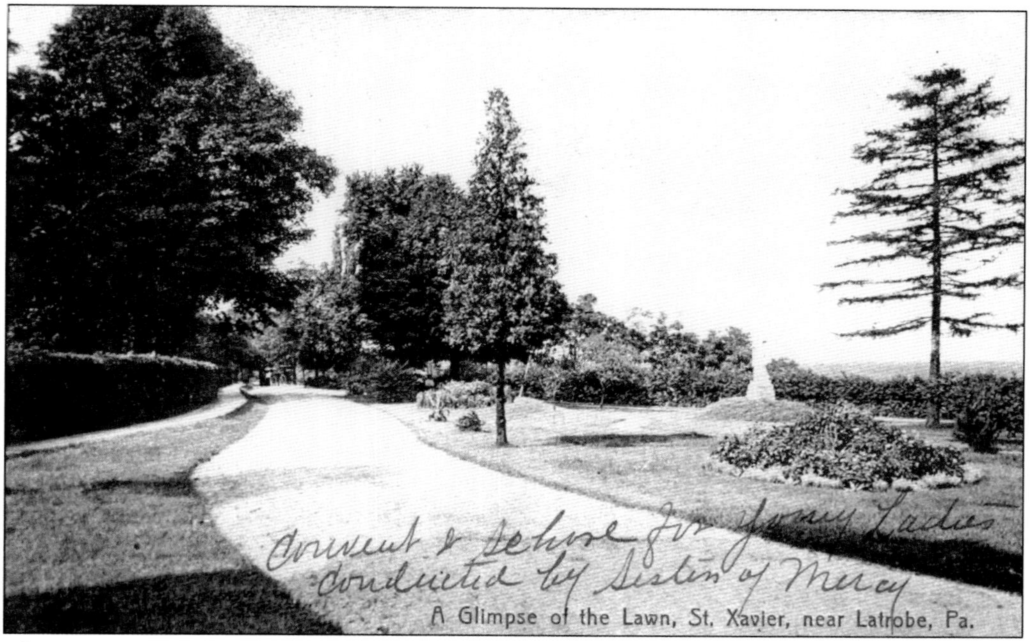

The St. Xavier convent and academy is the oldest institution of the Sisters of Mercy who came from Ireland in 1843.

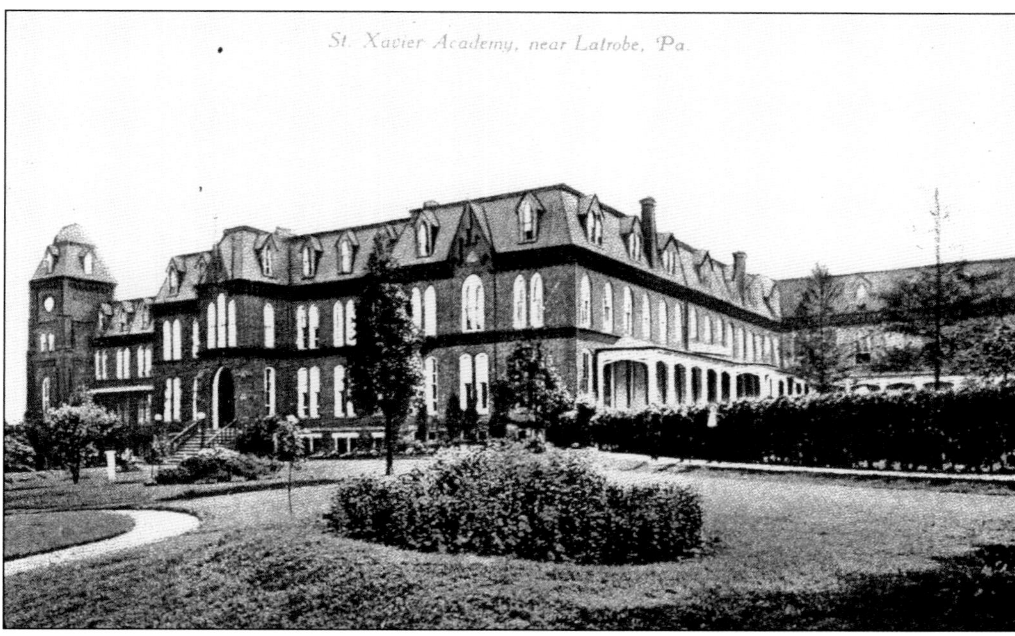

St. Xavier Academy served as an academy for girls and elementary-age boys. St. Xavier had a close relationship with the prep school at St. Vincent, with the St. Xavier girls cheering at the St. Vincent Prep games and the two schools going to dances together.

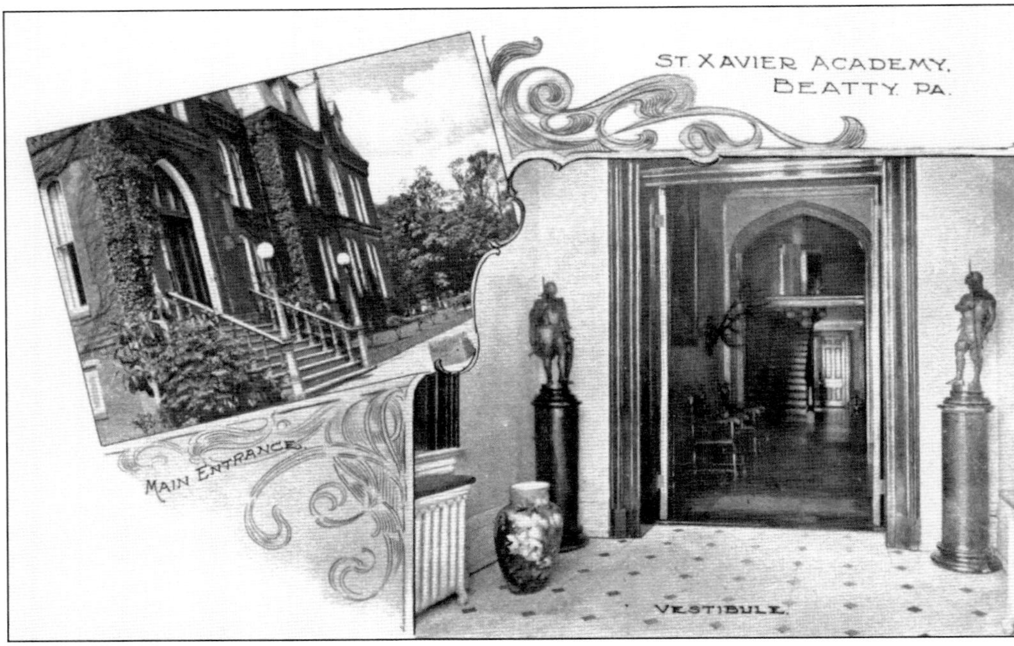

On March 17, 1972, St. Xavier Academy suffered a devastating fire, which burned the academy to the ground. After the fire, the academy never reopened, and no trace of the building remains.

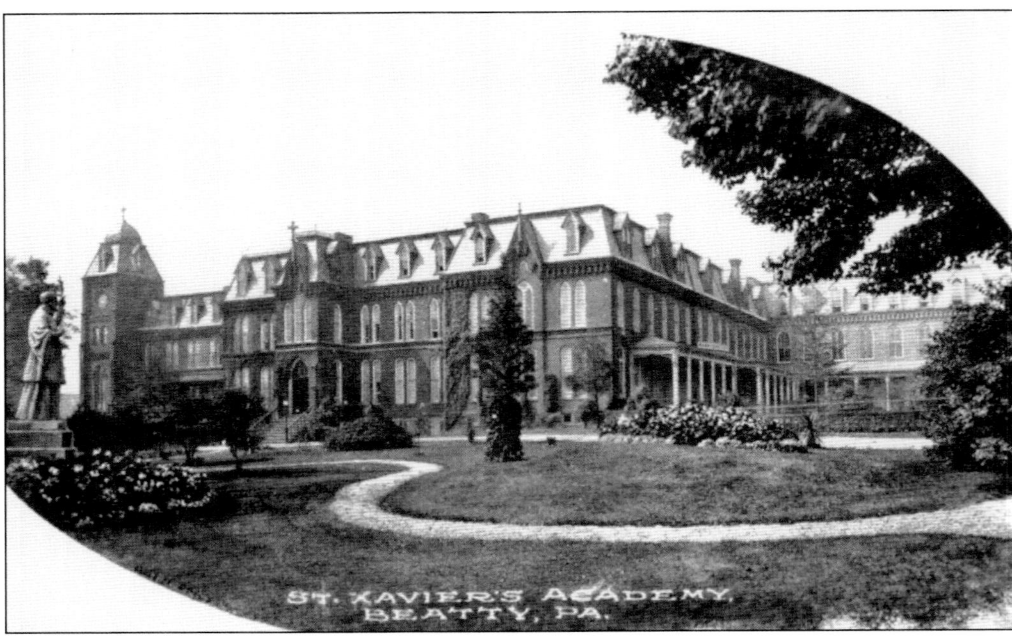

With all traces of the academy on the St. Xavier grounds just a memory, the land is still used for the Sisters of Mercy cemetery and farmlands.

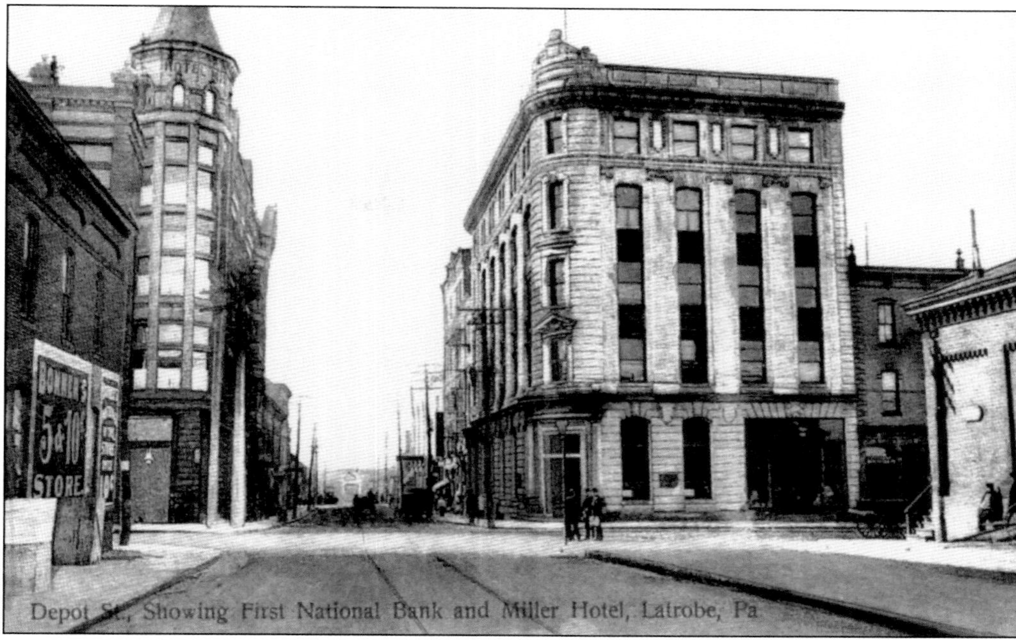

Bonner's 5 and 10, located on the corner of Depot Street, advertised nothing over 10¢. Bonner's would later become the Eisaman's 5 and 10.

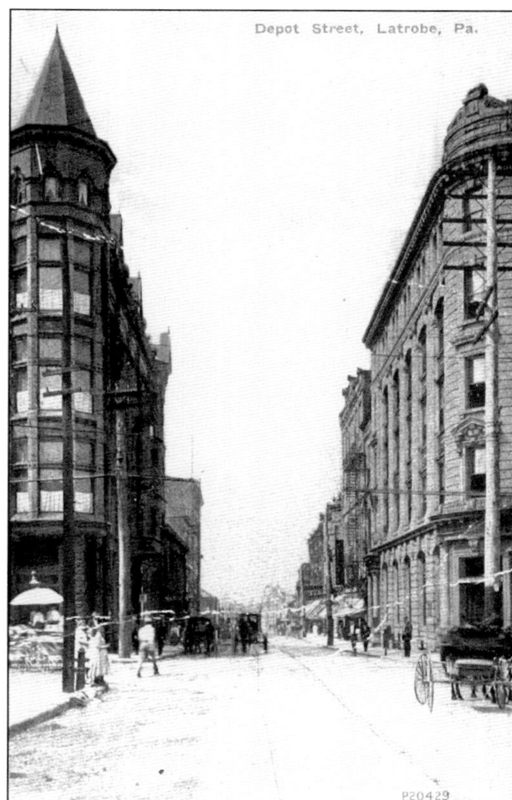

The First National Bank, shown on the right, housed Showalter's Drug Store on the first floor. Showalter's would later become Sun Drug. The First National Bank was torn down in 1976 to make way for several businesses. The Miller Hotel, shown on the left, burned down in 1974 and is now the site of the Mears, Smith, Houser, and Boyle Law Offices.

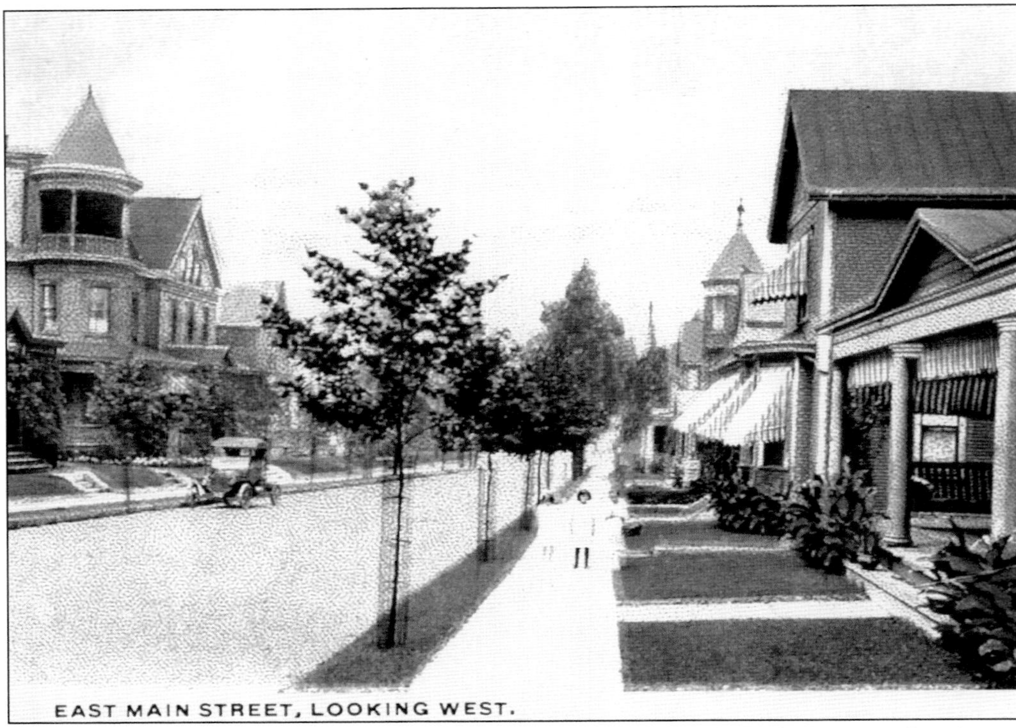

The wealthy residents of Latrobe lived on "the hill" in the residential sections of Main and Weldon Streets. The bankers, industrialists, and business owners all owned homes in these sections of town.

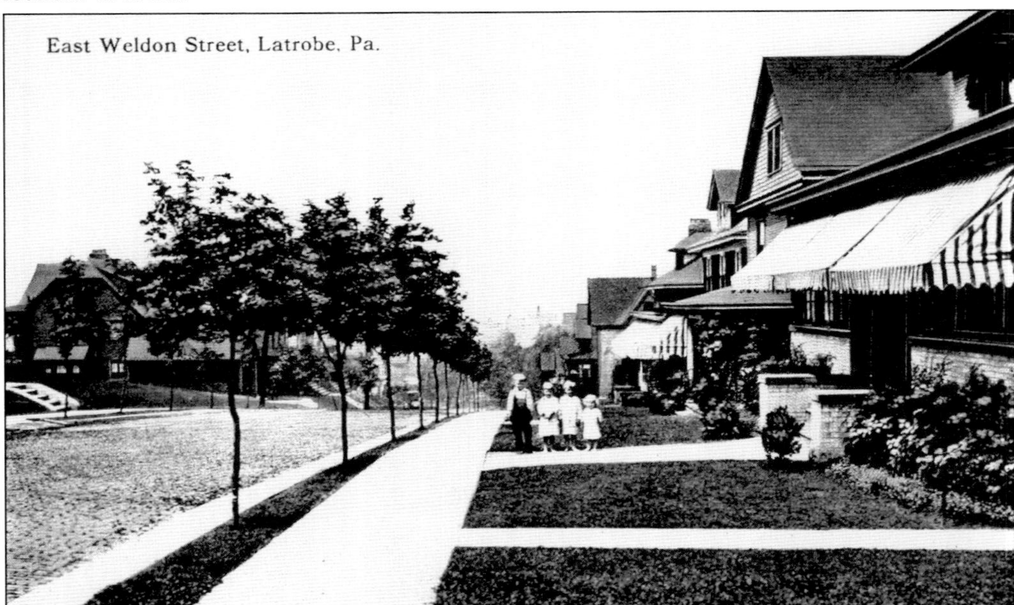

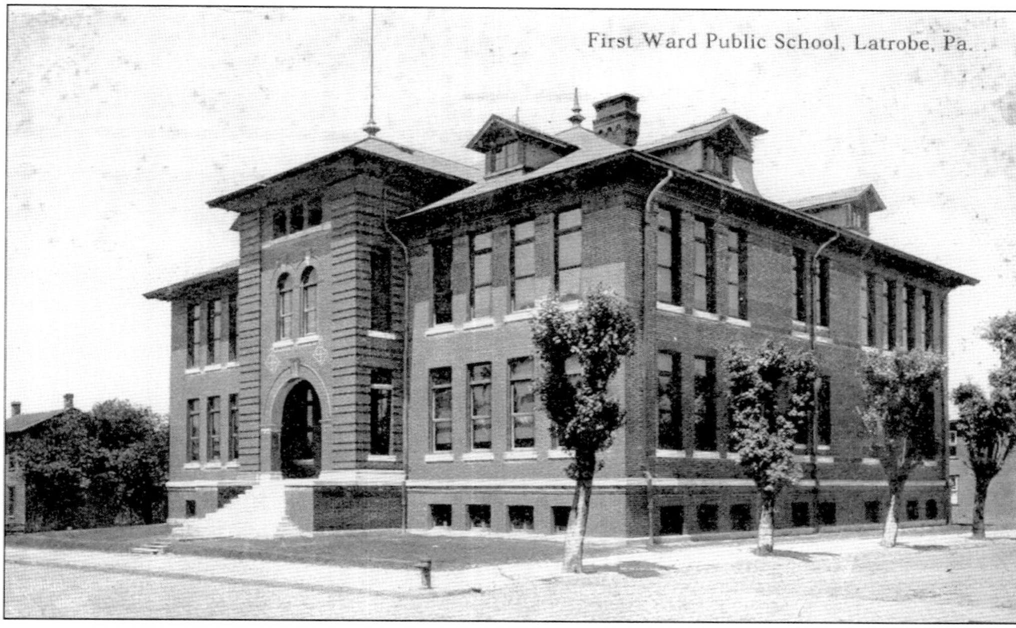

Located on the corner of Ligonier and Washington Streets, the First Ward School was built in 1909 as an elementary school, and the building functioned for its first five years as a high school. Now the building is privately owned.

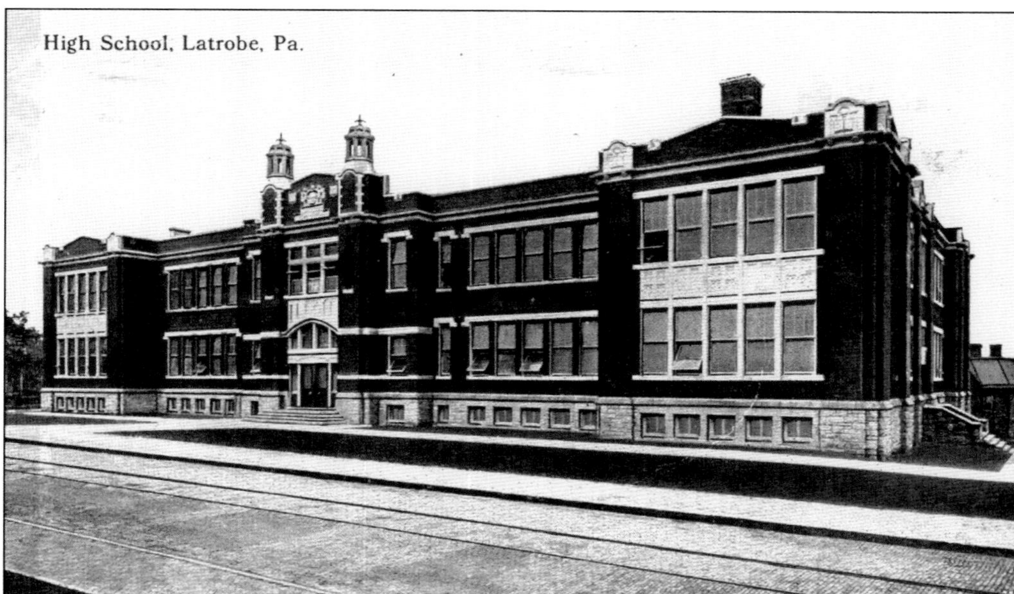

Built in 1914, Latrobe High School was added on to in 1936 and then converted to junior high use in 1966. The school is now used as the Latrobe Elementary School.

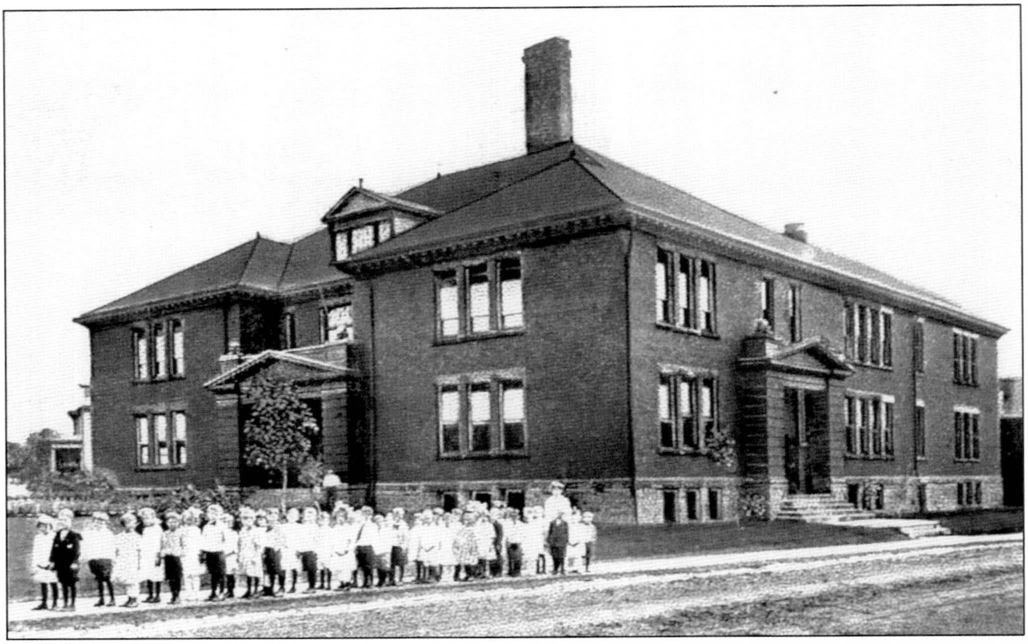

Built in 1901, the Fourth Ward School was one of several school buildings in the district. The school is still in existence, but it has been remodeled and is now used as an apartment building, which opened on December 16, 1983.

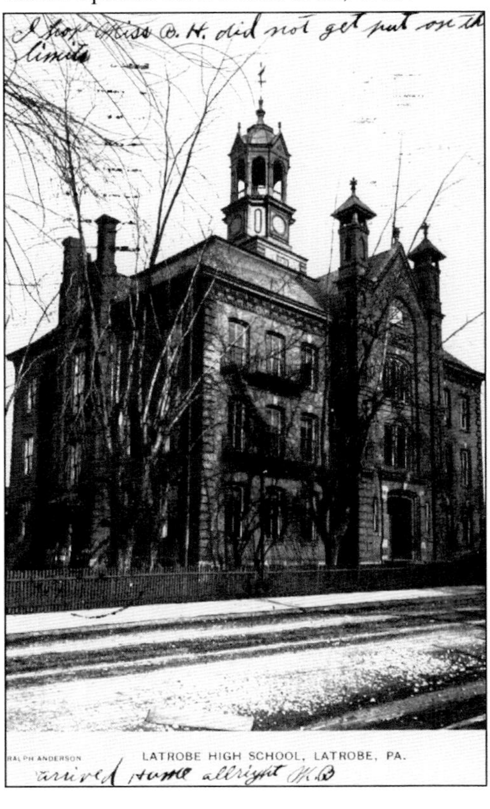

Built as Latrobe's first high school in 1882, the Second Ward School building is now used as the district's administration building. The center turret has been removed, as have the columns around the entrances.

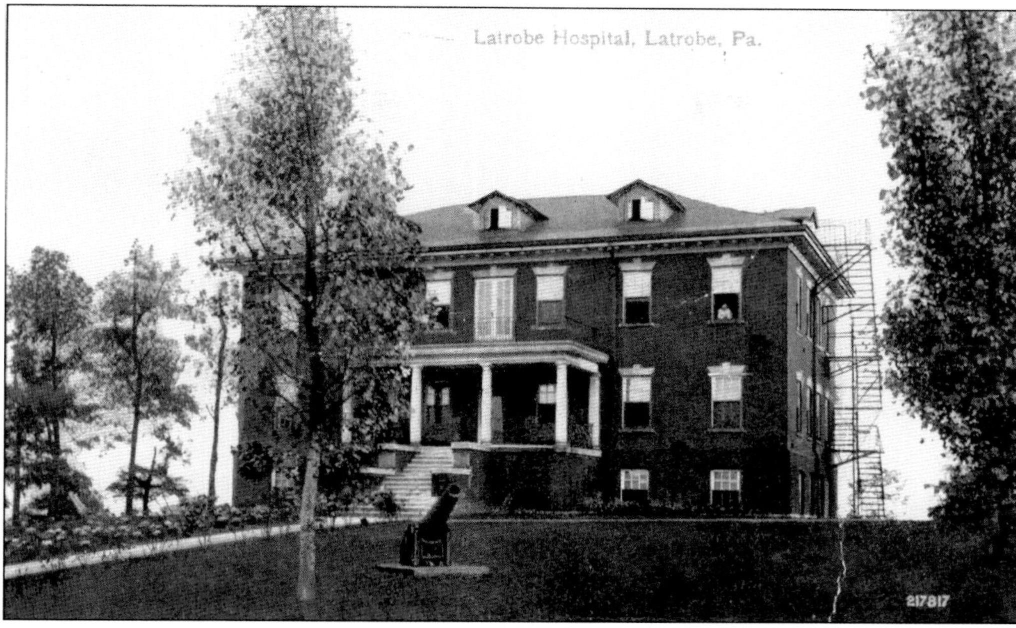

The Latrobe Area Hospital was built in 1909 on land donated by the Grand Army of the Republic (GAR). The hospital was originally run on donations and subscriptions. Over the years, many changes would come to the hospital, and many of the buildings seen in the picture no longer exist.

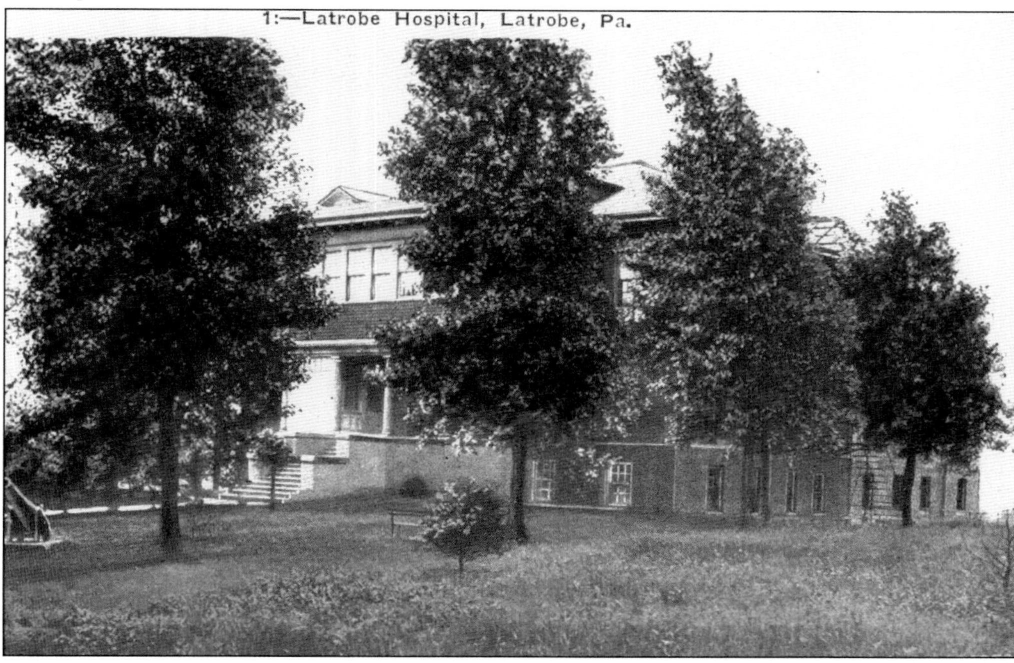

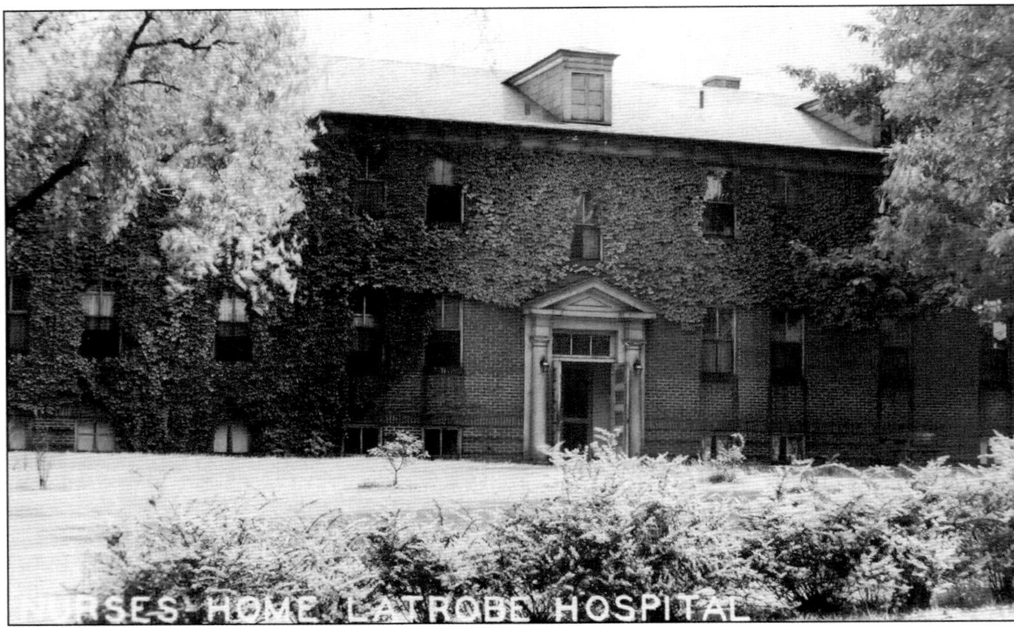

The School of Nursing was developed in 1910 to help staff the new hospital. At the time few women had the opportunity to pursue a career in medicine. The nurses' home was located next to the hospital. The school was closed in 1970 and was later torn down.

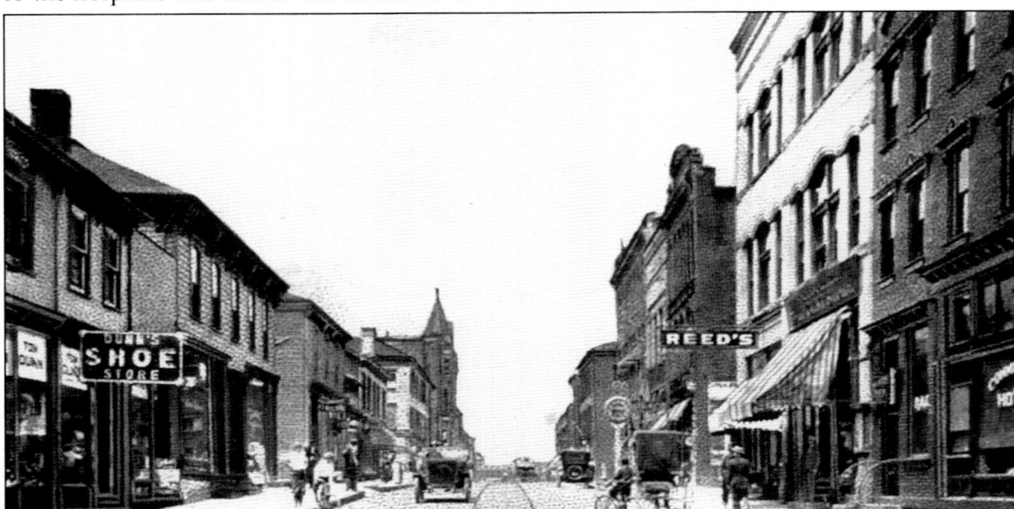

Visible on the right-hand side of the street is Reed's Department Store. Originally Reeds and McLaughlin's, Reed bought out McLaughlin to become Reed's. The store would later move across the street and eventually become Troutman's.

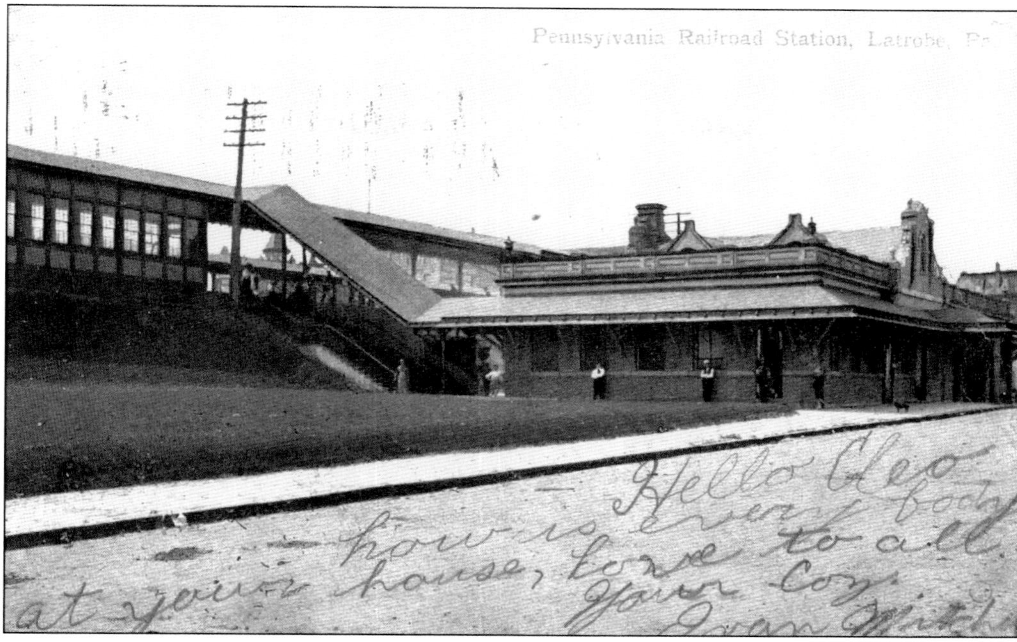

Built in 1903, the Pennsylvania railroad station in Latrobe was then known as the Latrobe train station. It functioned as a train station until 1970, when other modes of transportation became more popular.

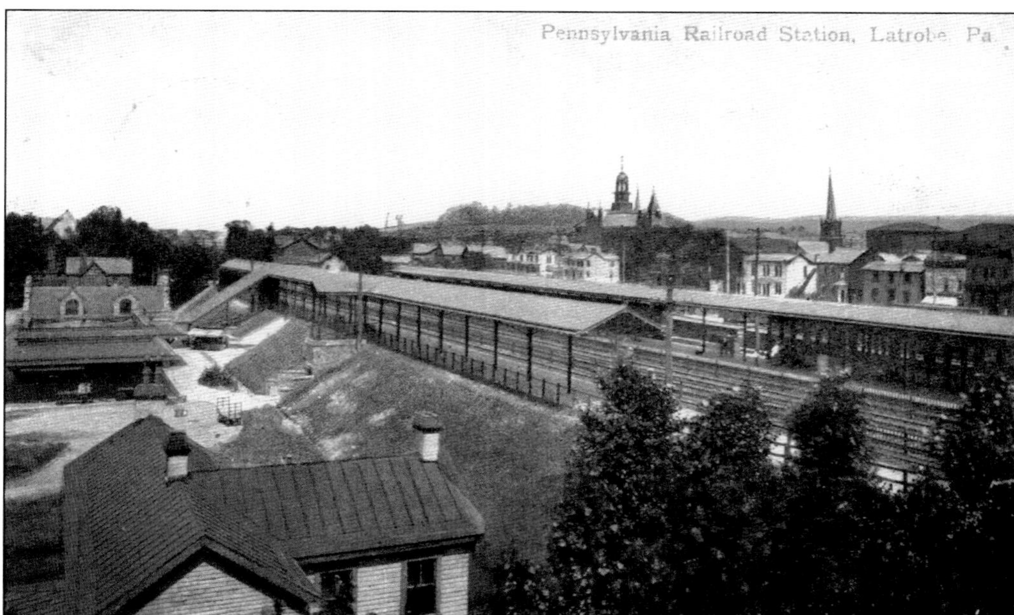

After the 1970 closing of the Latrobe train station, the station was abandoned and fell into disrepair. In 1980, the station was restored, and in 1986, it was placed on the National Register of Historic Places.

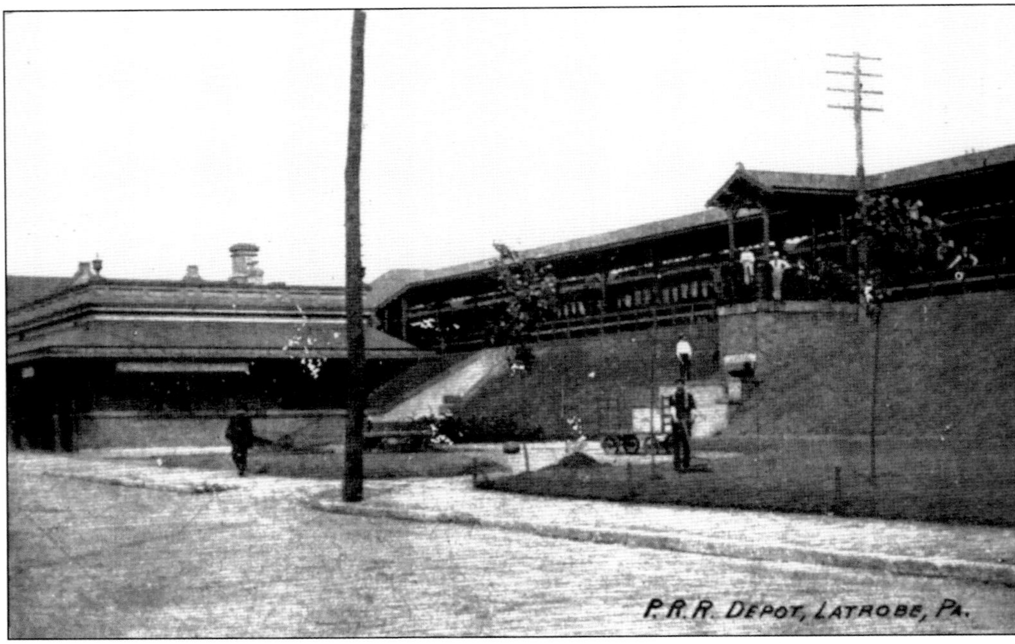

In 1989, the DiSalvo family bought the Latrobe train station and added a gourmet restaurant. Now travelers can depart from the station and catch a train heading west or east on one of the major Amtrak lines.

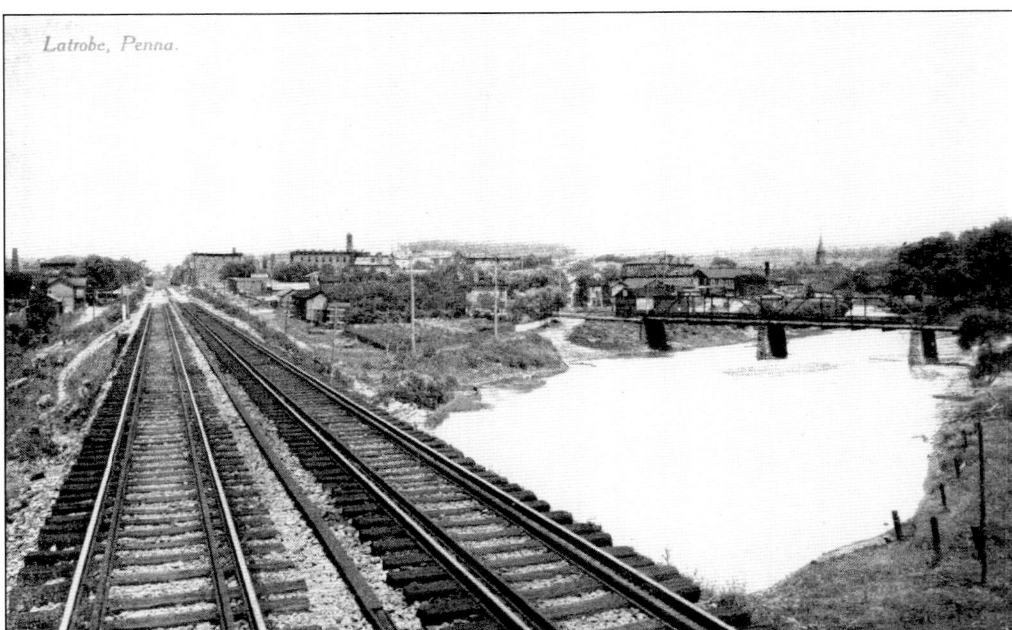

The railroad tracks were raised in 1902 and expanded to include four sets of rails instead of just two.

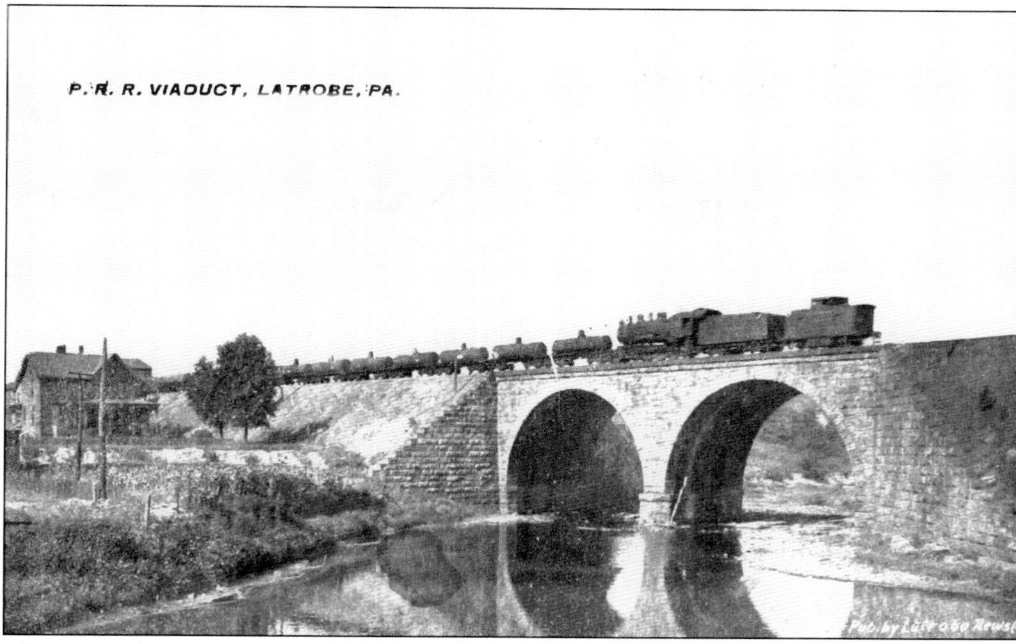

The Pennsylvania Railroad viaduct crossed the Loyalhanna Creek to bring railroad traffic into Latrobe.

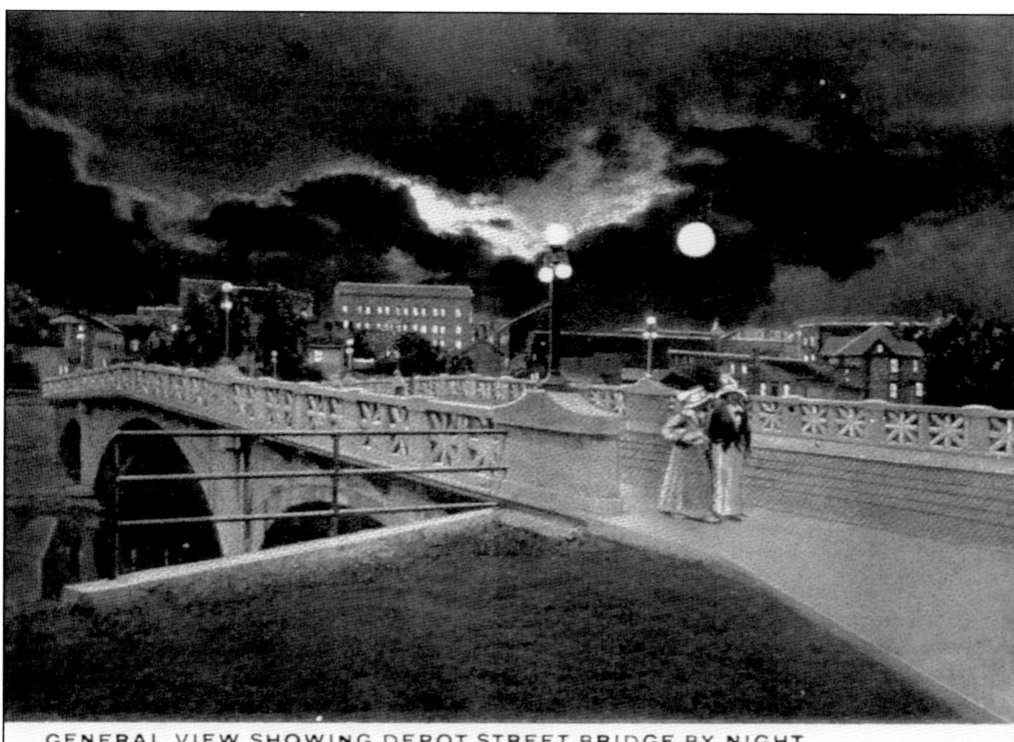

This postcard shows a couple enjoying an evening walk over the new Depot Street Bridge.

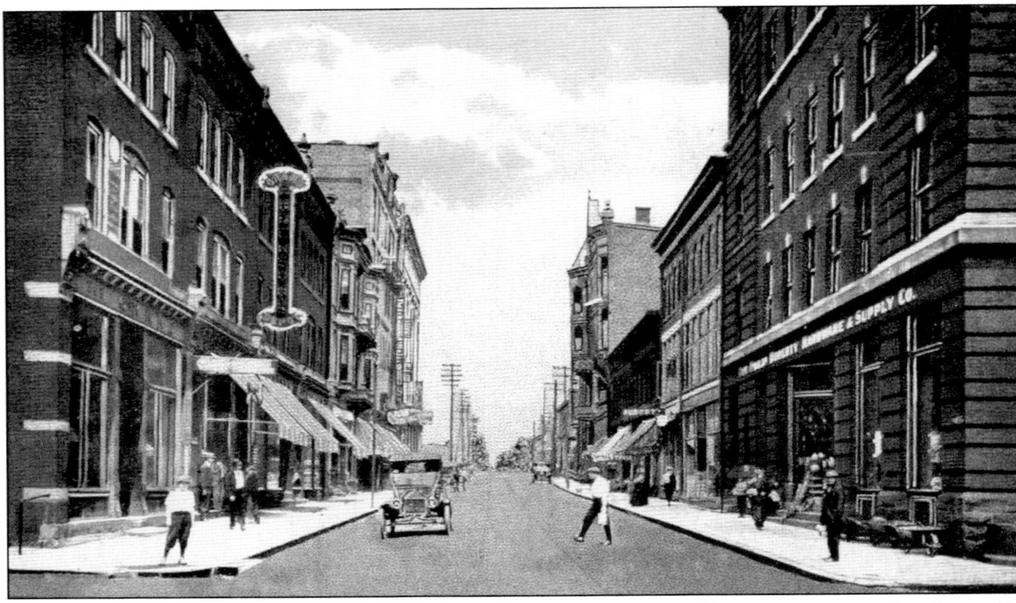

Doherty Hardware was located on the corner of Depot Street and Jefferson Street. Farther down the street was Stader Furniture. On the left-hand side of the street is Anderson's Grand Depot. Anderson's was originally Lowenstein's Department Store until 1920 before becoming Anderson's.

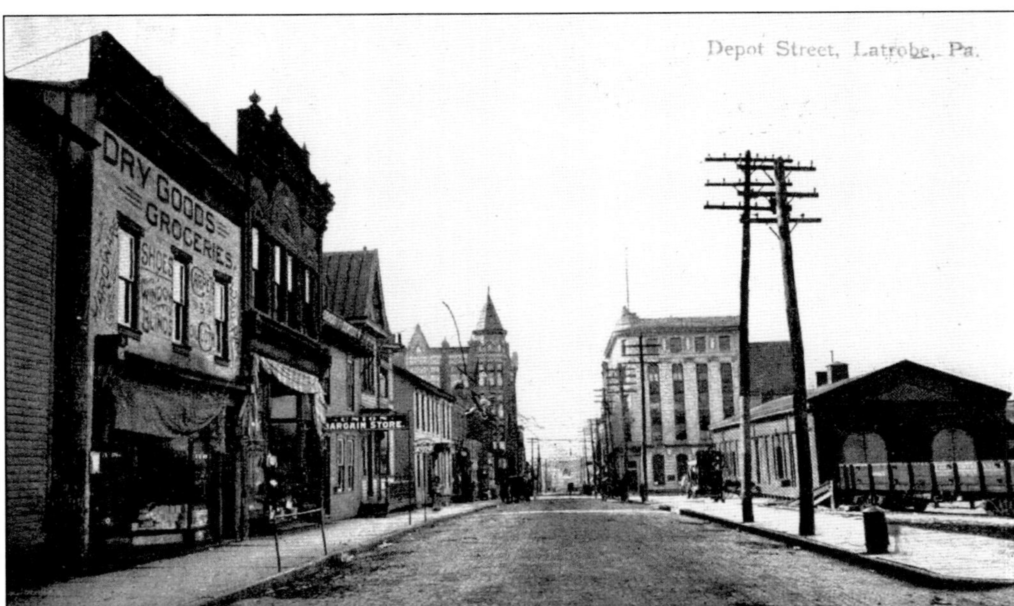

Located on the far left is Albert's Dry Goods. Also visible is the Union Bargain Store. On the right is the freight station, which was torn down in the 1950s.

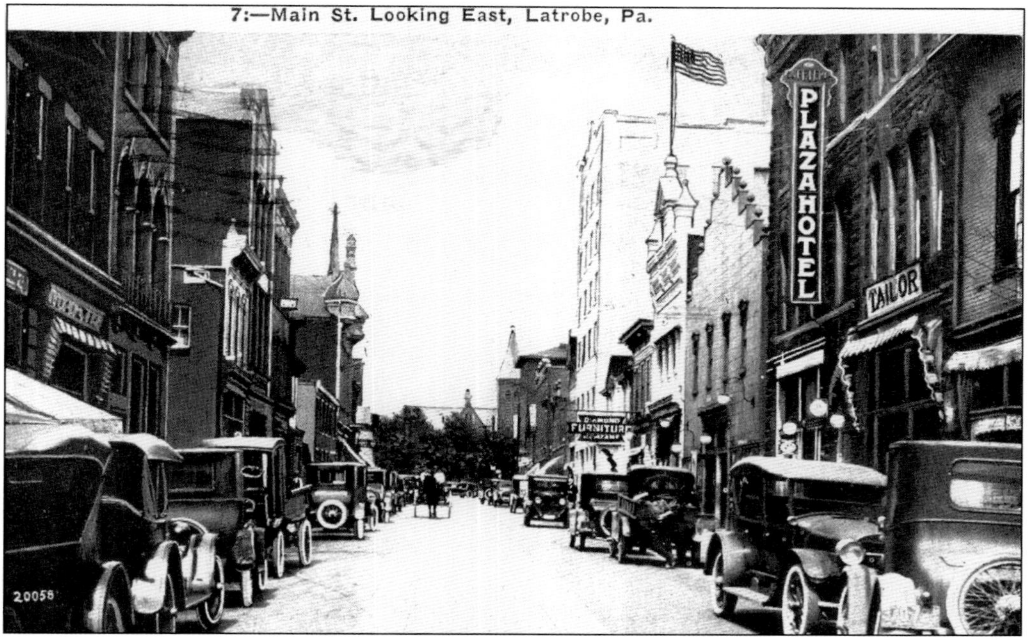

The Realty Building on the left housed Showalter's Drug Store and Meat Market on the first floor and real estate offices on the upper floors. The Mozart House can be seen farther down the street. On the left is the Plaza Hotel. Originally known as the Mahaney Hotel, the building is now part of Commercial National Bank.

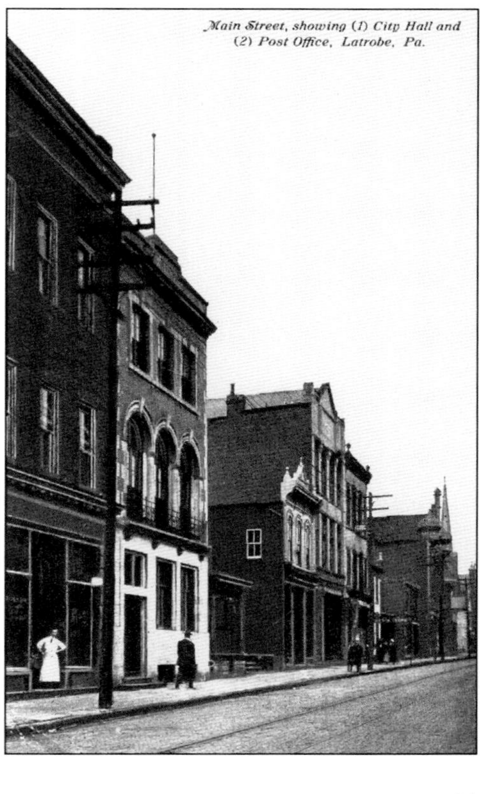

Showalter's Meat Market is visible on the far left of this card with the butcher standing out front, complete with the white butcher's apron. Beside the meat market is the old city hall, which was built in 1904. Also visible is the old post office building, which would later house Torris Drug Store and eventually a bank.

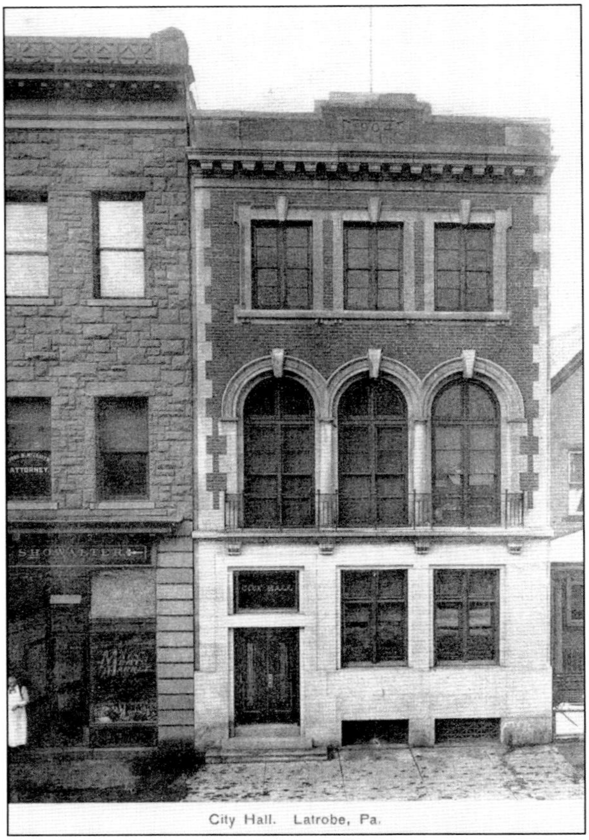

The old city hall building was torn down in the late 1970s, when the new municipal building was built. Also visible on the left is Showalter's Meat Market, with the butcher still standing out front.

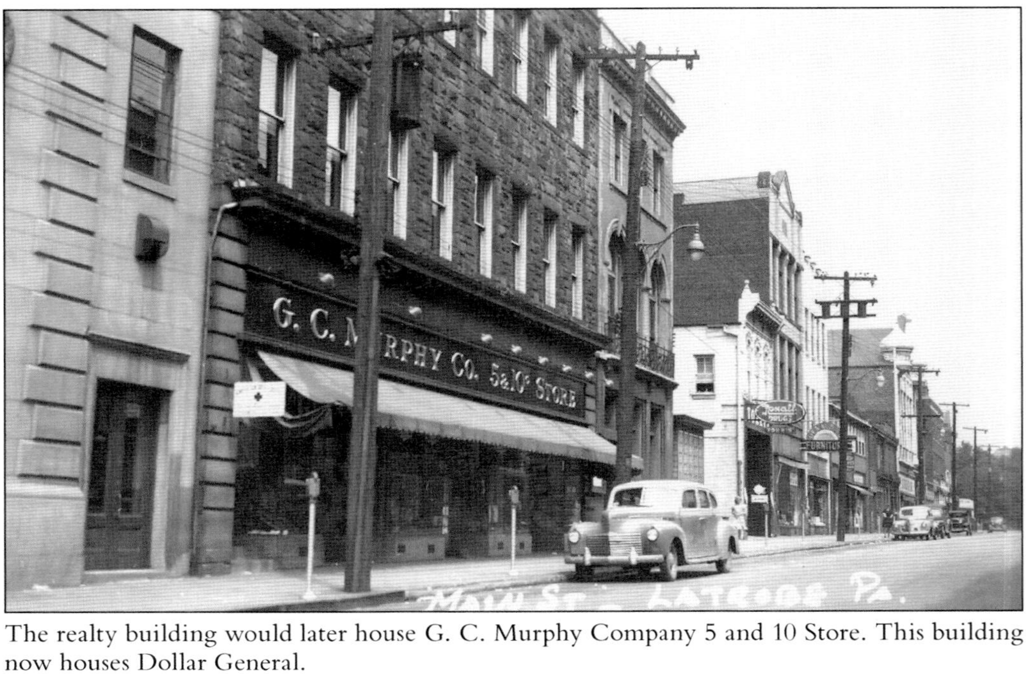

The realty building would later house G. C. Murphy Company 5 and 10 Store. This building now houses Dollar General.

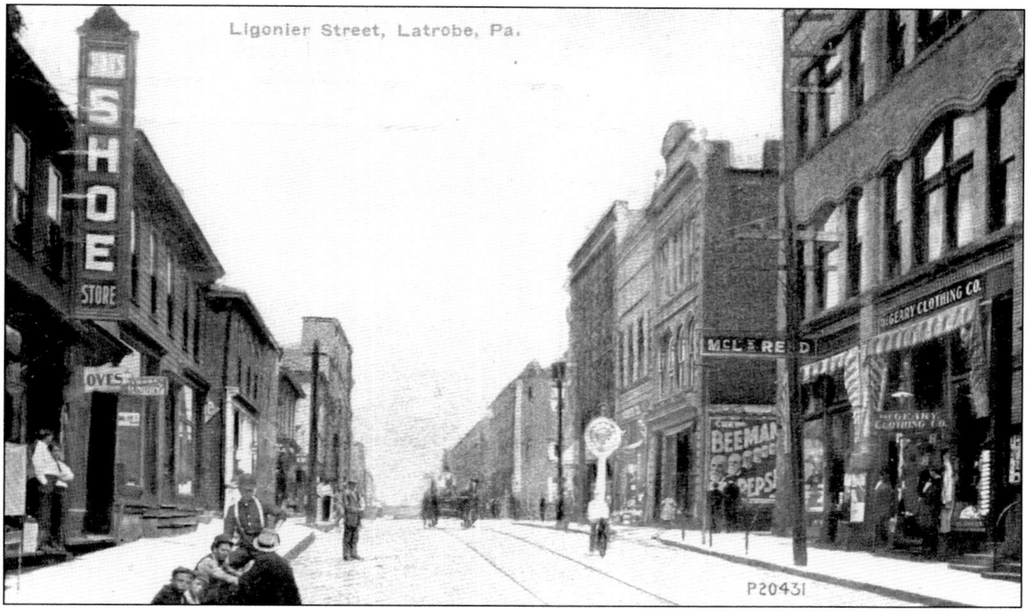

On the left is Dunn's Shoes store, which was started in the 1880s. Geary's Clothing Company is on the right-hand side of the street. The building with the decorative facade is Columbus Hall, which was home to Potthoff Jewelers.

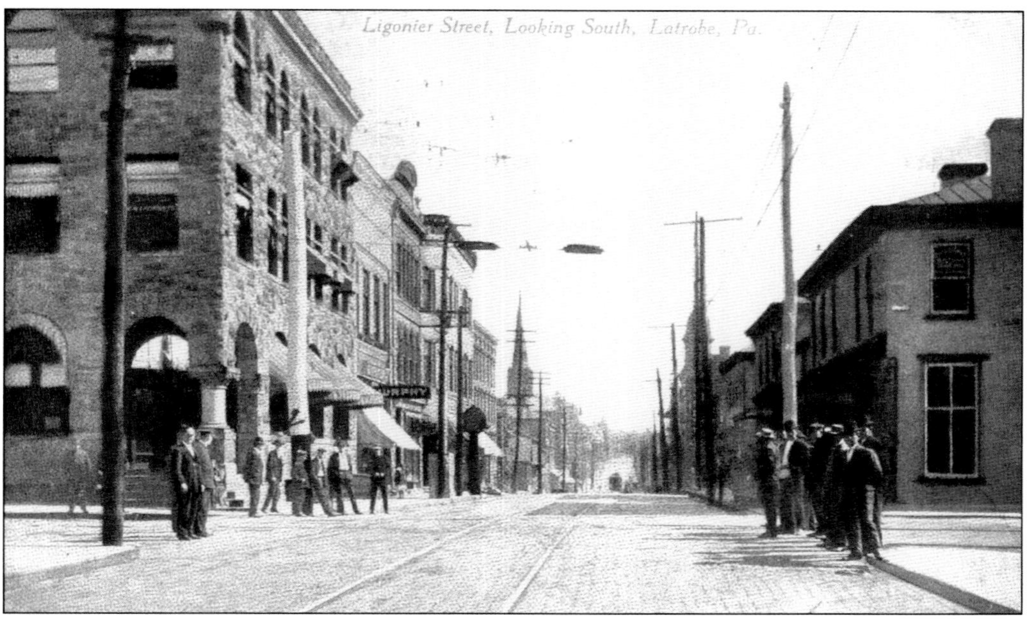

This postcard features the People's National Bank, the Murphy Building, and Columbus Hall.

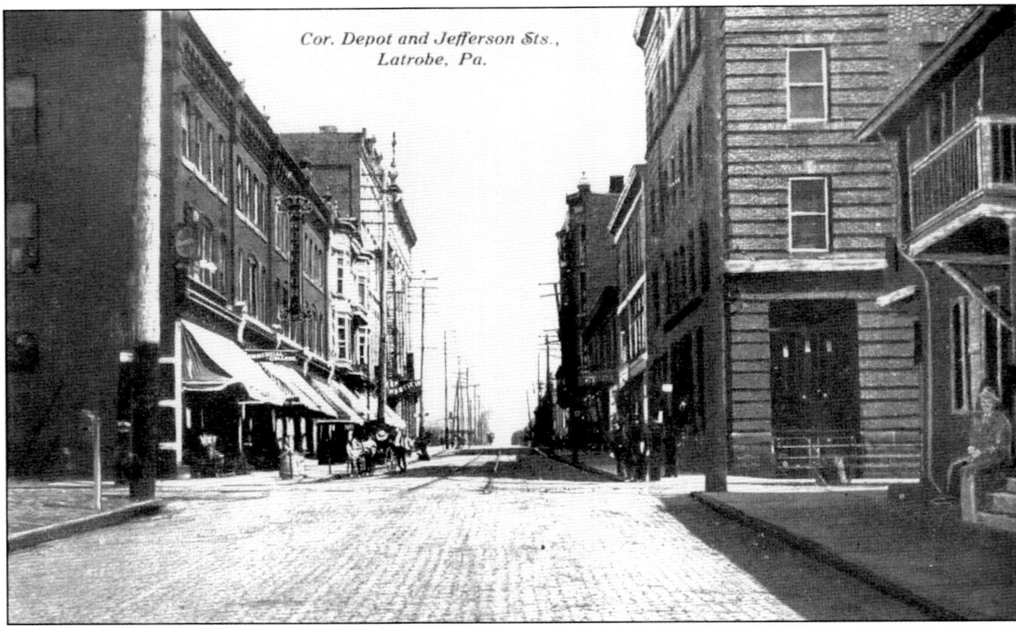

On the lower right-hand corner is the Abbaticchio Building. This building had several uses, including serving as a hotel. The new municipal building is located there now.

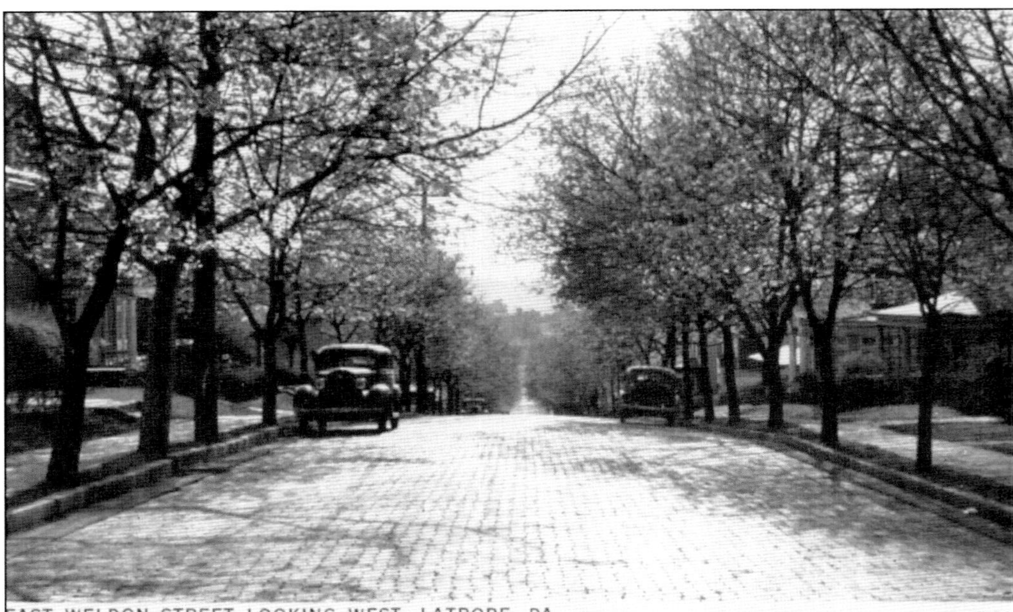

This view of East Weldon Street shows fine houses, tree-lined streets, and nice cars. These are indications that these were the homes of the town's wealthy.

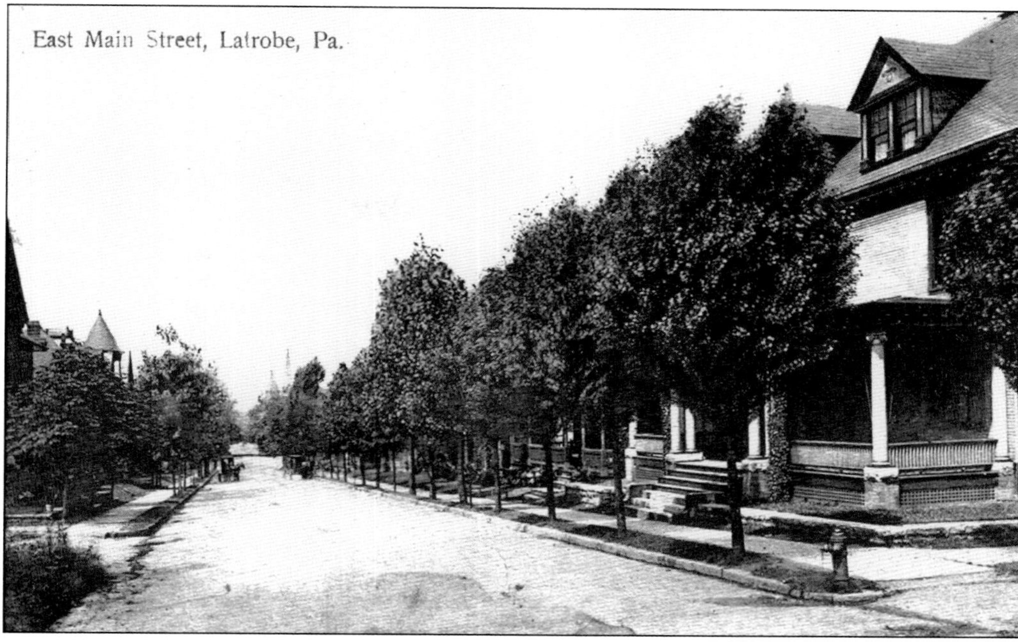

These cards show additional views of the residential sections of Main Street.

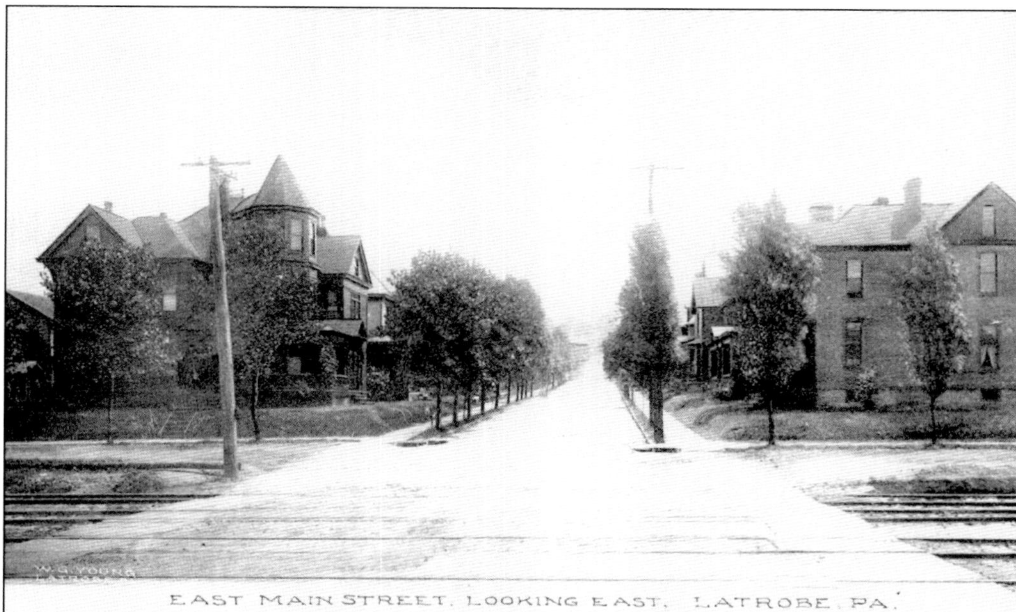

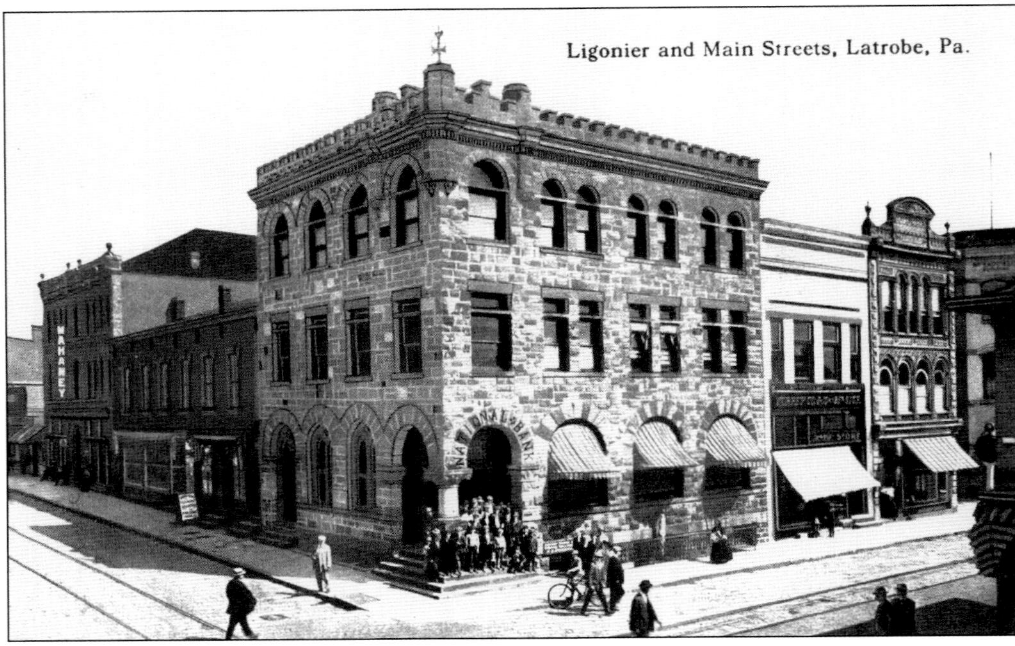

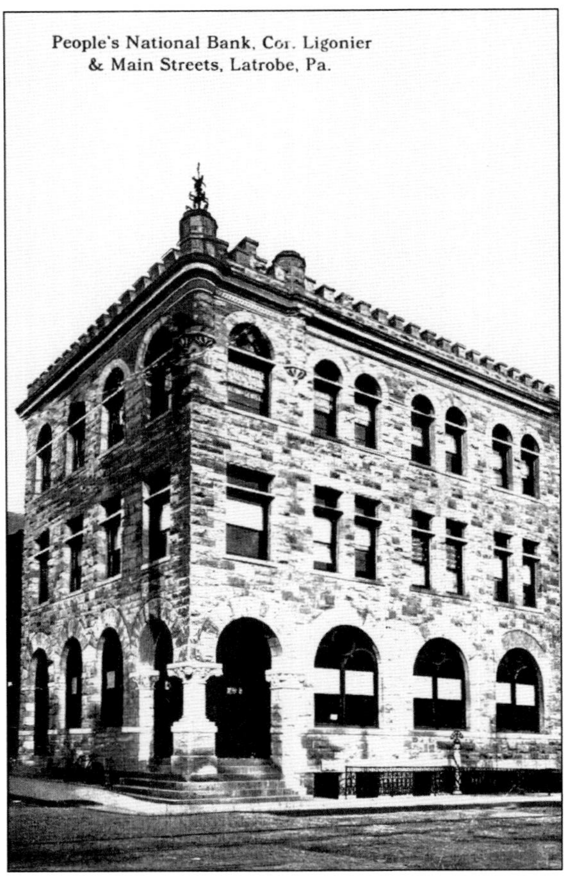

The People's National Bank stood on the corner of Ligonier and Main Streets from 1901 until 1926, when it was torn down and replaced with the Commercial National Bank, which is still standing today. The Plaza Hotel, located on the far left of the upper card, is now part of the Commercial National Bank. During the renovation of the hotel, a secret room was found under the alley, which had been used during the Prohibition era to make whiskey and hide the stills.

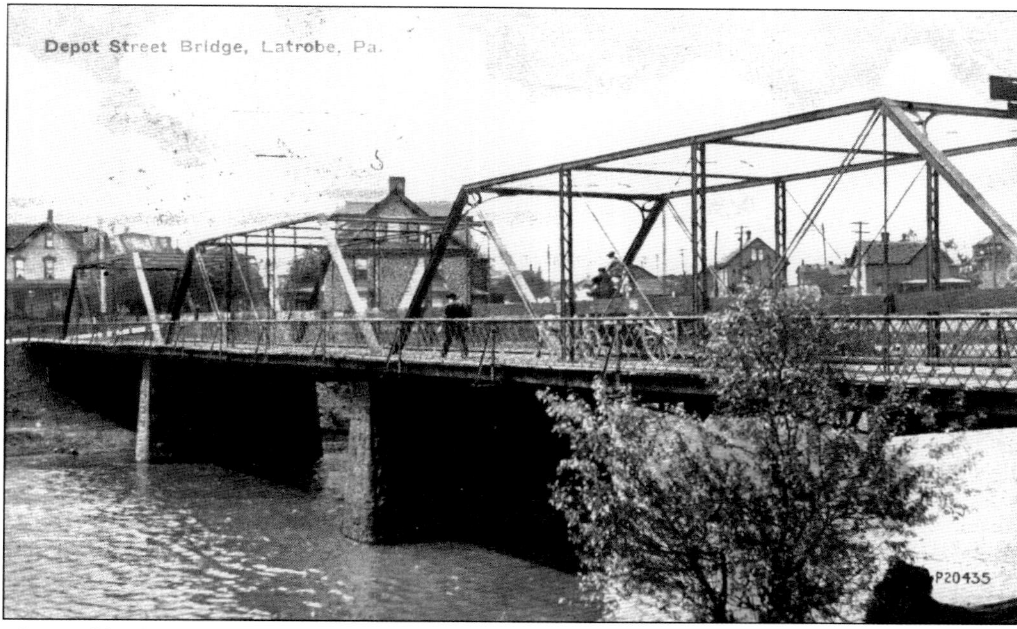

The steel bridge on Depot Street ushered both residents and visitors alike into Latrobe. Spanning the Loyalhanna Creek, the steel bridge functioned up until 1914, when it was replaced with a new concrete bridge.

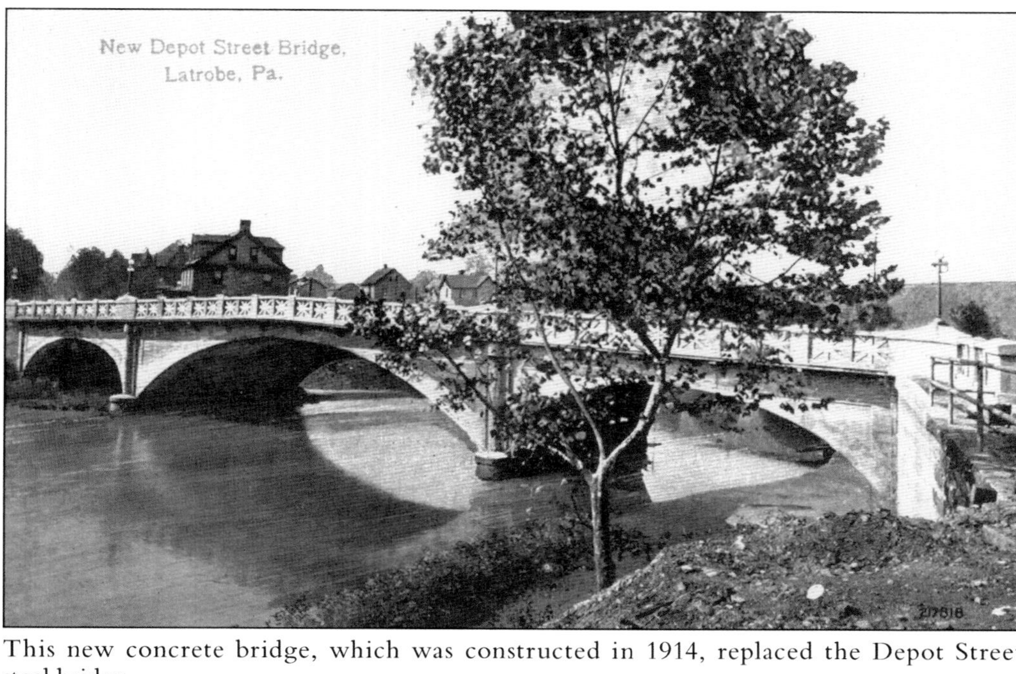

This new concrete bridge, which was constructed in 1914, replaced the Depot Street steel bridge.

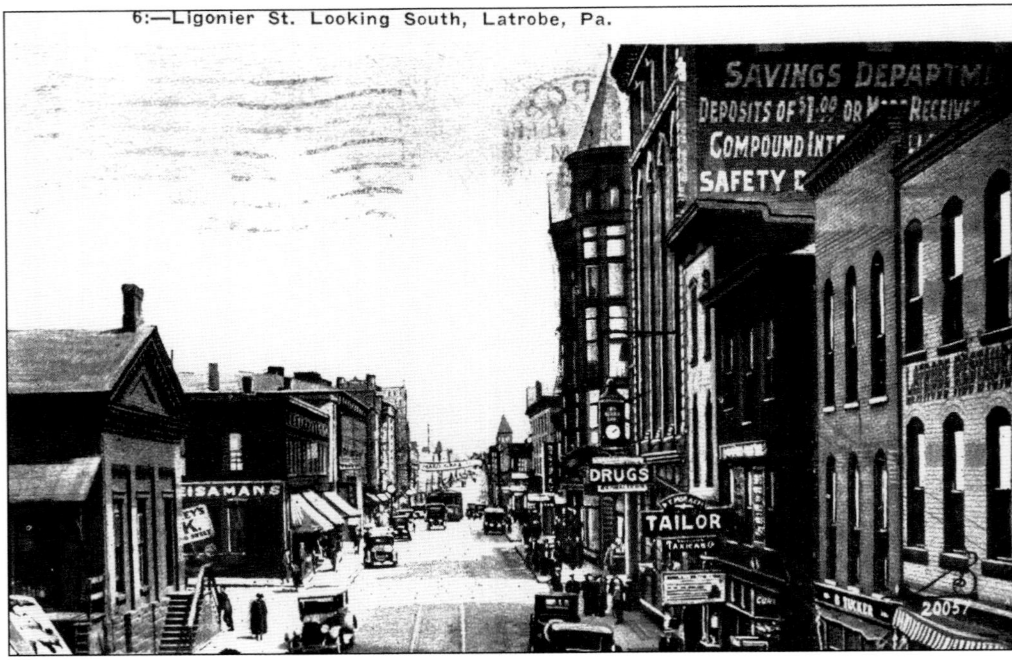

Eisaman's 5 and 10 is visible on the left-hand side of the street along with the freight station. In the lower right-hand corner are the Latrobe Restaurant, B. Tucker Clothing, and Showalter's Drugs. In the distant background is the turret of the Hill House.

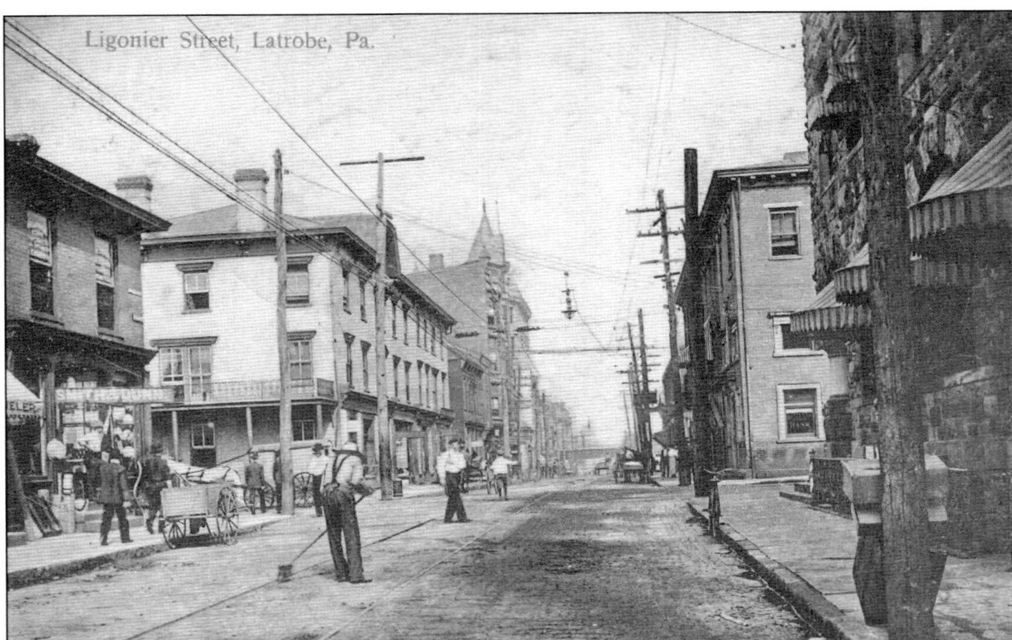

This postcard shows a busy scene on Ligonier Street. Visible on the left is the Parker House Hotel. The hotel was torn down in the 1940s. In the lower right-hand corner Murphy's is also visible.

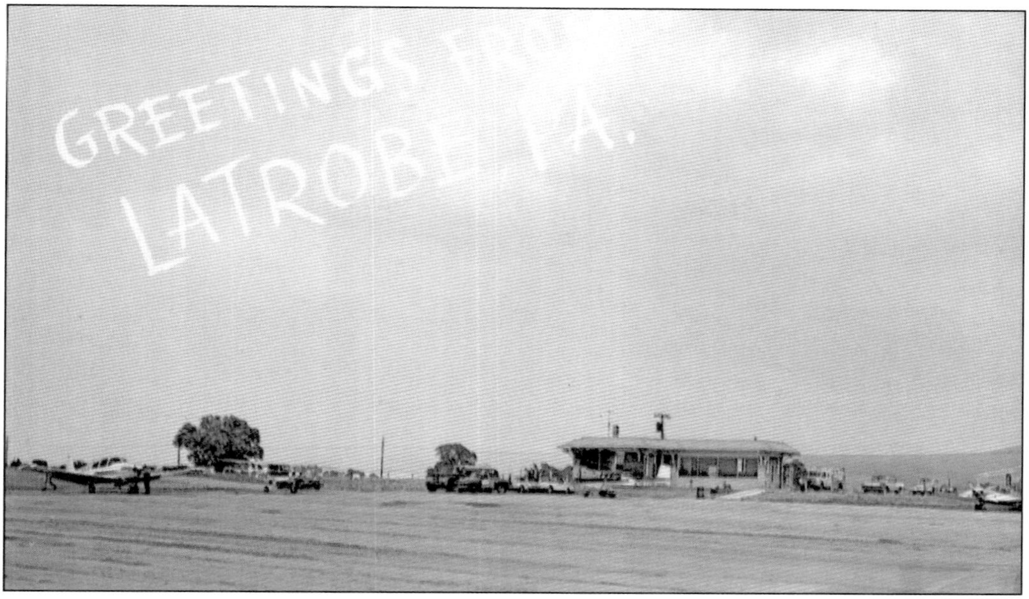

In 1924, Charlie Carroll opened the Longview Flying Field, which would eventually become Latrobe Airport and in 1999 was renamed Arnold Palmer Regional Airport. In 1974, the first official air show, organized by the Westmoreland County Airport Authority, debuted at the airport.

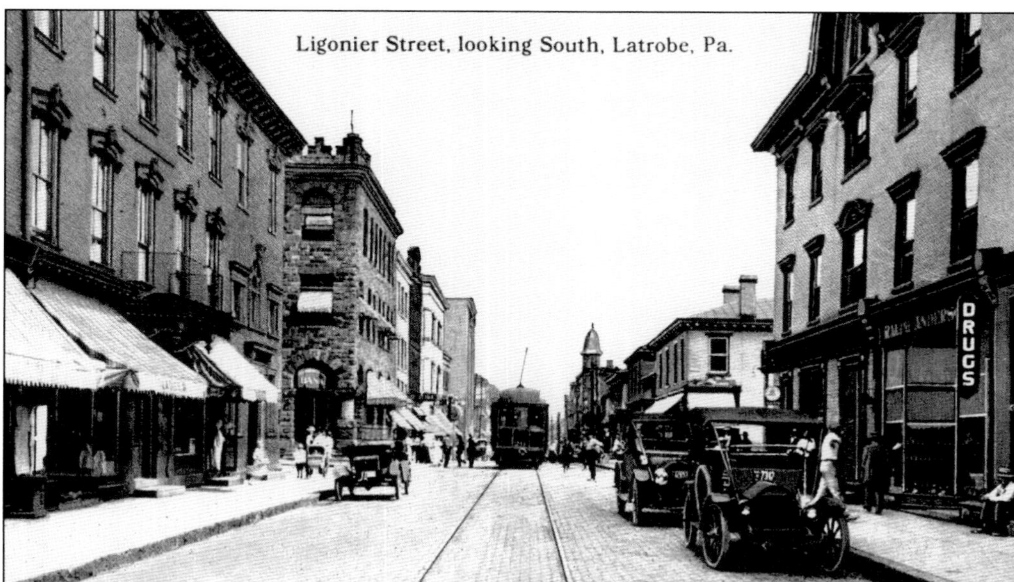

The People's National Bank Building, seen on the left, stood on the corner until 1926, when it was torn down and replaced with the Commercial National Bank Building. Citizens Bank is now housed there.

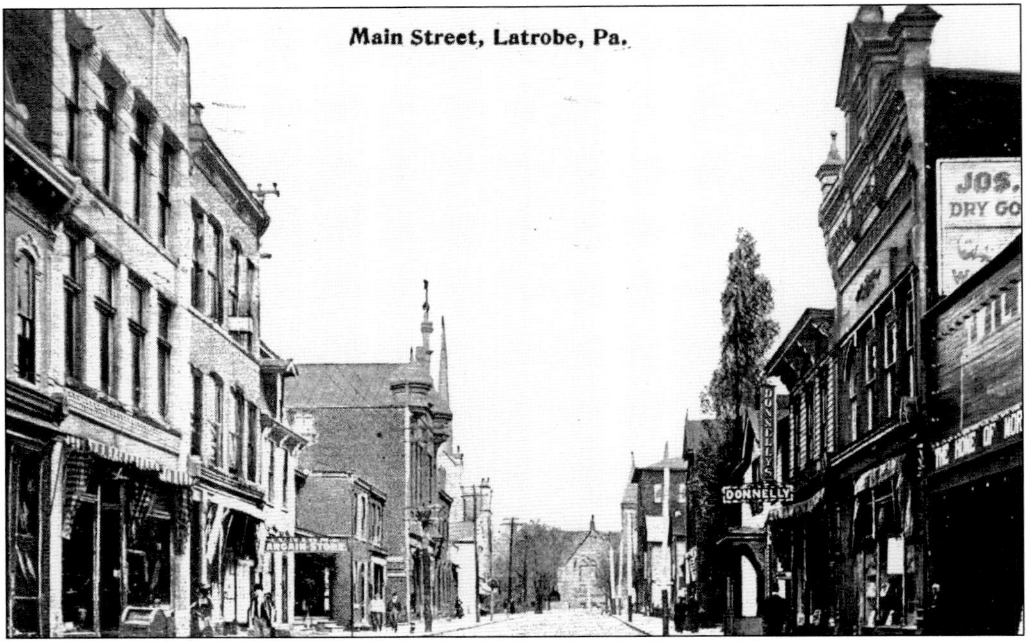

A publication prepared for the centennial celebration listed businesses and stores on Ligonier Street, Main Street, and other areas of Latrobe in the 1940 borough directory. There were 55 food stores, 36 of which were in the immediate downtown area. In addition to food stores, there were many physicians, beauty shops, barbers, hotels, restaurants, and bars.

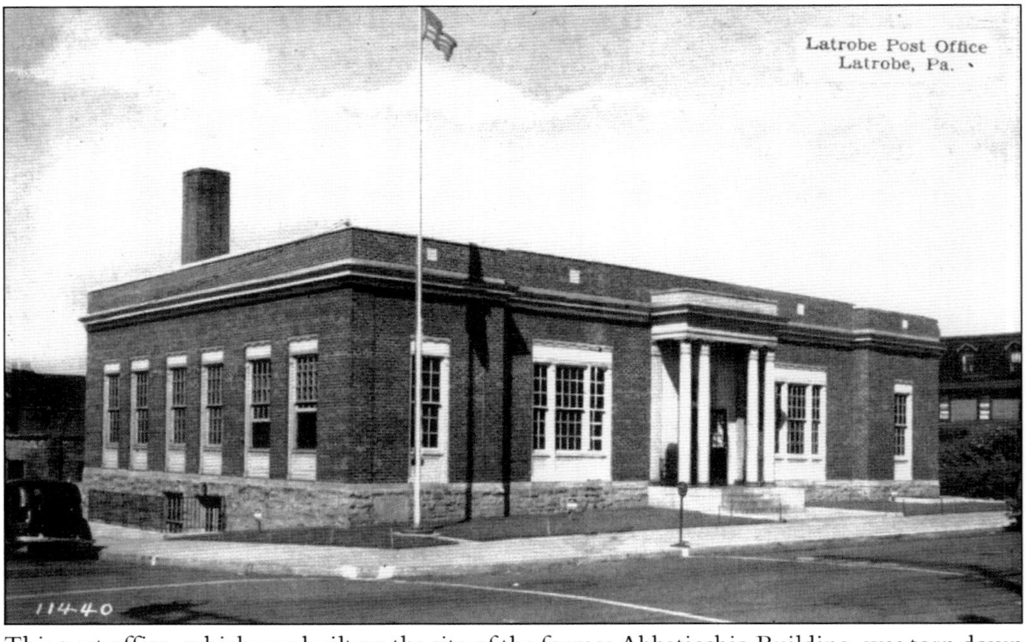

This post office, which was built on the site of the former Abbaticchio Building, was torn down in the late 1970s. The current post office is now located next door to the site of this building.

This postcard features both the former city hall on the right, and Ralph Anderson's Drug Store is located on the left.

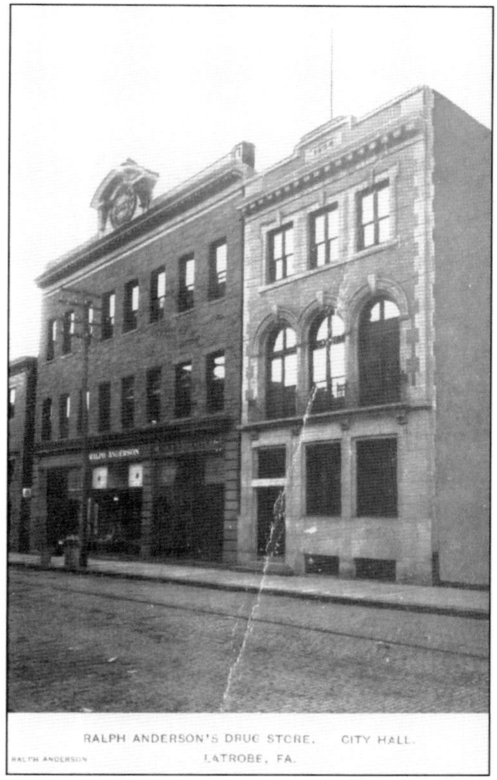

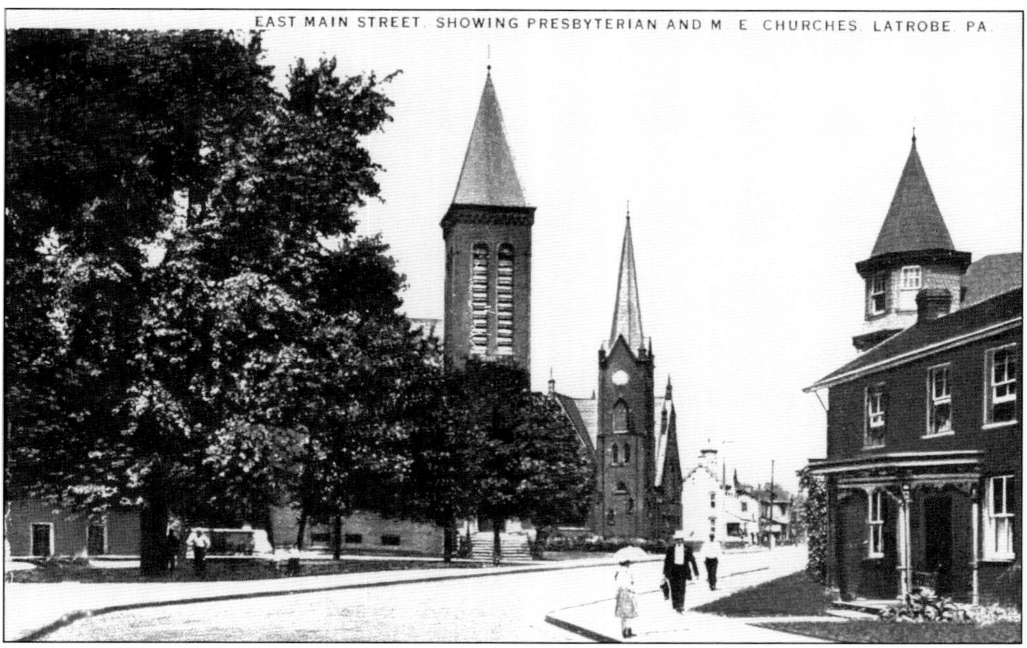

The dominating spires of both the Presbyterian and Methodist Episcopal churches are seen on this view of East Main Street. Residents of Latrobe had several choices of where to worship in the early 1900s.

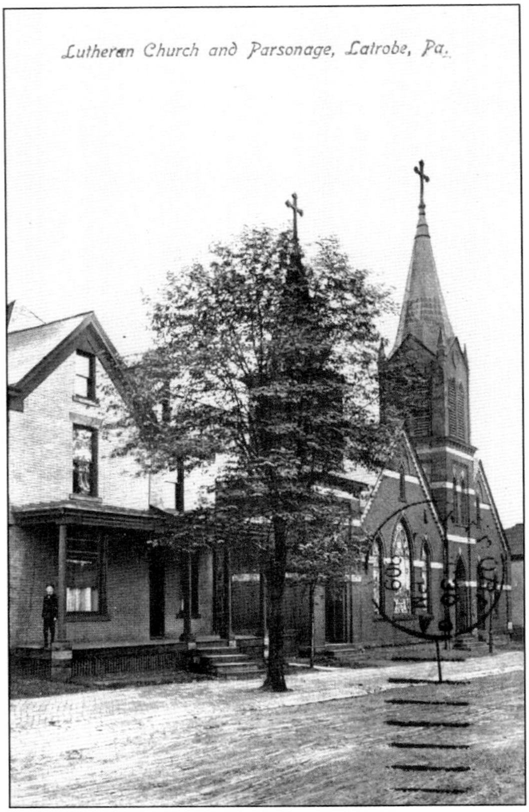

The Latrobe Lutheran Church was established in 1855. The current church, located on Weldon Street, was built in 1899 with the adjacent parsonage being added in 1901.

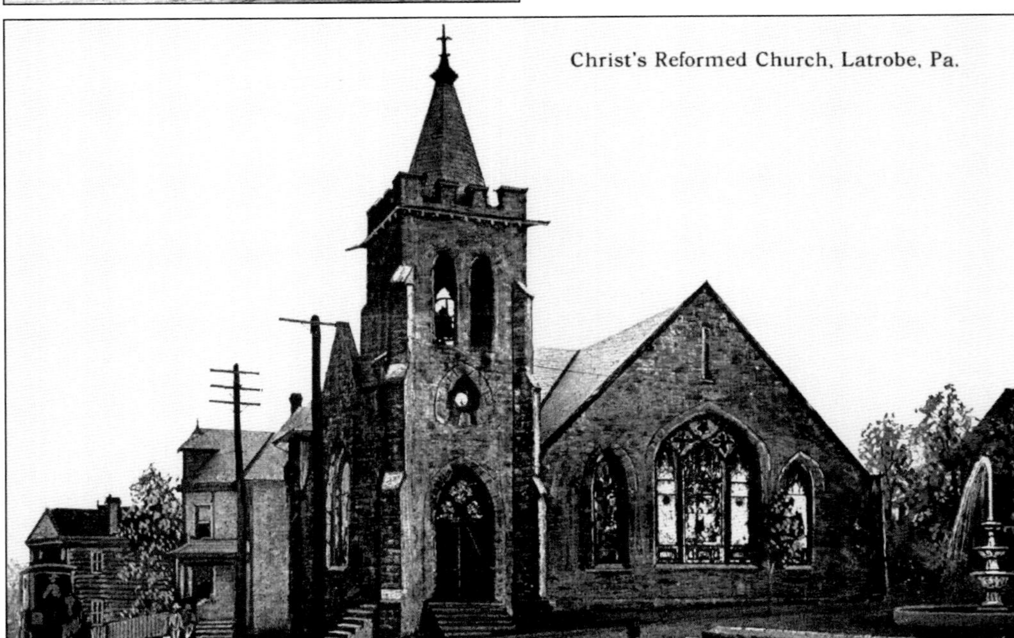

Originally connected with the Youngstown Reformed Church, the Latrobe congregation built the church shown in this postcard in 1902.

Prior to 1857, the Holy Family Catholic Church had been supplied with pastors from the nearby St. Vincent's. Located on Ligonier Street, the current church was built in 1907.

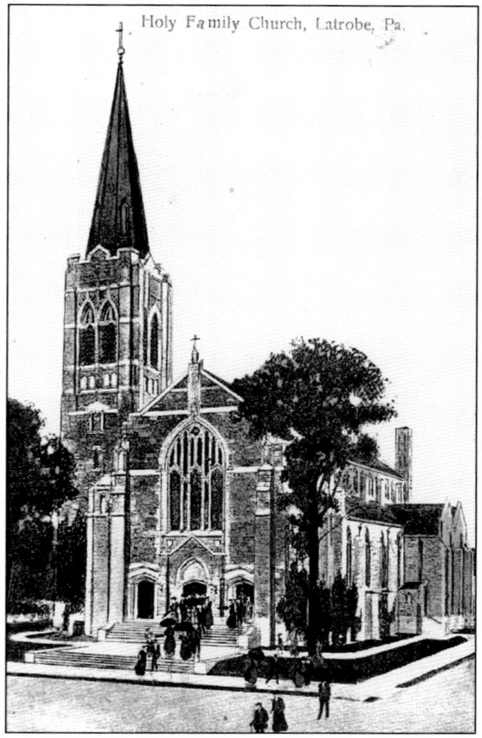

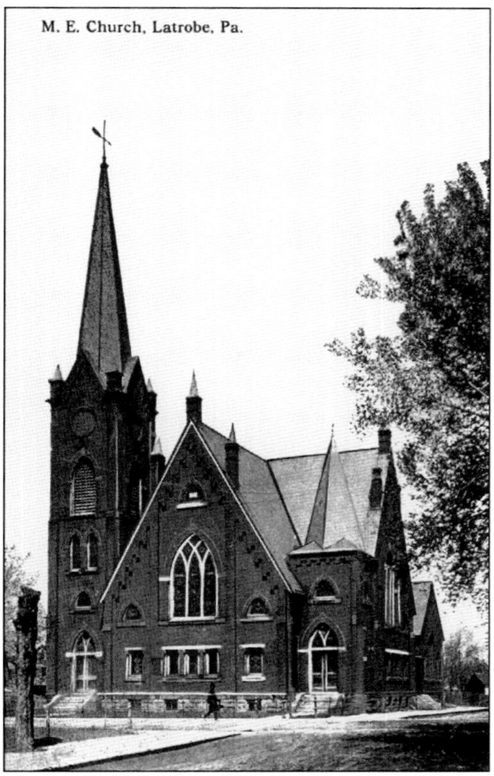

After initially holding services in the First Ward School, the Methodist Episcopal Church congregation built their current brick building in 1856. The building has gone through several renovations since then, but it has remained relatively the same.

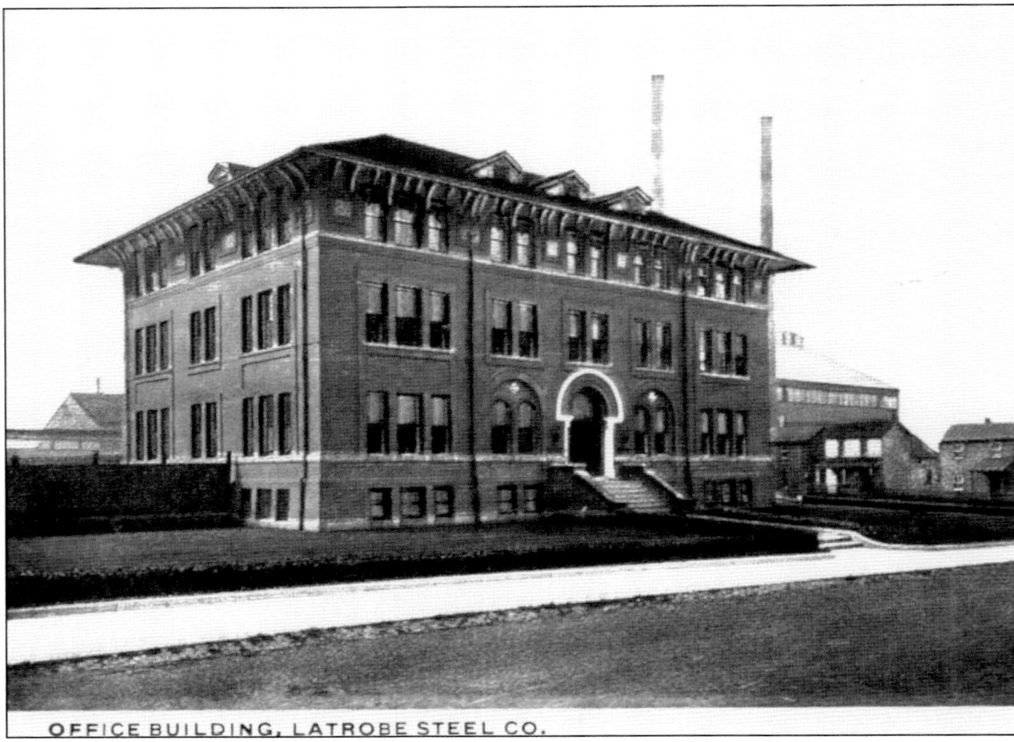

Standard Steel, which is now the oldest industrial plant still in operation in Latrobe, was founded in 1888 as Latrobe Steel Works.

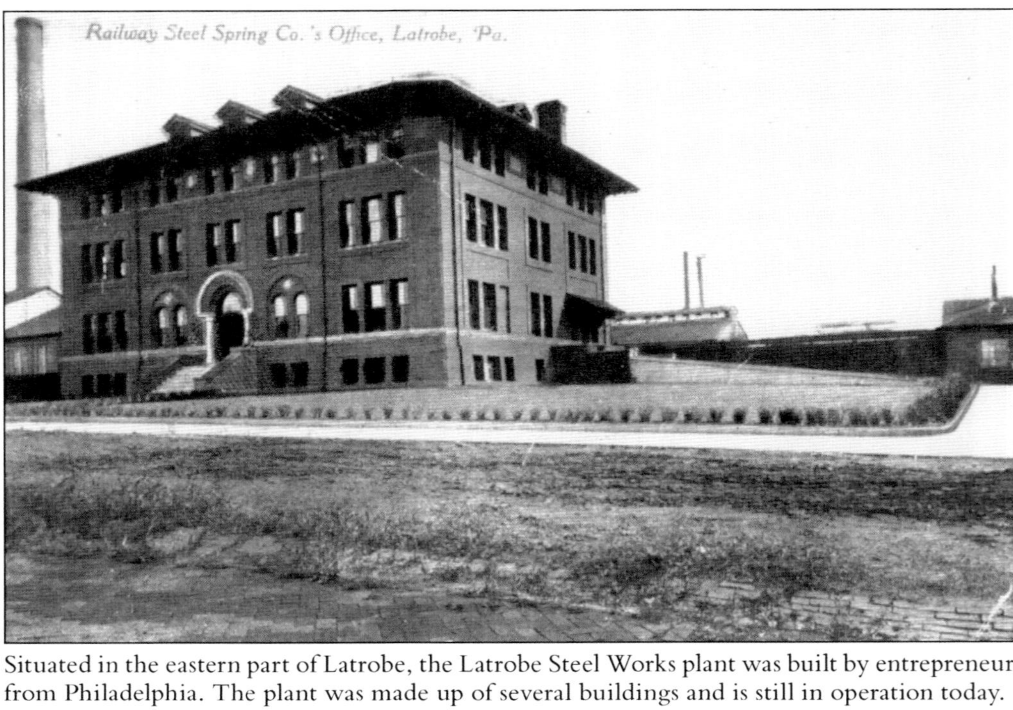

Situated in the eastern part of Latrobe, the Latrobe Steel Works plant was built by entrepreneurs from Philadelphia. The plant was made up of several buildings and is still in operation today.

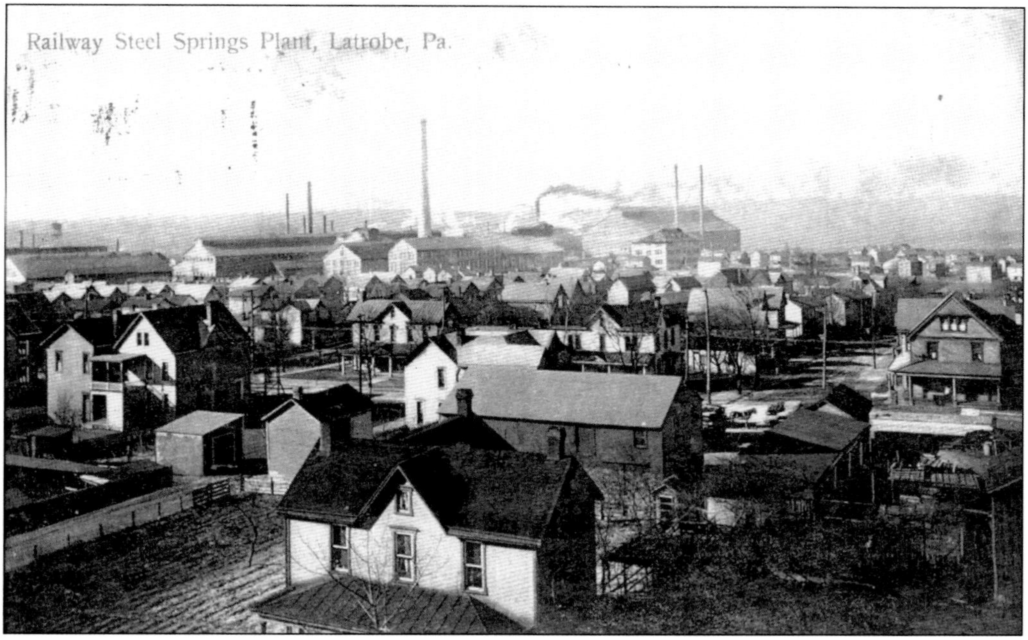

In the Latrobe area, the Ligonier Valley Railroad took on the role of an industrial switching operation, serving the Railway Steel Springs plant, Latrobe Steel, Vulcan Molf, Latrobe Foundry and Machine, and others.

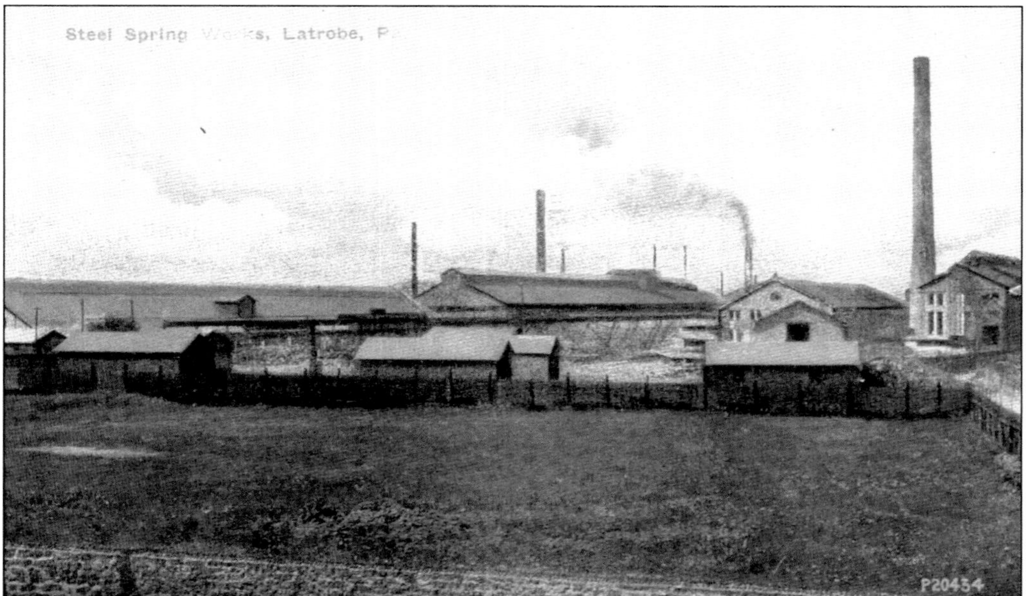

Founded in 1913 as Latrobe Electric Steel, the *electric* was dropped from the name in the 1950s. In 1998, the company officially changed its name to Timken Latrobe Steel.

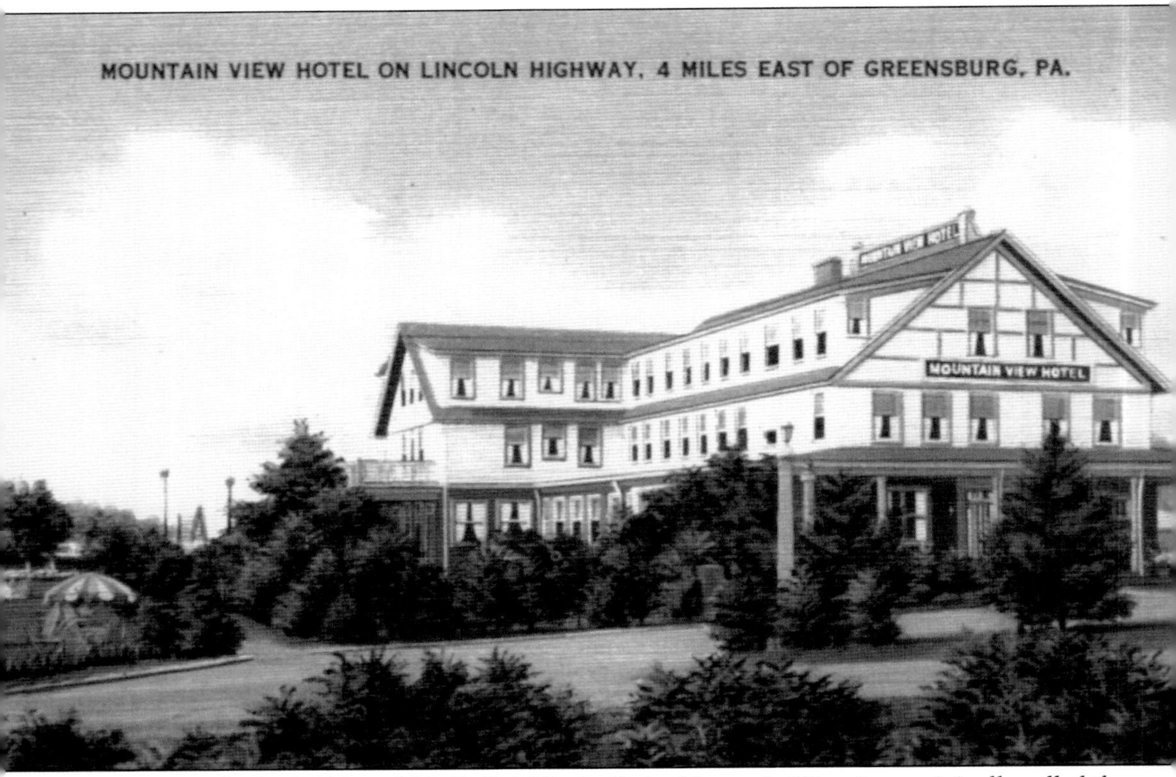

In 1924, Charles Wible and M. E. Strickler built the Mountain View Inn, originally called the Mountain View Hotel. Guests were treated to a swimming pool, sun deck, and boardwalk. After struggling through the Depression, the hotel was bought by the Booher family in 1940 and they have managed it ever since. The inn has hosted celebrities such as Pres. Ronald and Nancy Reagan, golfer Arnold Palmer, Harrison Ford, Bernadette Peters, and the Dalai Lama. The hotel is now part of the Historic Hotels of America and is one of the area's best-known inns.

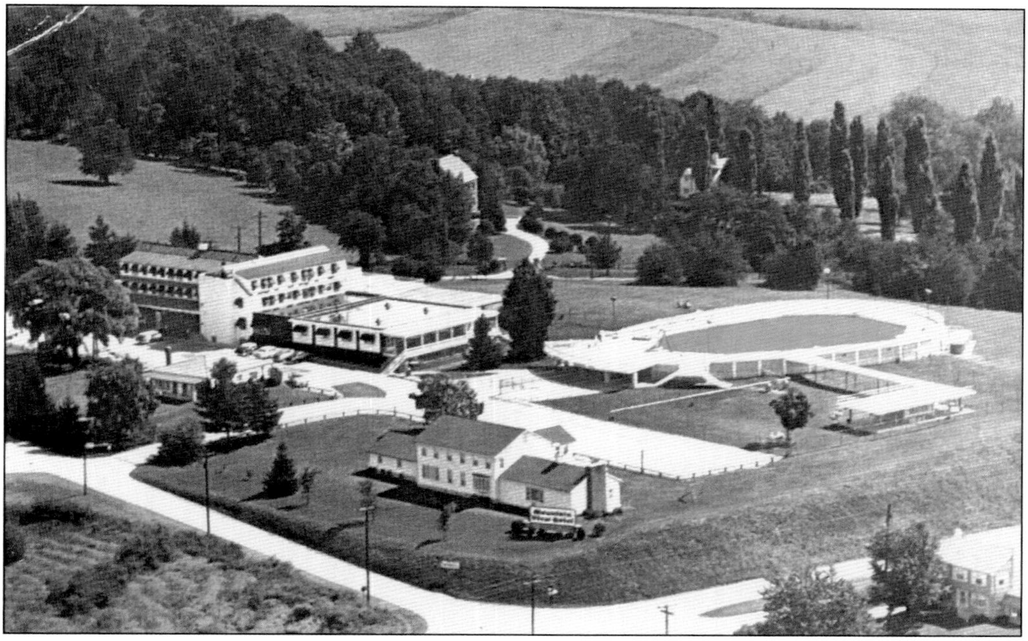

The swimming pool at Mountain View Inn was a popular summertime hangout during the 1950s and 1960s. The high dive was located at the fan-shaped end of the pool and the refreshment stand on the sun deck to the right. The pool was eventually torn down in the 1970s.

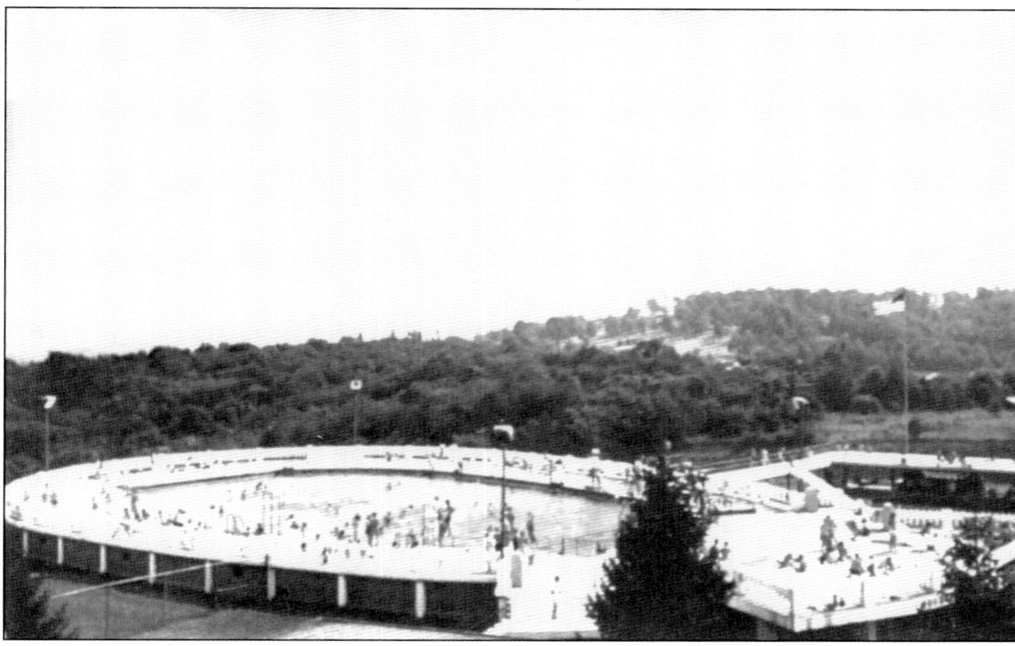

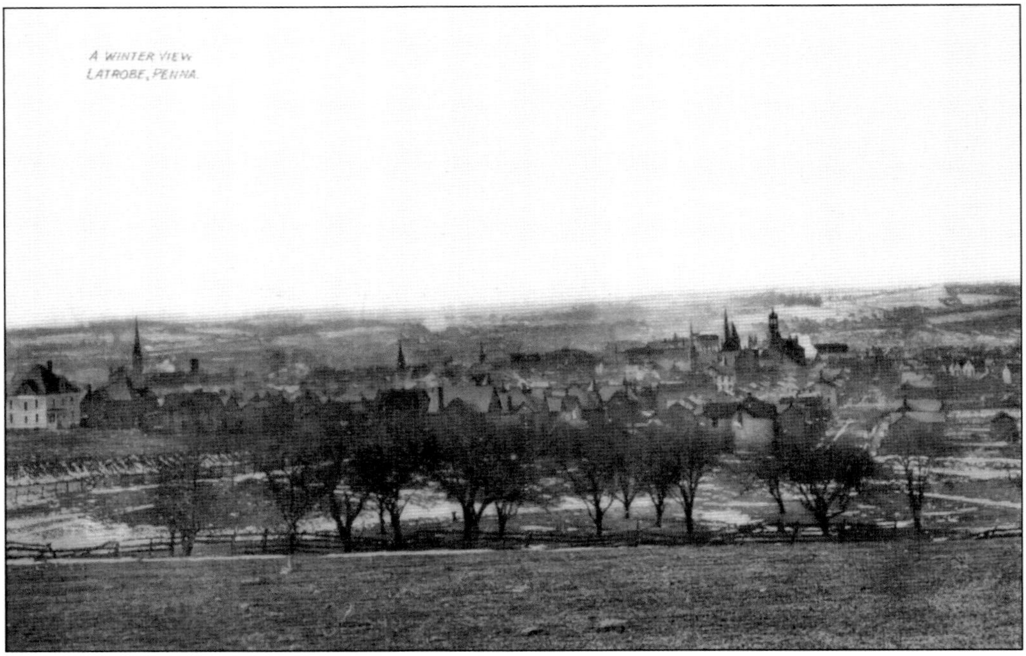

This scenic card shows a winter scene in Latrobe.

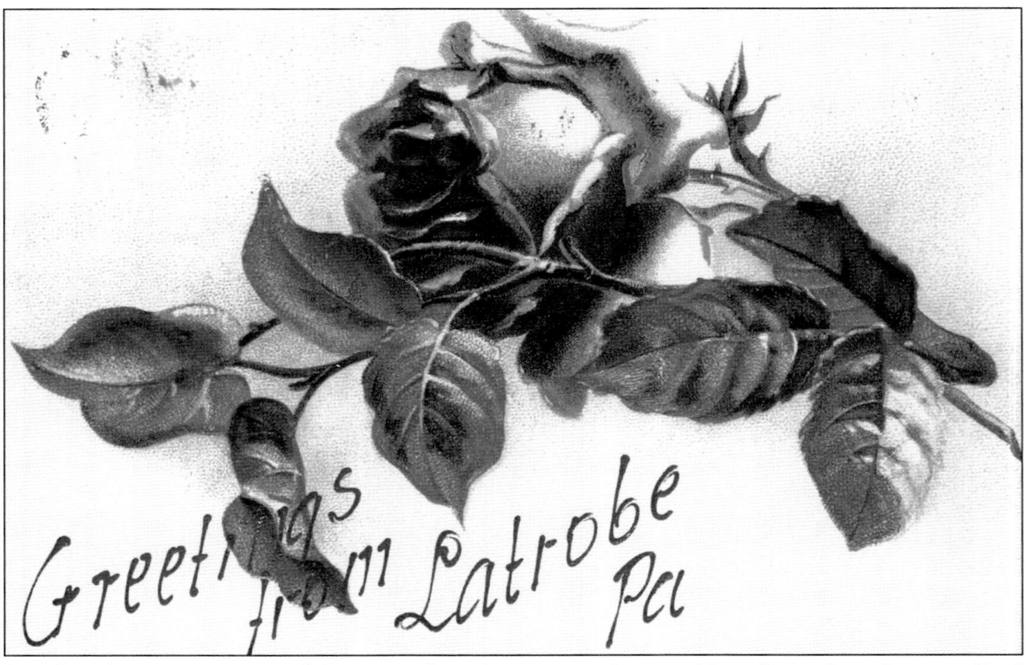

Seen here is a generic postcard from Latrobe. Many postcards were able to be made and personalized with the town's name where they were sold. This card was done using eye-catching glitter.

Two

LIGONIER

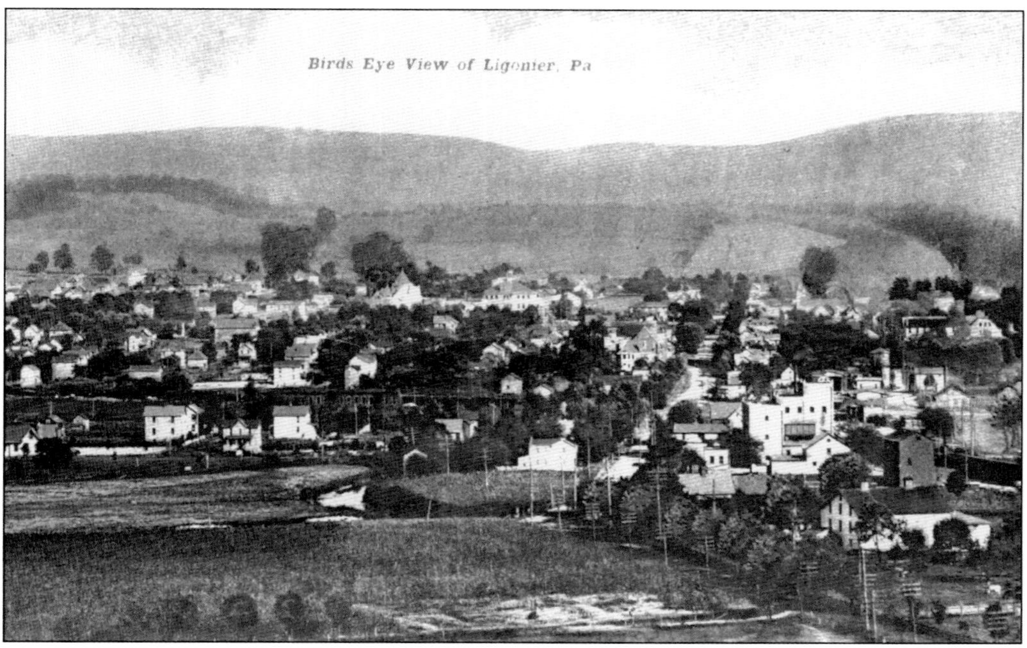

This bird's-eye view of Ligonier shows the town in its early days. In 1834, Ligonier was incorporated as a borough, and through most of the 1850s, most of Ligonier's growth occurred along Main Street, referred to as the "turnpike corridor."

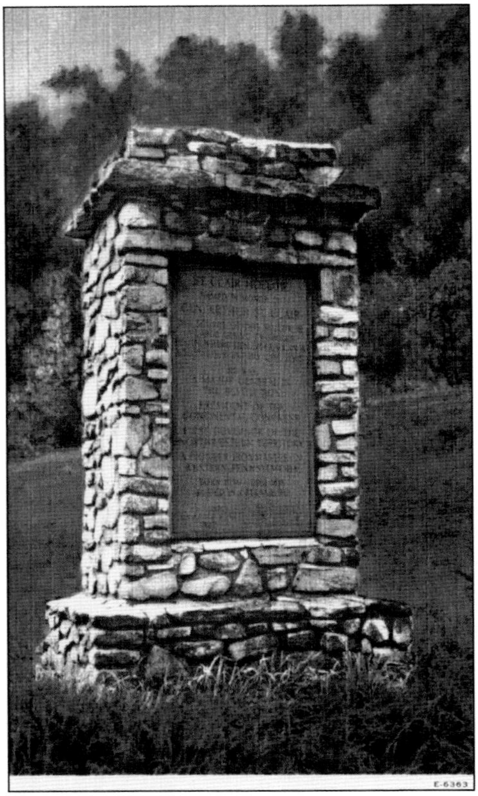

This marker, located in St. Clair Hollow, was named after Gen. Arthur St. Clair. The land was granted to St. Clair in September 1783 by the General Assembly of Pennsylvania. This monument marks the location of the log cabin where St. Clair lived during his later years.

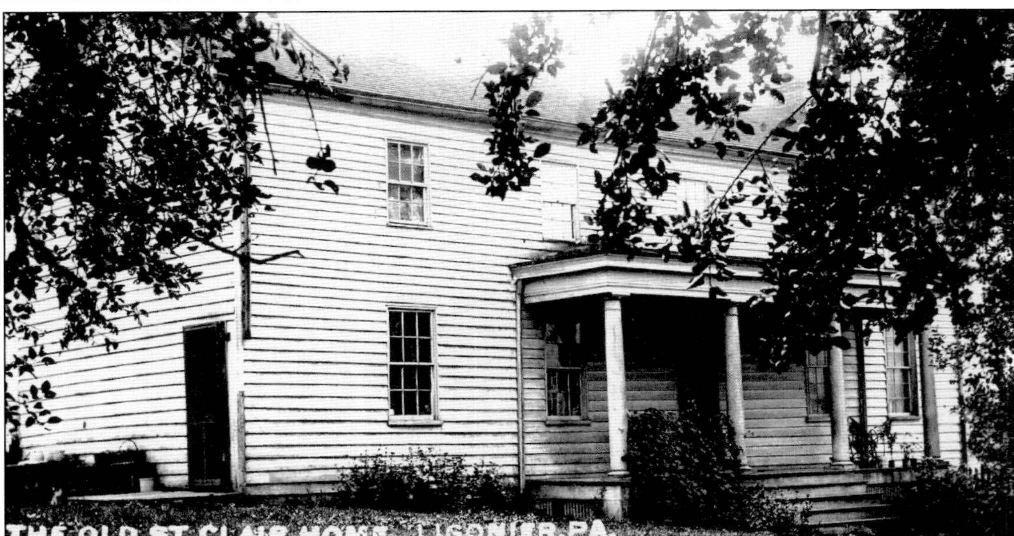

The Arthur St. Clair home, called the Hermitage, was built on several hundred acres near Ligonier. Often St. Clair had to finance his own governmental appointments, including financing his troops in the Northwest Territories. Although he was promised repayment, the money never came. Eventually St. Clair's properties, including the Hermitage, were sold at sheriff's sales to repay creditors. Nothing remains of the house today.

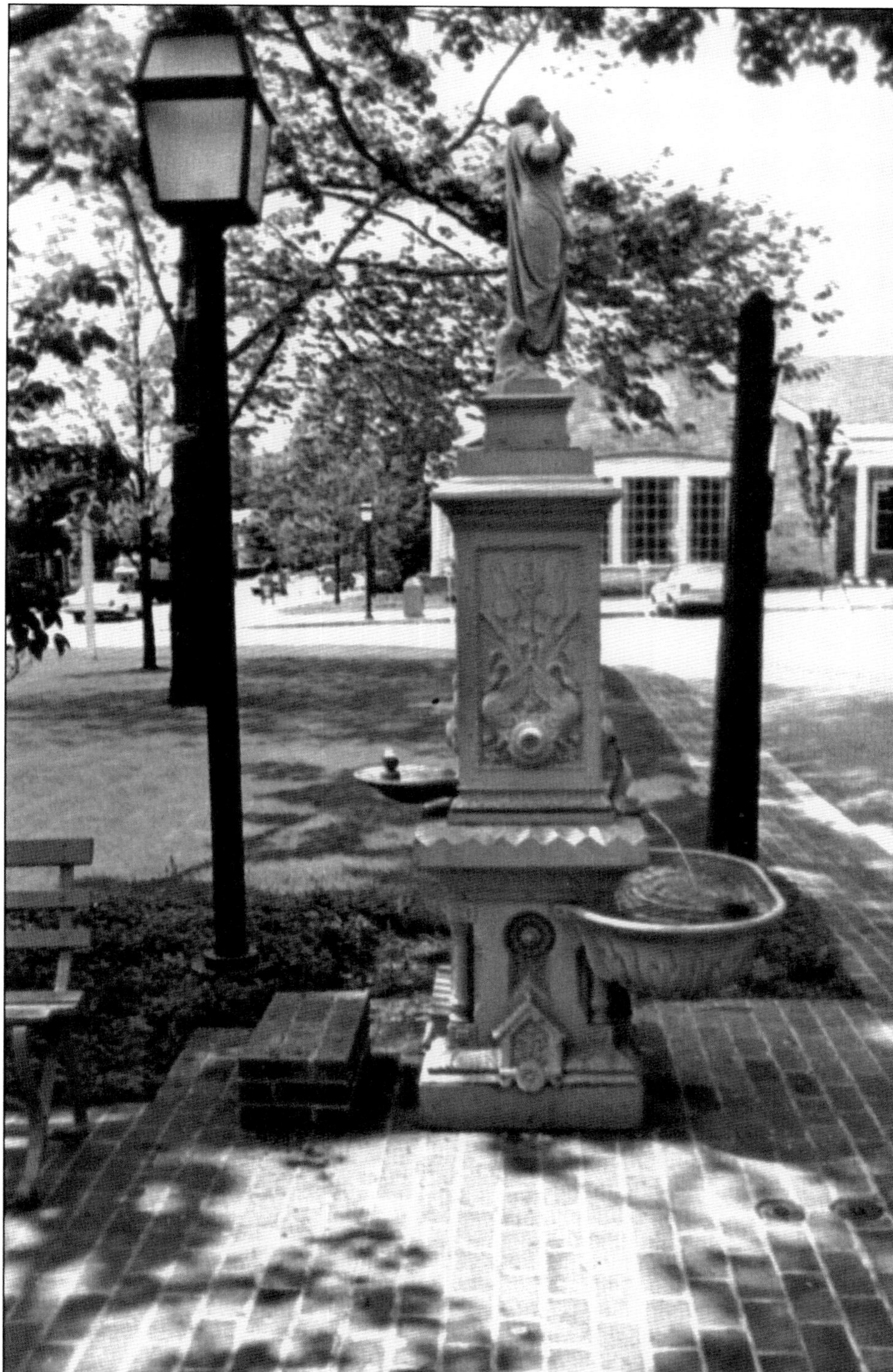

The fountain on the Ligonier diamond, which was built at the beginning of the 19th century, features three troughs—one for horses, one for humans, and one for dogs.

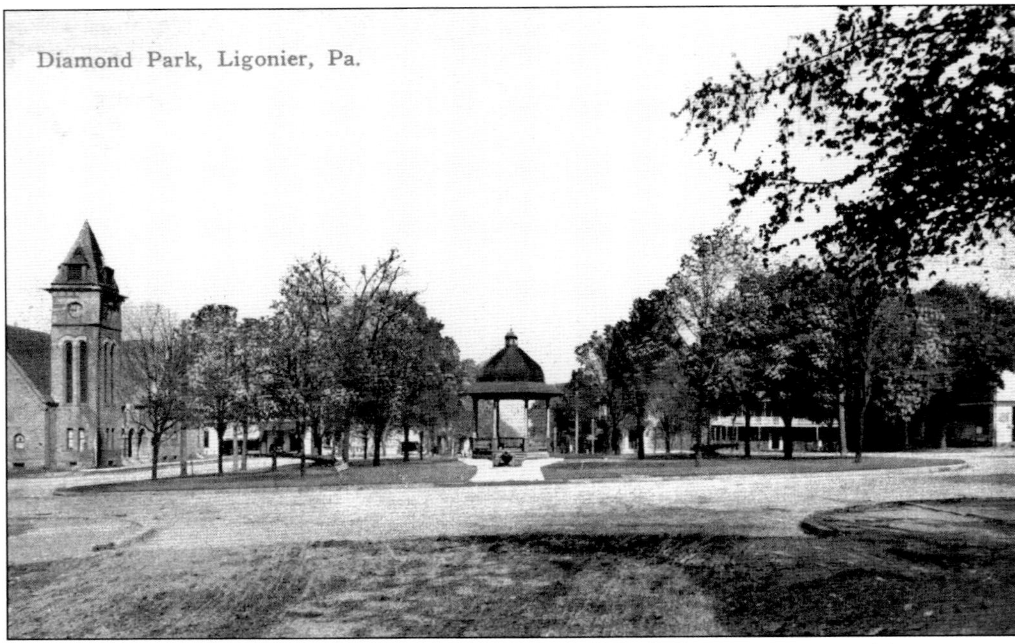

The original plan for Ligonier, developed by John Ramsey, was based on his public square, or diamond plan. This original plan consisted of about four blocks. The town square eventually became the hub of social and business activity.

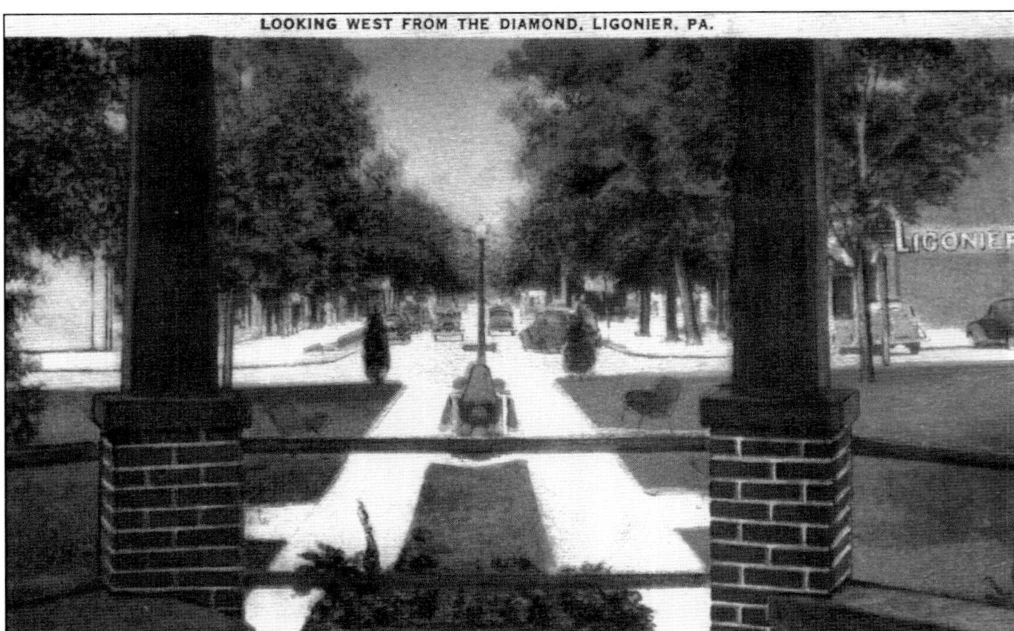

As one of Ligonier's most prominent landmarks, many postcards have been printed of the diamond over the years.

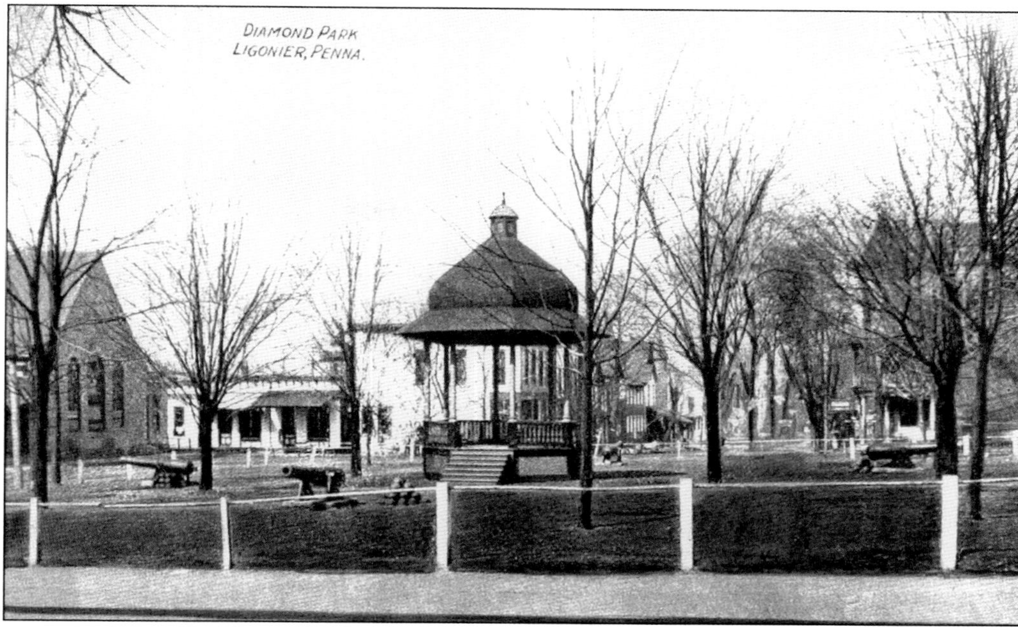

The Civil War cannons pictured in the foreground were donated by Congressman George F. Huff to the Ligonier GAR post. The guns remained on the diamond until World War II, when they were donated to the war scrap effort.

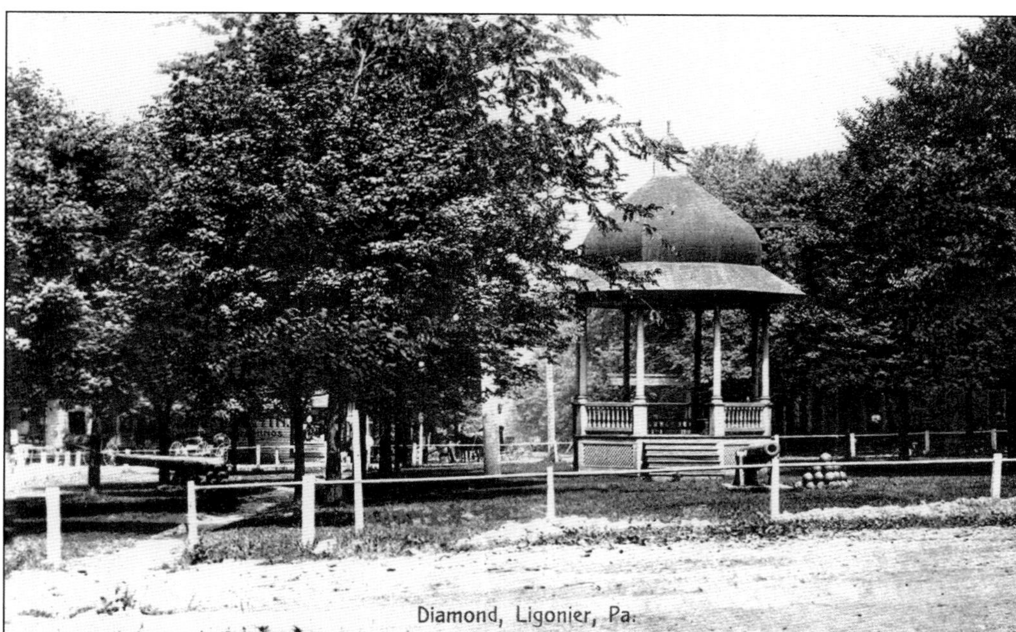

The Ligonier diamond is now purely decorative, but at one time coaches and wagons could park there for the night and the diamond even had a corral with hitching posts for livestock.

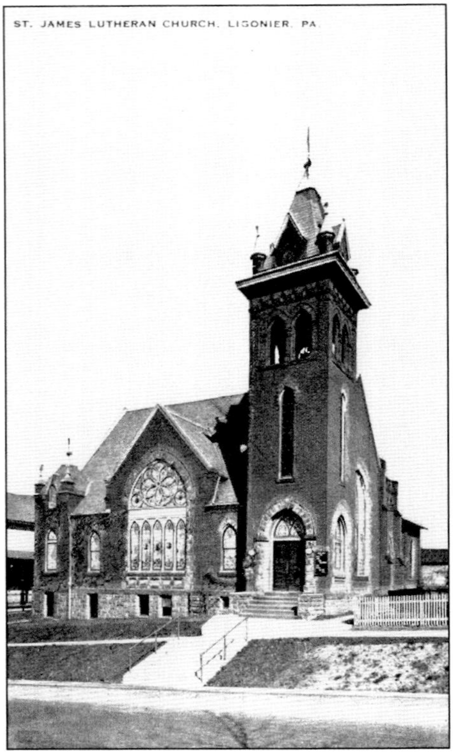

The St. James Lutheran Church was dedicated in 1851 on West Main Street. In 1882, a parsonage was added to the church. In 1898, the present church was built, utilizing some of the original church's walls. A new parsonage was added in 1958.

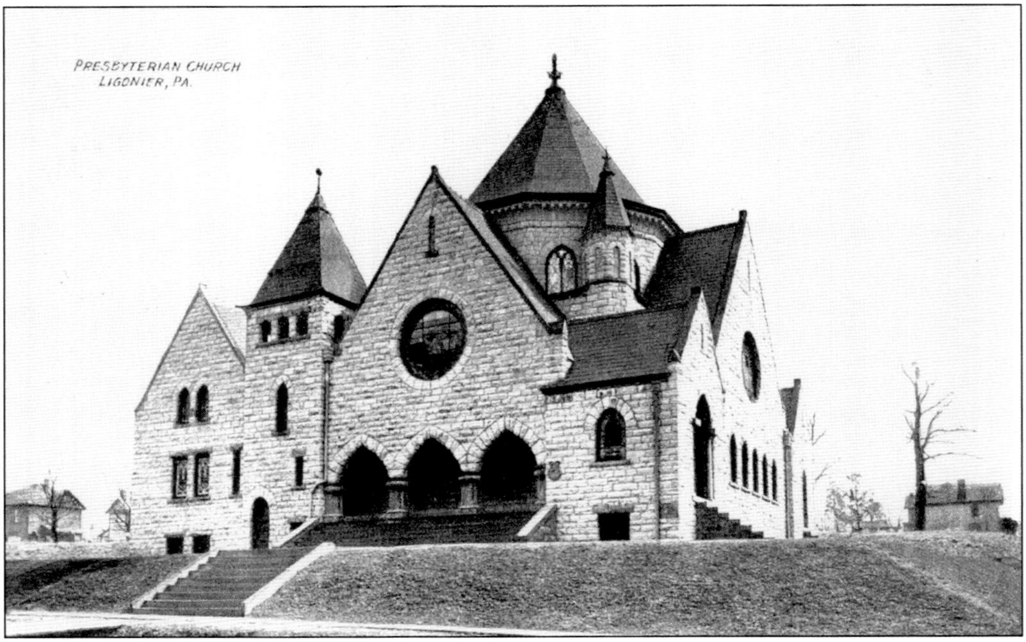

In 1817, the Covenant Presbyterian Church formed, building first a small, brick building in 1820. In 1847, the congregation built a larger facility. The cornerstone for the present church was laid in 1902. Constructed from sandstone from the McCance quarries, the church was dedicated in 1904.

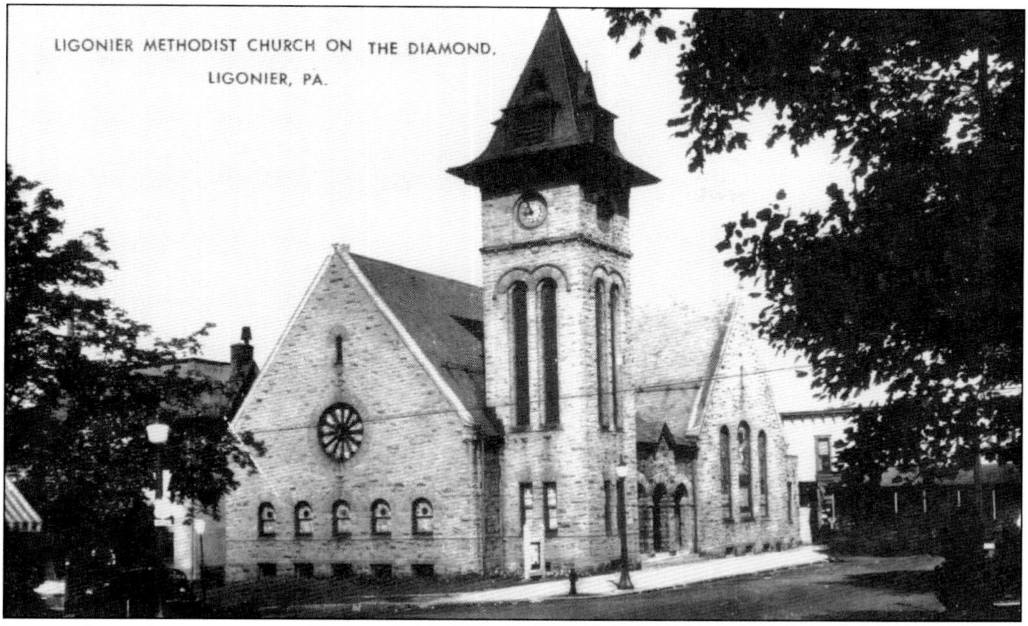

Located on the Ligonier Diamond at West Main and South Market Streets, the Methodist congregation moved to a brick church and parsonage at this location in 1857. The brick church was torn down in 1902.

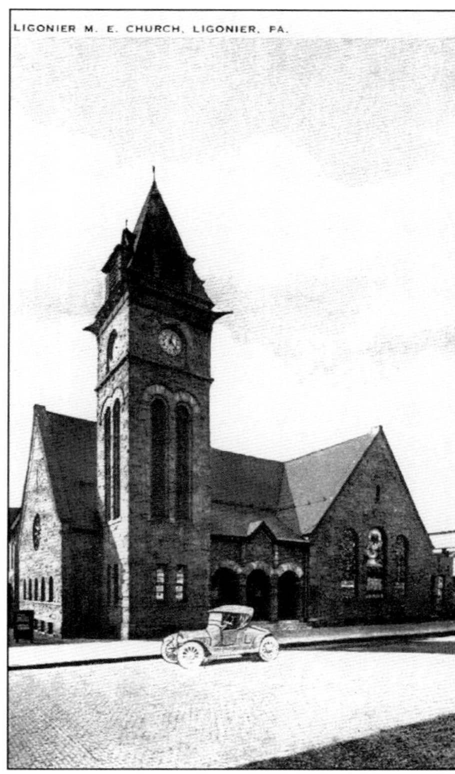

Built of bluestone obtained from the Byers and Denny families, who were members of the congregation, this new building replaced the Methodist Church's former brick building. Built in the same location on West Main and South Market Streets, the building was dedicated in 1903.

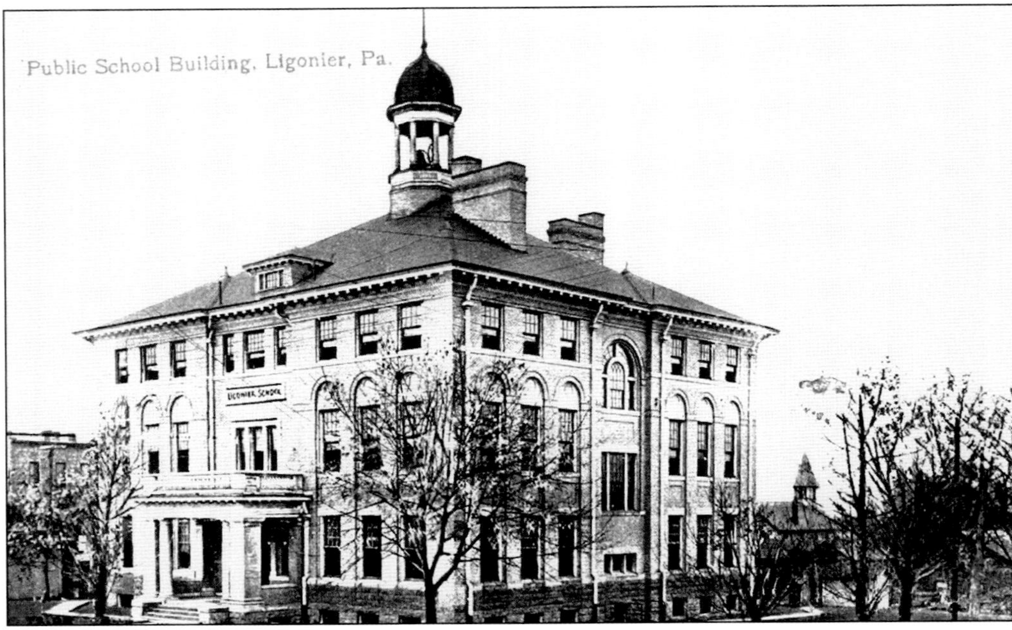

The first public school in Ligonier Borough was built on Church Street and was located between the Methodist and Presbyterian churches. The Dickinson School, which is shown in this picture, was built in 1903. The school has since been torn down and is now a municipal parking lot.

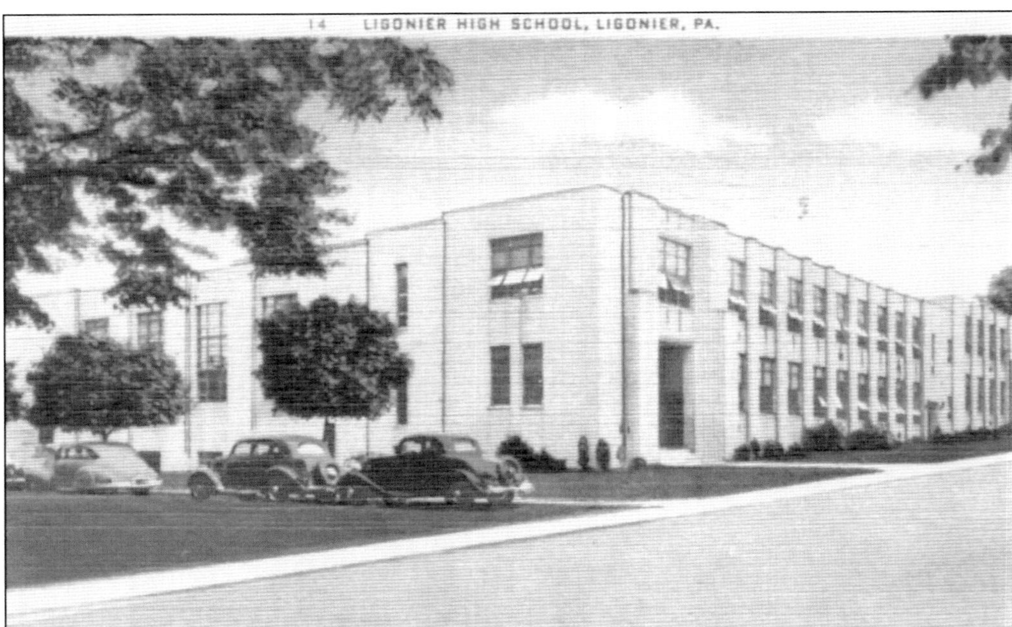

Ground was broken for a new high school in 1923. In 1932, the first section opened with six classrooms and an auditorium. A gymnasium and eight additional classrooms were added in 1936. Today the old high school serves as the home for the YMCA.

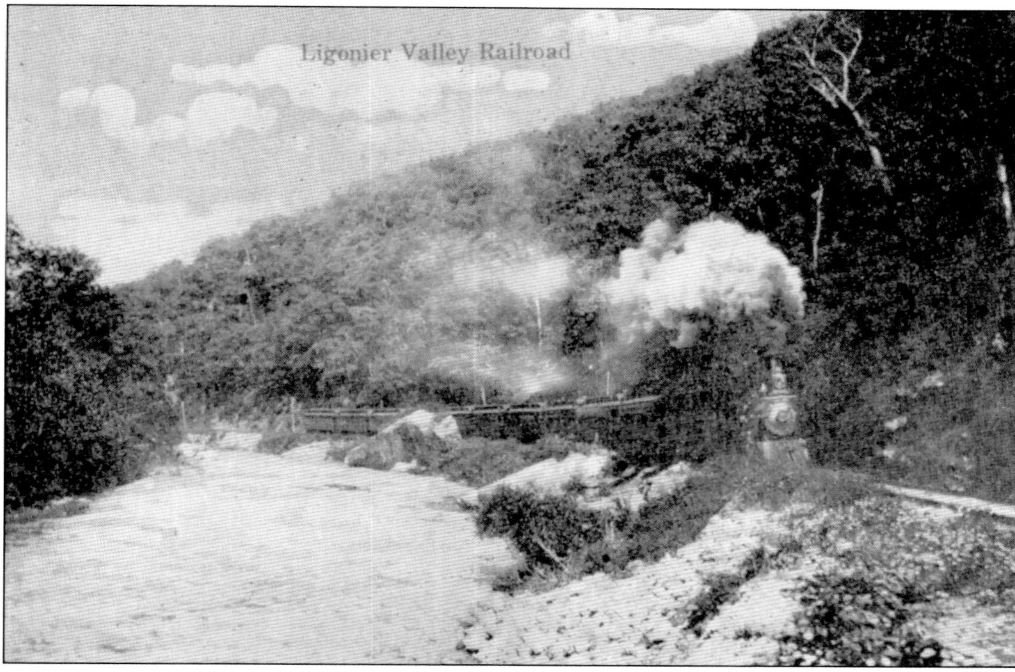

The Ligonier Valley's lumber, stone, and coal resources lead to the development of the Ligonier and Latrobe Rail Road in 1853. The line connected to the Pennsylvania Railroad main line in Latrobe.

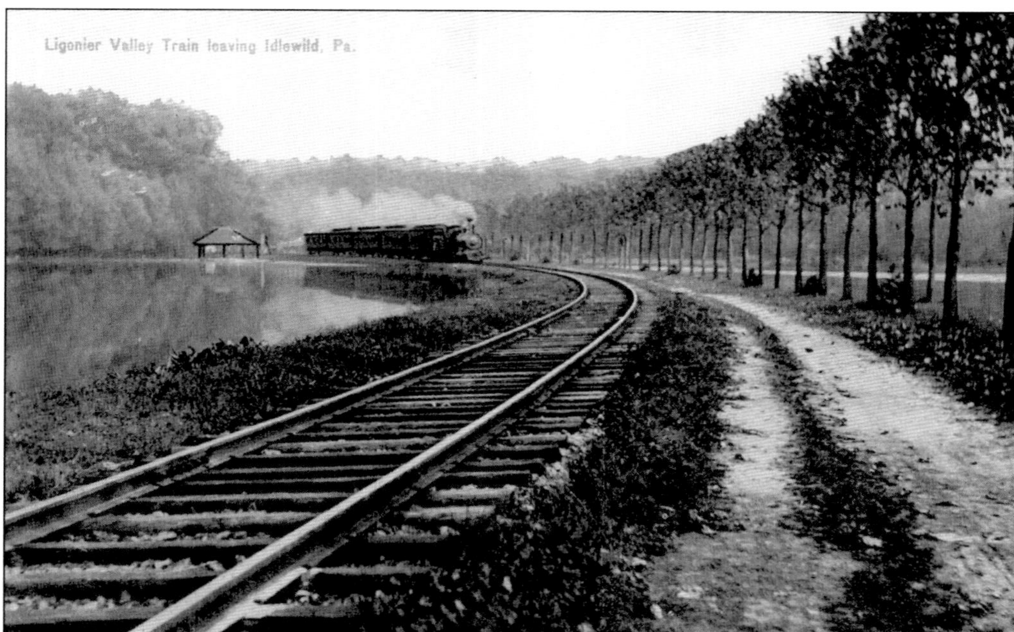

Judge Thomas Mellon bought the Ligonier and Latrobe Rail Road in 1871 when the line was still incomplete. Mellon changed the name to the Ligonier Valley Railroad and completed the line in 1877. The railroad operated under that name until its last run in 1952.

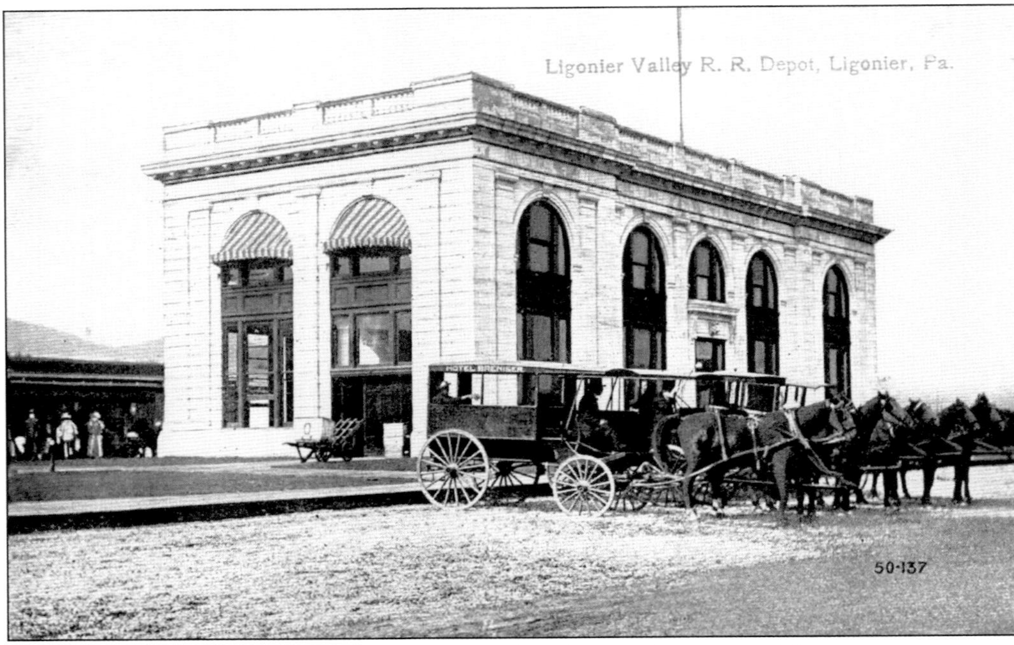

This postcard featuring the Ligonier Valley Railroad depot shows several livery wagons waiting to transport passengers to the local resort hotels. The railroad's new stone building held ticket offices, a baggage room, and waiting rooms on the first floor. On the second floor were the railroad offices.

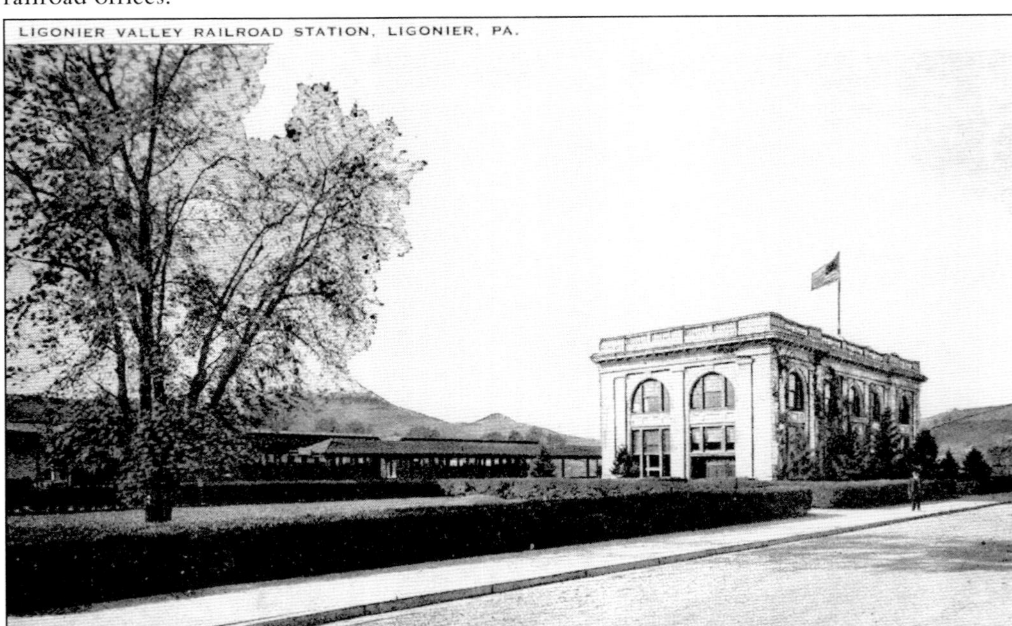

Part of the Ligonier Valley Railroad, this was Ligonier's second railroad station. The first was a wood frame building off Main Street. In 1910, the depot was moved to the more spacious stone building. After the railroad's last run in 1952, the Pennsylvania Game Commission purchased the building for its offices.

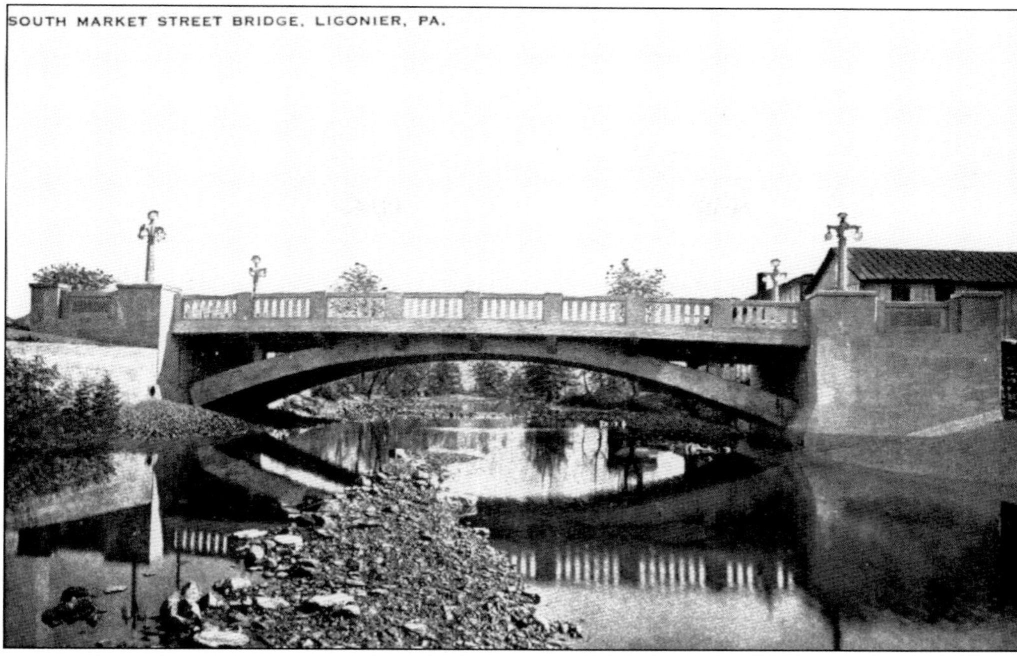

This postcard shows the South Market Street Bridge crossing the Loyalhanna Creek before Route 30 was improved.

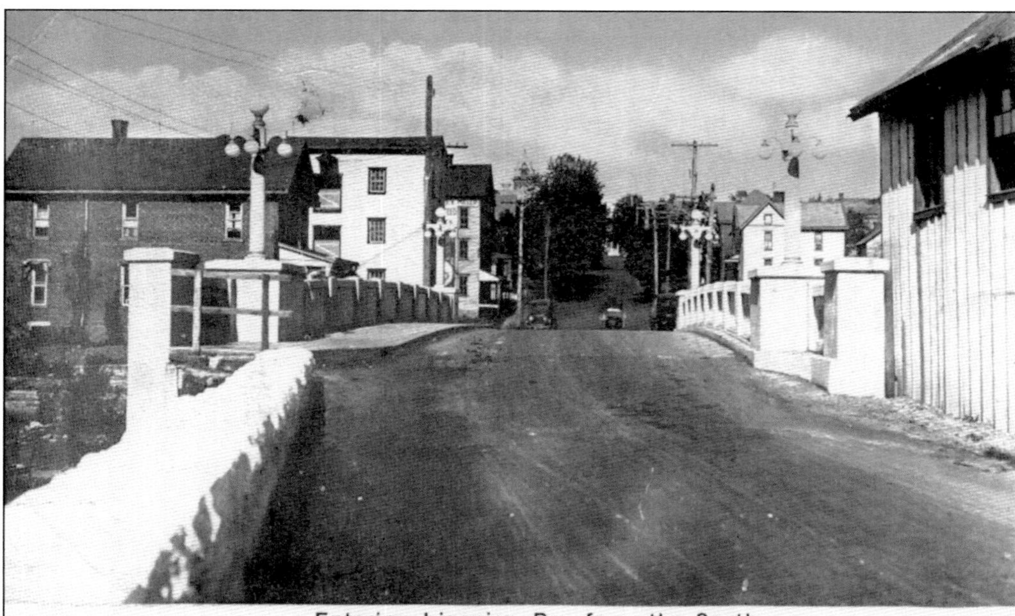

Visitors to Ligonier crossed the South Market Street Bridge. The bridge was adorned with globe light fixtures. Many of the buildings in this postcard are no longer standing or have undergone renovations.

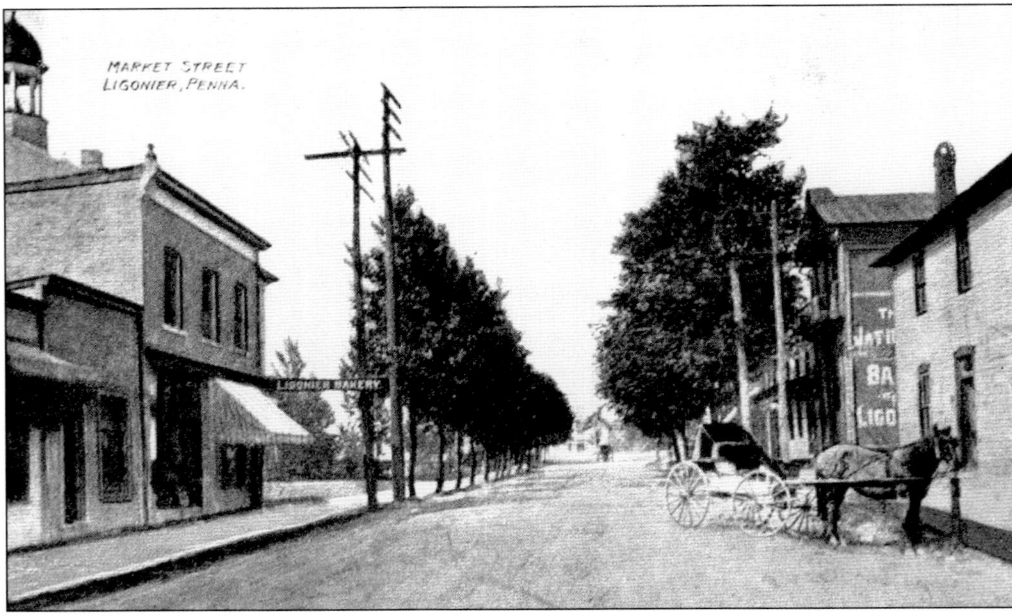

Visible on the left of this postcard is the Ligonier Bakery. The tower to the public school is also visible on the far left. The municipal parking lot is now where the school once stood.

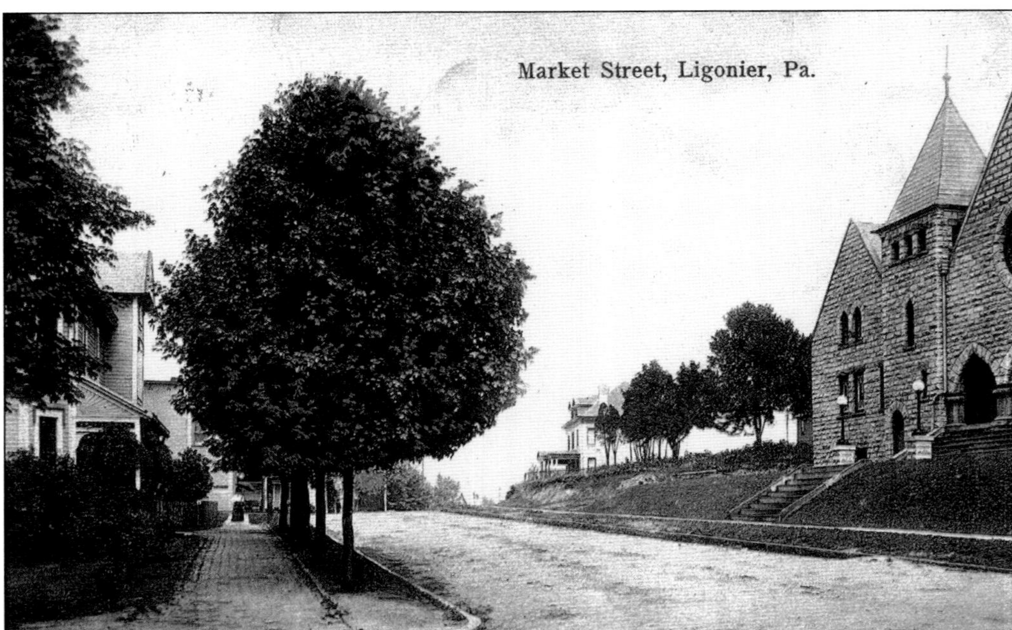

This postcard shows a view of North Market Street with the Covenant Presbyterian Church on the right.

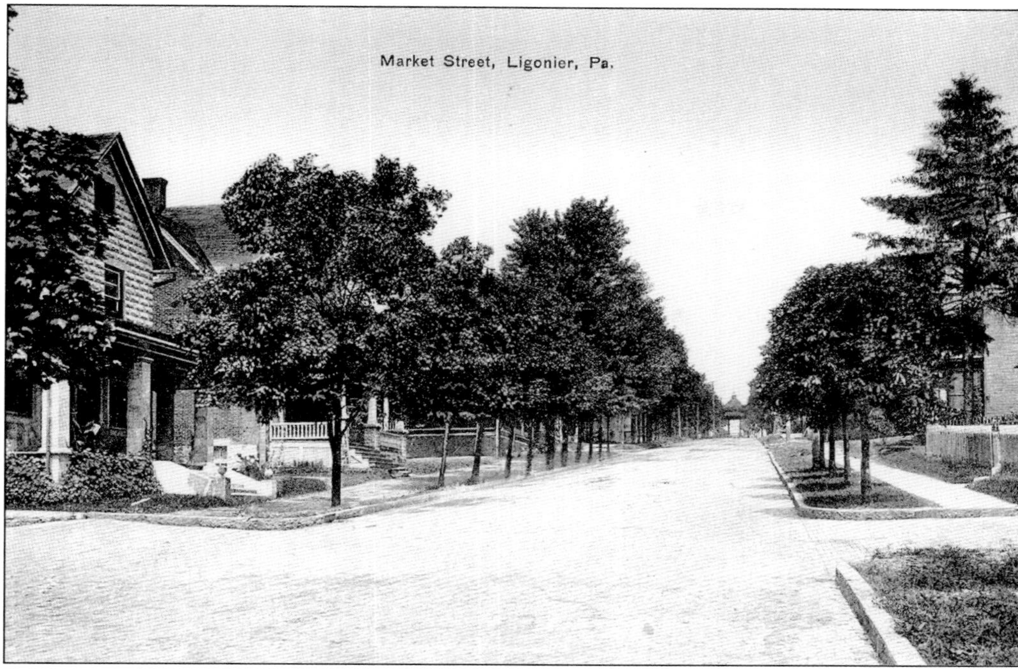

This view of Market Street shows the tree-lined streets leading up to the Ligonier Diamond. Many of these houses have been converted into shops and offices since the days that this postcard was taken.

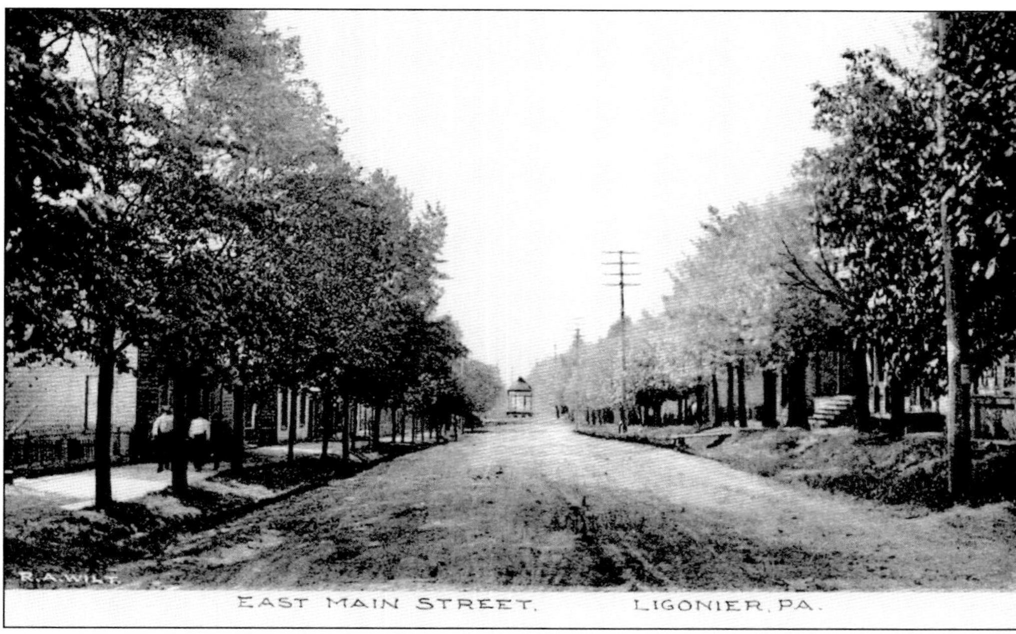

The view of East Main Street is looking west toward the Ligonier Diamond. At that time the road was unpaved, as can be seen by the buggy tracks. Today many of these houses contain specialty shops.

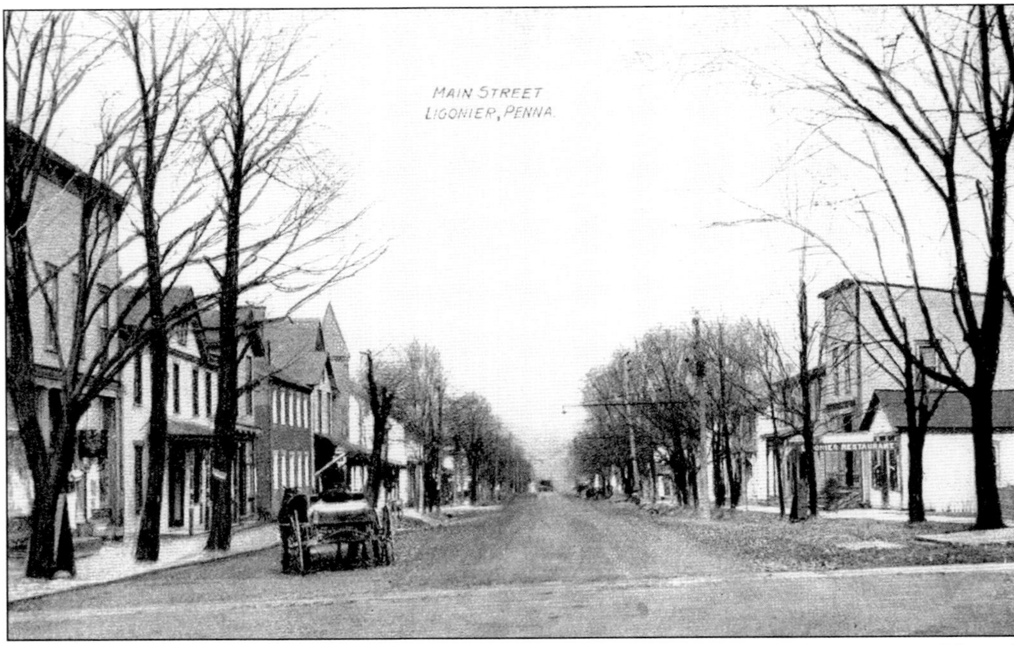

This view of Main Street shows the Ligonier Restaurant on the right side of the street. Although the streets are still unpaved and the method of travel is still horse and buggy, the town has been wired with electricity, as is evidenced by the streetlamp.

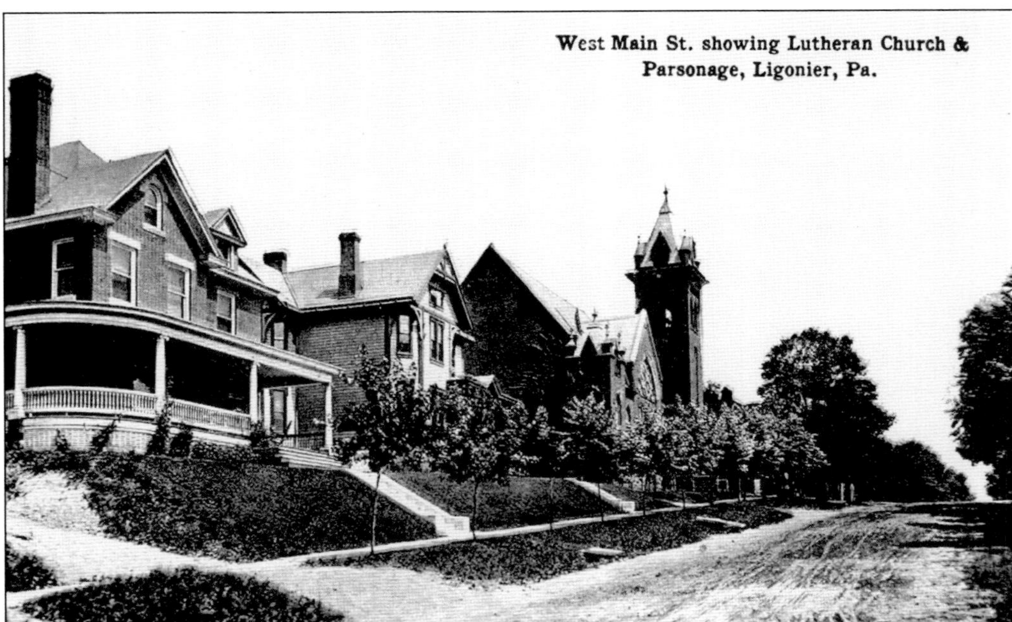

This view of West Main Street shows the tree-lined streets and fine houses of Ligonier's wealthy. On the corner, farther up the street is the Lutheran church and parsonage.

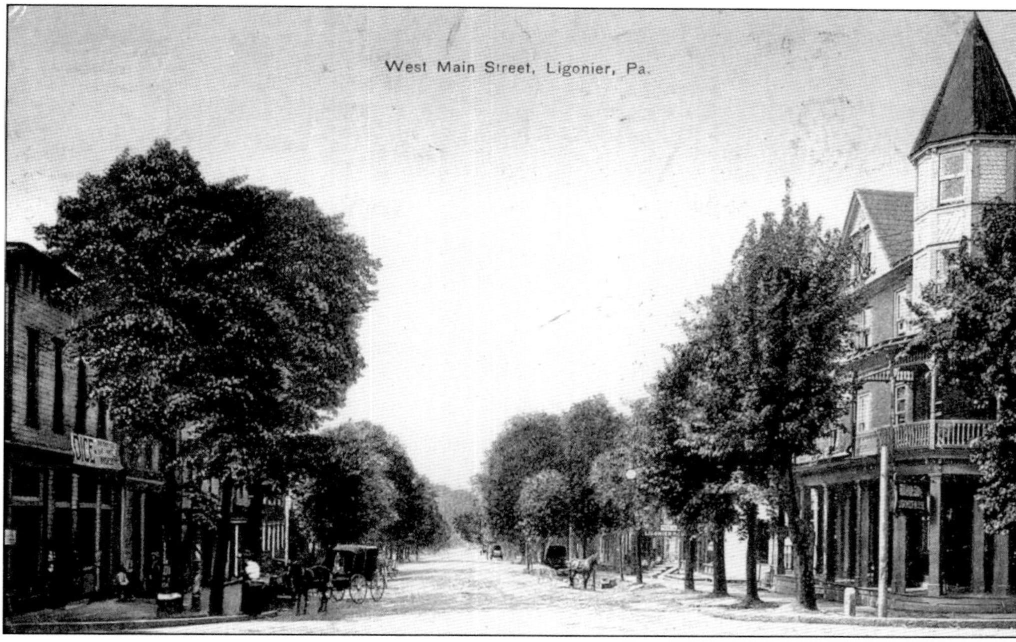

This view looking west from the Ligonier Diamond shows the Frank Building on the left. Built in the 1860s, the building was bought by Benn Kline in 1915, and the family ran a store there for years. Sam Dice also owned a barbershop in the same building.

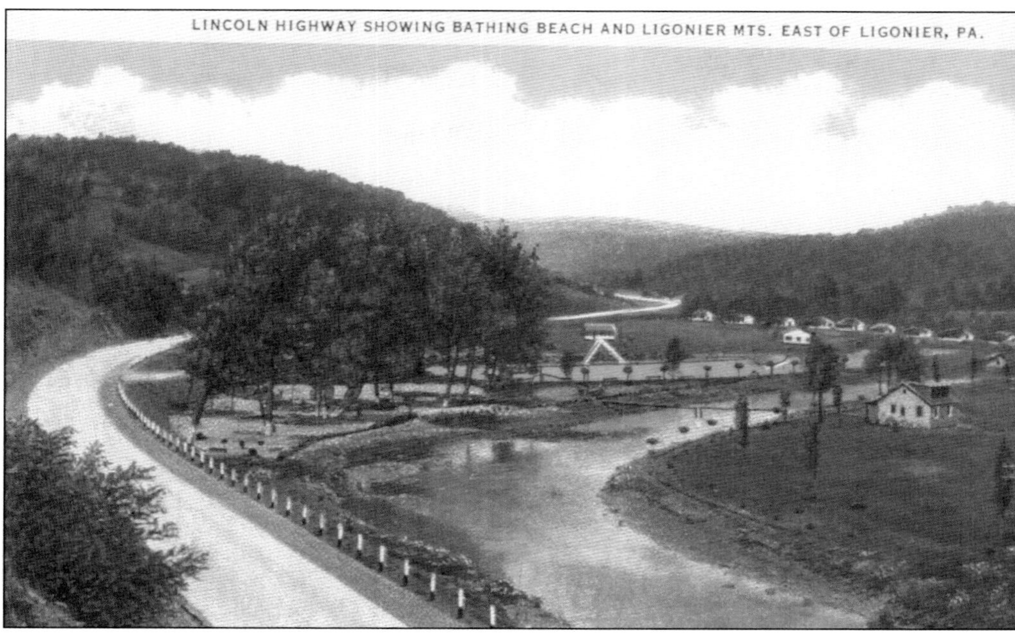

In 1908, the front page of the *Greensburg Daily Tribune* featured an item warning local citizens to beware of a "Sun-Tatooing" fad in which young women were wearing peek-a-boo blouses with arrows, hearts, flowers, and other designs burned into their otherwise beautiful white shoulders through the openings in their blouses.

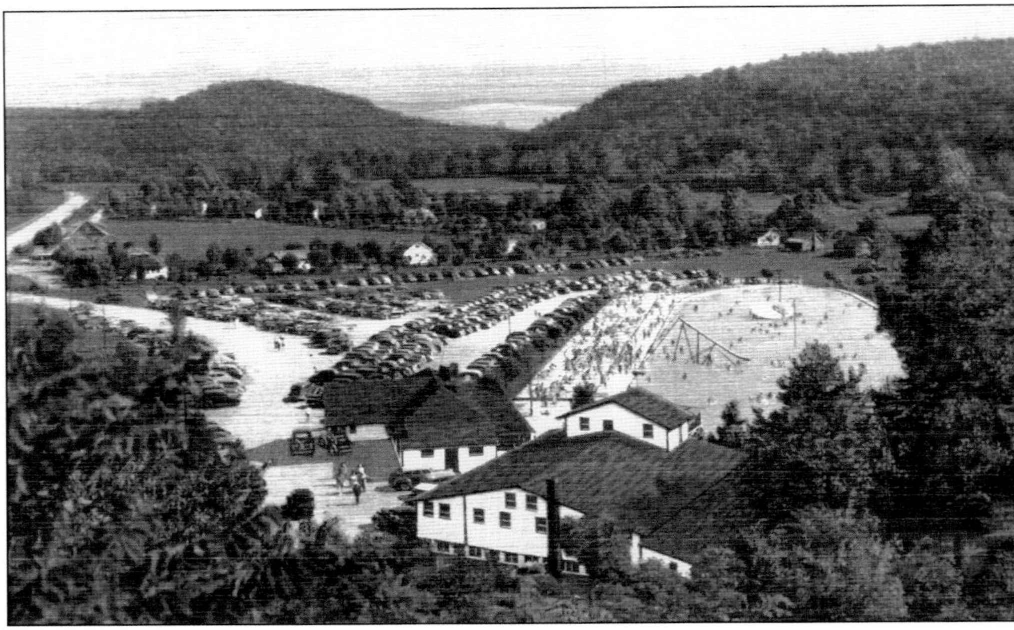

The Ligonier Valley Bathing Beach opened on July 4, 1925. It is 400 feet long and 125 feet wide and features a man-made sand beach, a slide, and a dance pavilion. Steps used to access the pool and beach before the Lincoln Highway was rerouted. Before becoming famous under the name Dean Martin, Dino Crocetti performed there.

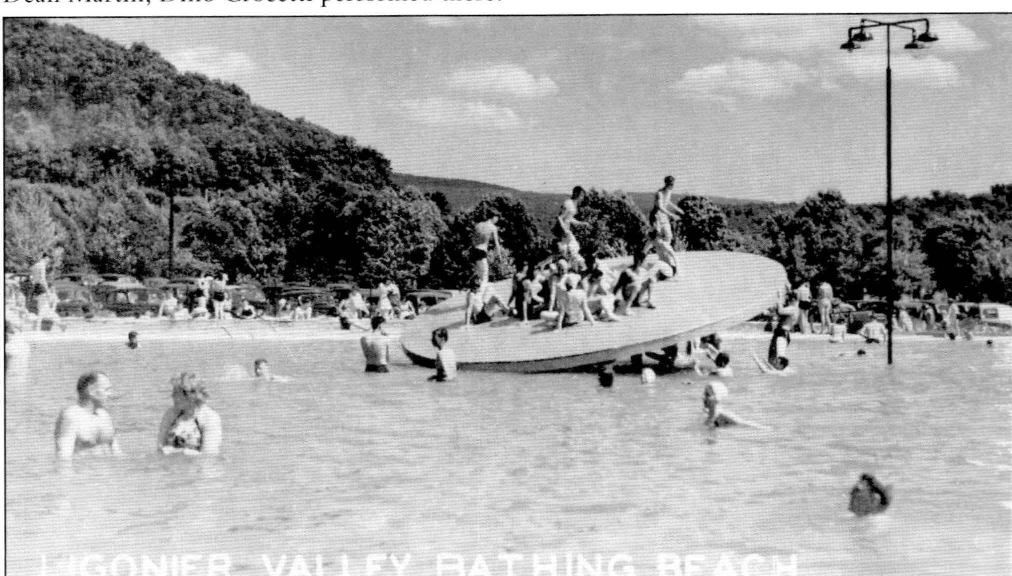

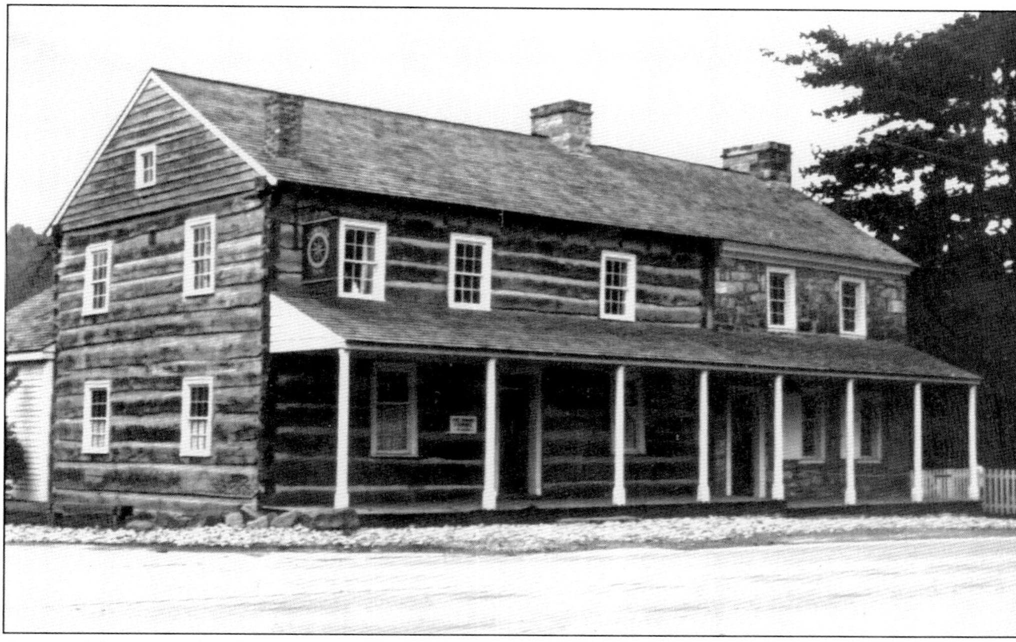

A Laughlintown landmark since 1799 when Phillip Freeman bought the land from Robert Laughlin, the Compass Inn served the area until 1862 when the introduction of the railroads cut into turnpike travel. The inn was then converted into a family home. Eventually it was sold to the Ligonier Valley Historical Society, which restored it to its original 1830 appearance as a stagecoach inn.

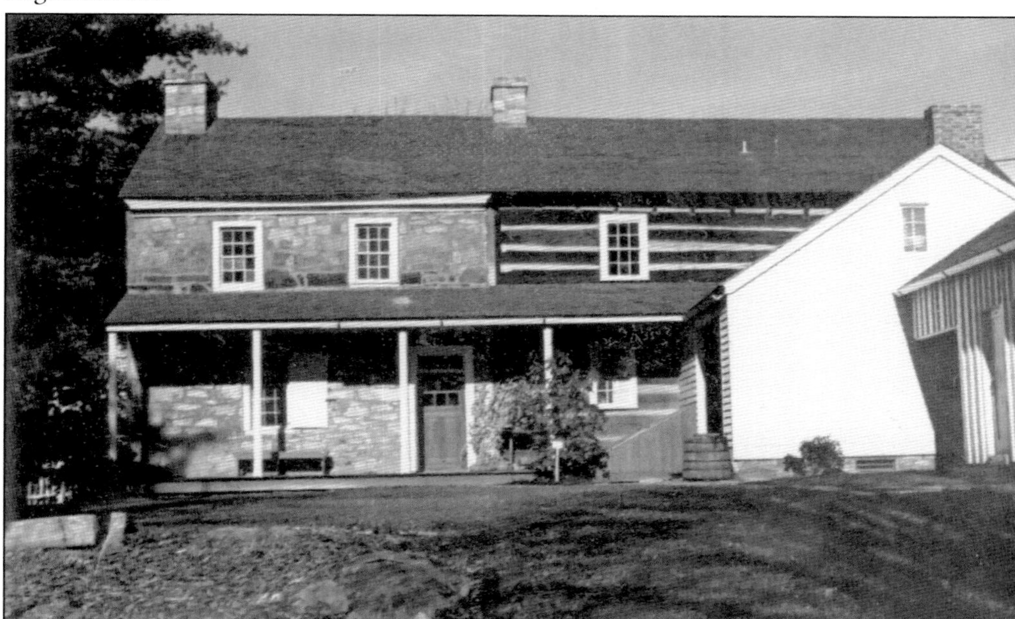

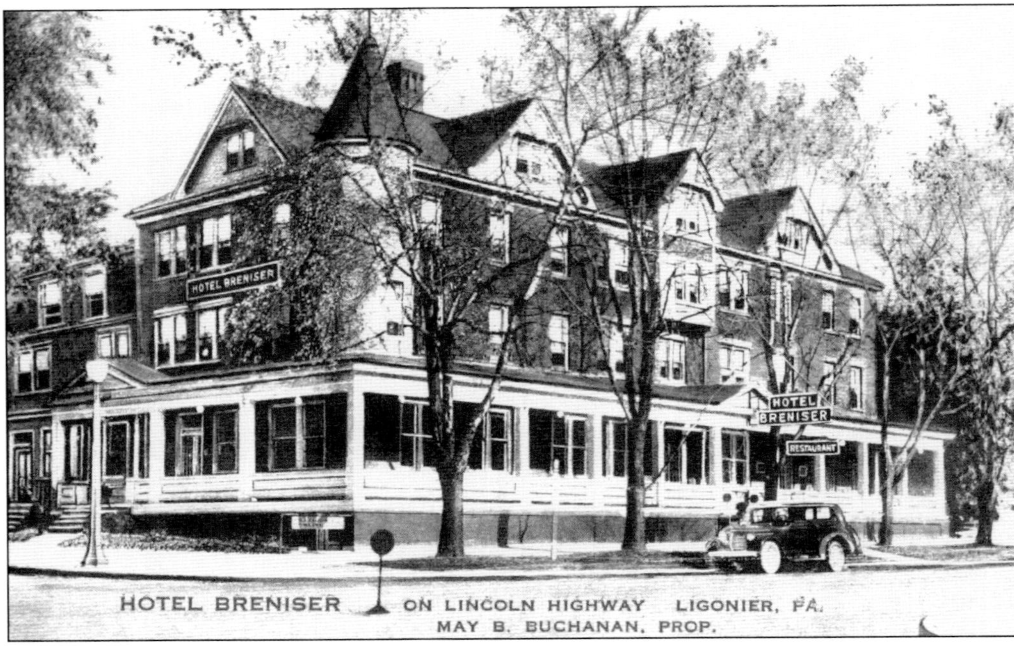

Located on the diamond, the Hotel Breniser was built in 1900 by Pete Breniser and was billed as being one of the finest and most modern hotels in town. After over 60 years of heavy use and several owners, the hotel was beginning to show its age.

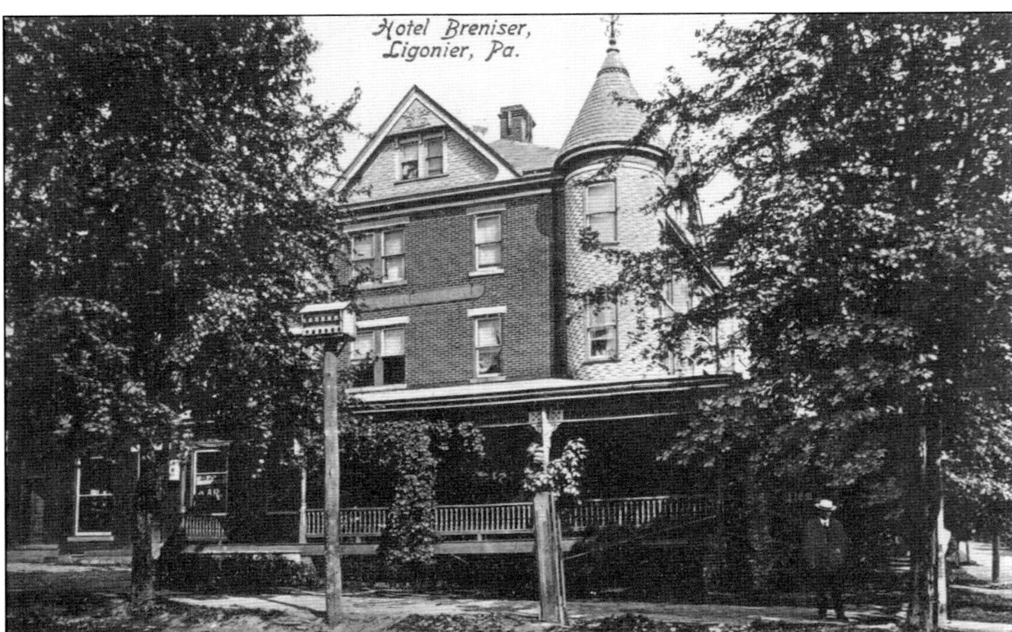

In 1967, the Hotel Breniser was torn down by the Noralco Corporation of Pittsburgh to make room for a new community building.

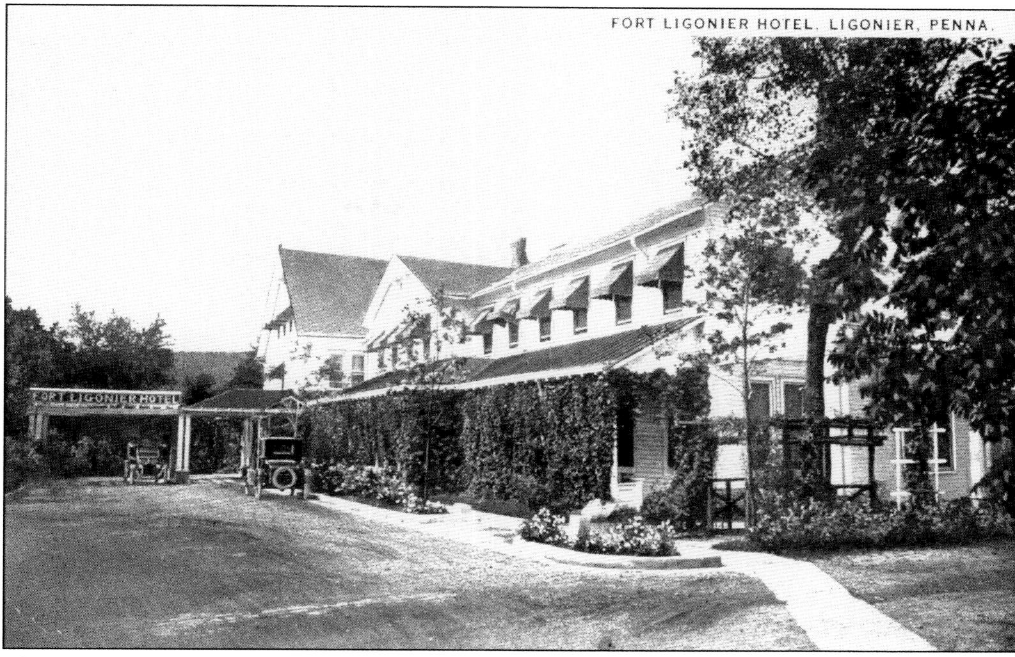

This Ligonier hotel was at one time Frank's Hotel before becoming the Hoffman Hotel and finally the Fort Ligonier Hotel. The Fort Ligonier Hotel was owned by John H. Frank, a railroader and banker from Ligonier.

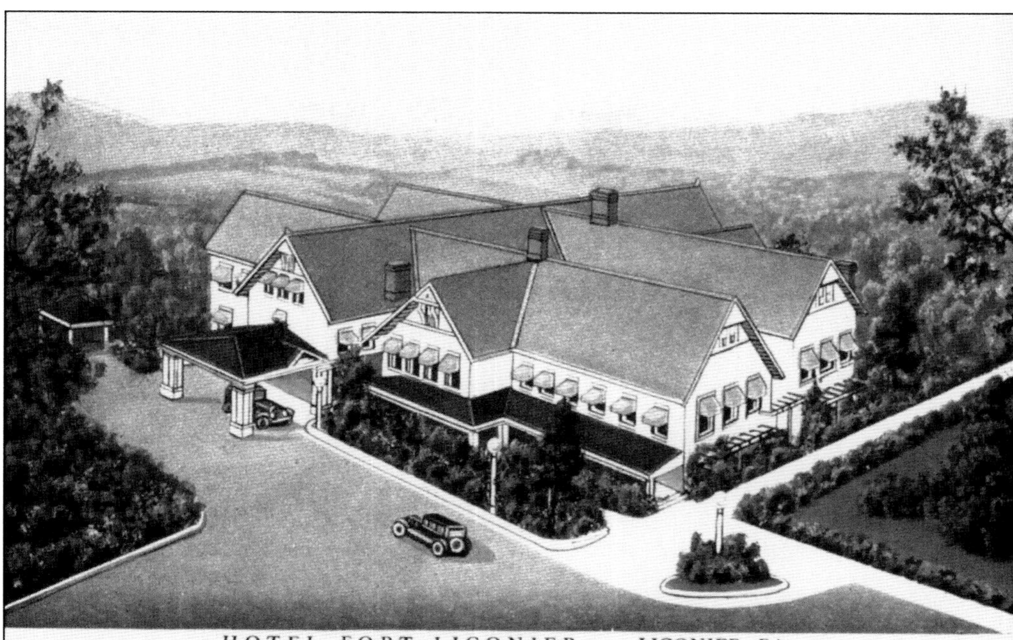

The Fort Ligonier Hotel burned down in the 1960s. Once the structure was torn down, a Holiday Inn was constructed, which in turn became Lord Ligonier Inn. It is currently a Ramada Inn.

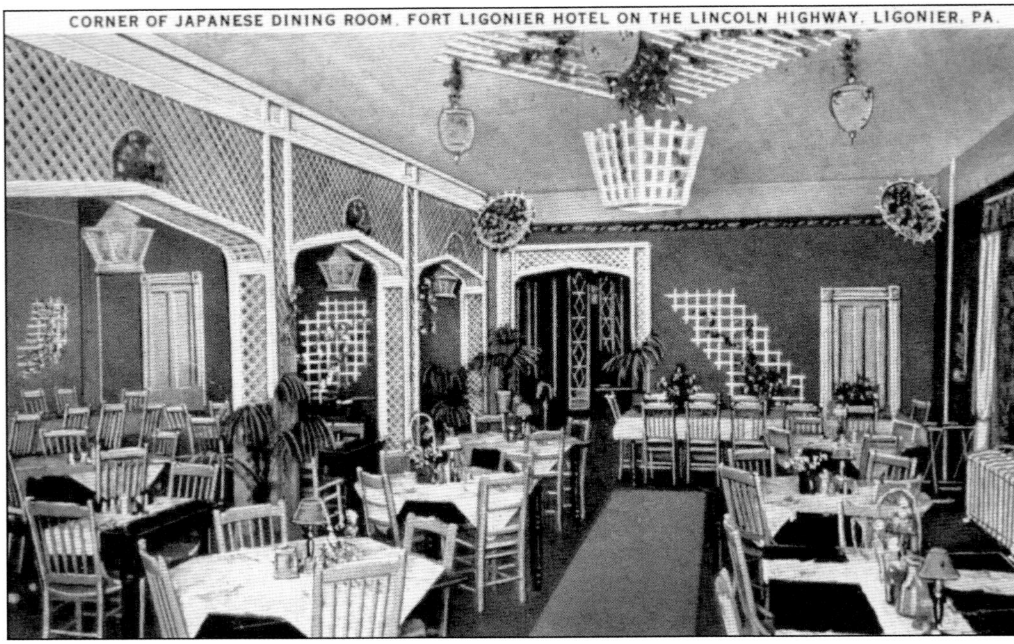

The Fort Ligonier Hotel offered elaborate accommodations and fine dining for guests, as can be seen in these views of the Japanese dining room and the lobby.

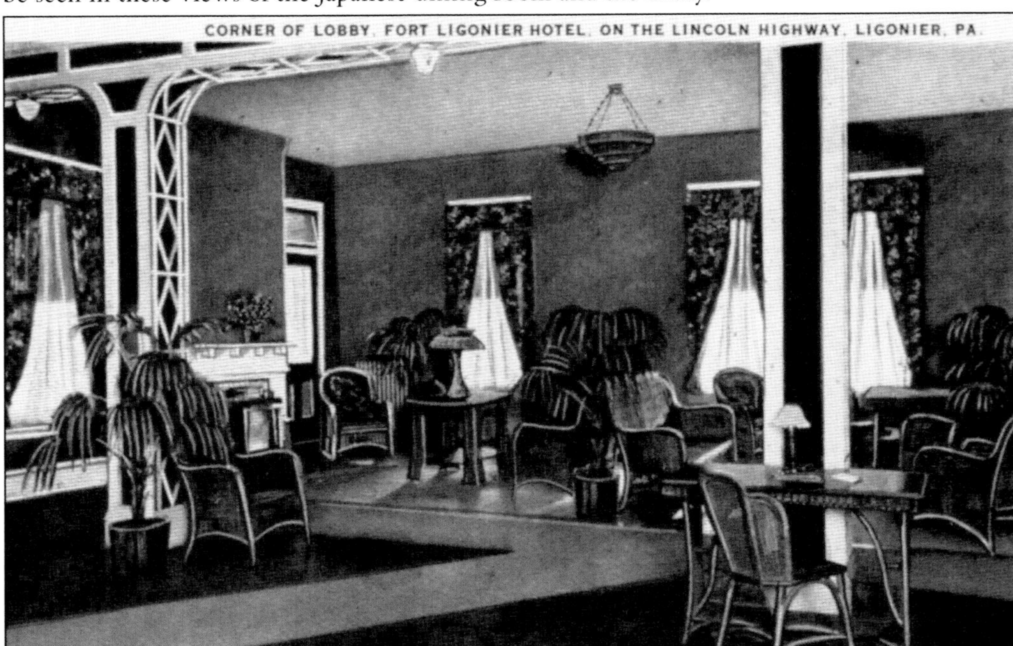

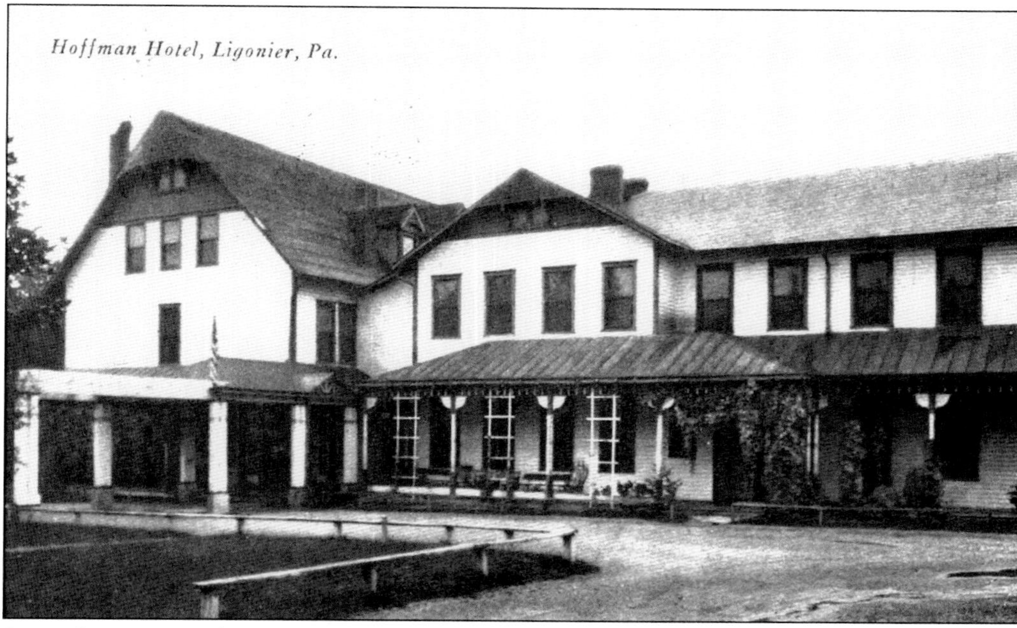

Later known as the Fort Ligonier Hotel, this hotel was previously known as the Hoffman Hotel.

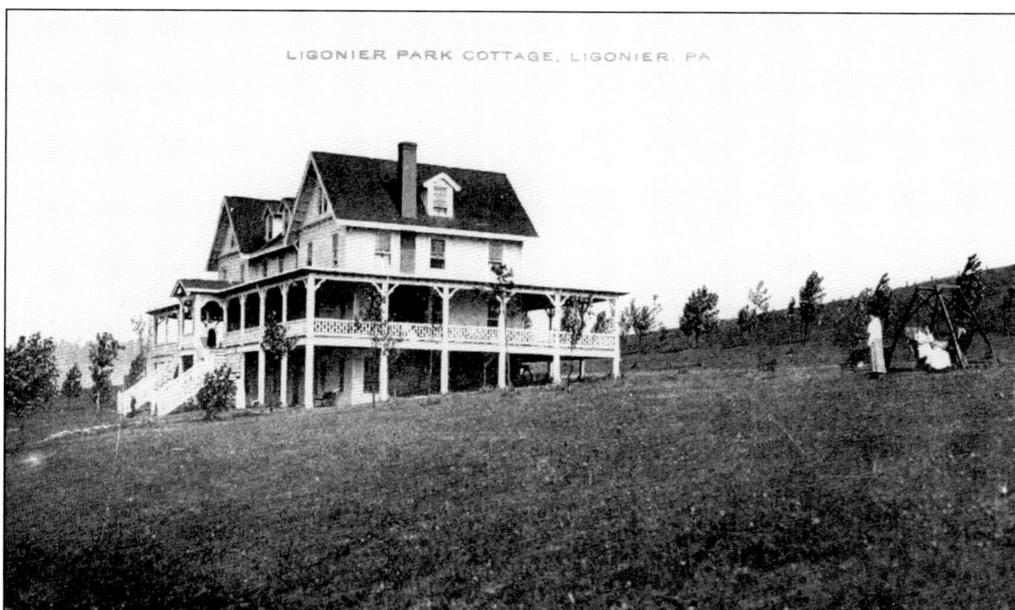

The Ligonier Park Cottage was built on the land of George W. Deeds in 1906. Despite the spectacular view, fine food, and accommodations, the resort never caught on with summer tourists. During the influenza epidemic of 1918, the cottage was converted into a hospital. Eventually the Ligonier Park Cottage became a charitable home for orphans, dependents, and the elderly.

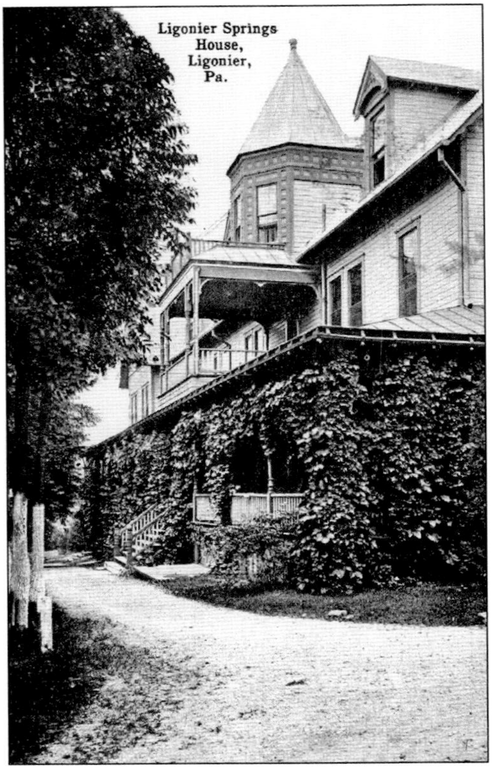

The Ligonier Springs were located between Loyalhanna Street and Route 30 below what is currently the Ramada Inn. The springs drew many hotels to this area, including the Ligonier Springs Hotel (pictured), the Hoffman Hotel, and the Fort Ligonier Hotel.

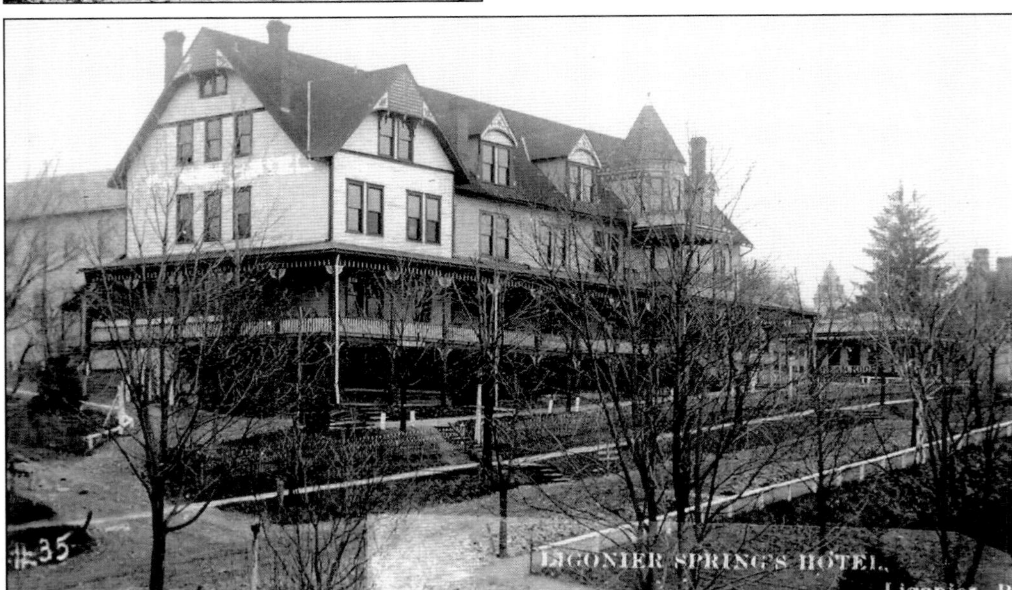

The Ligonier Springs Hotel was operated as a sanitarium from 1903 to 1905 by Dr. E. M. Clifford and Edward C. Price. In 1904, Clifford was advertising the hotel/sanitarium for those suffering from illnesses such as rheumatism, neuralgia, and other chronic diseases. Patients who were not confined to their rooms were welcome to come to the hotel for baths or treatments without having to reside at the hotel.

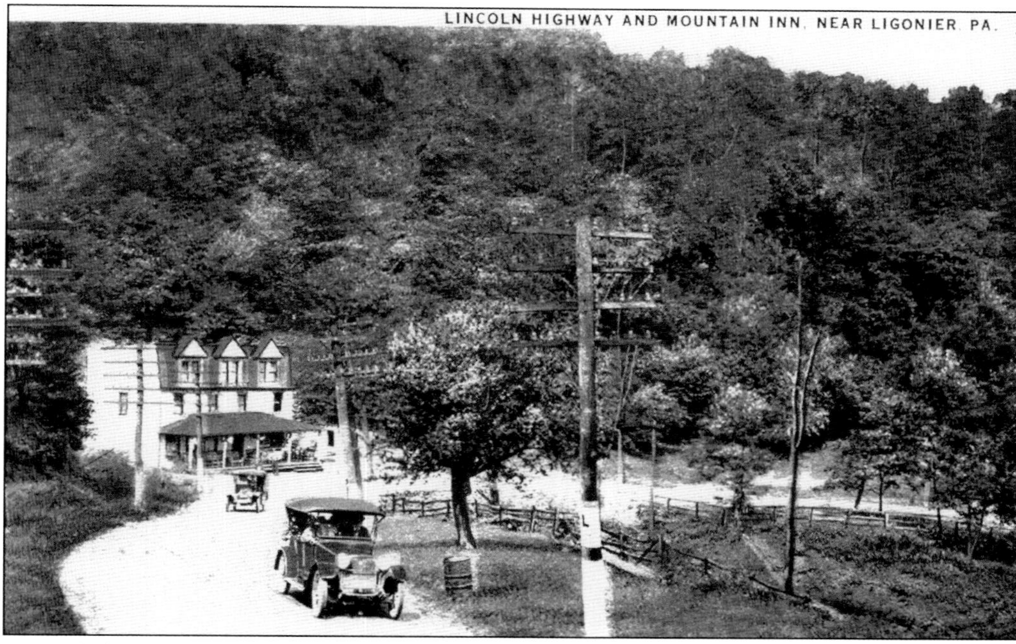

Located along the Lincoln Highway on the steep western slope of Laurel Ridge was the Mountain Inn. The inn, which was about halfway up the mountain and on a sharp curve, served travelers whose cars had overheated or brakes needed a rest.

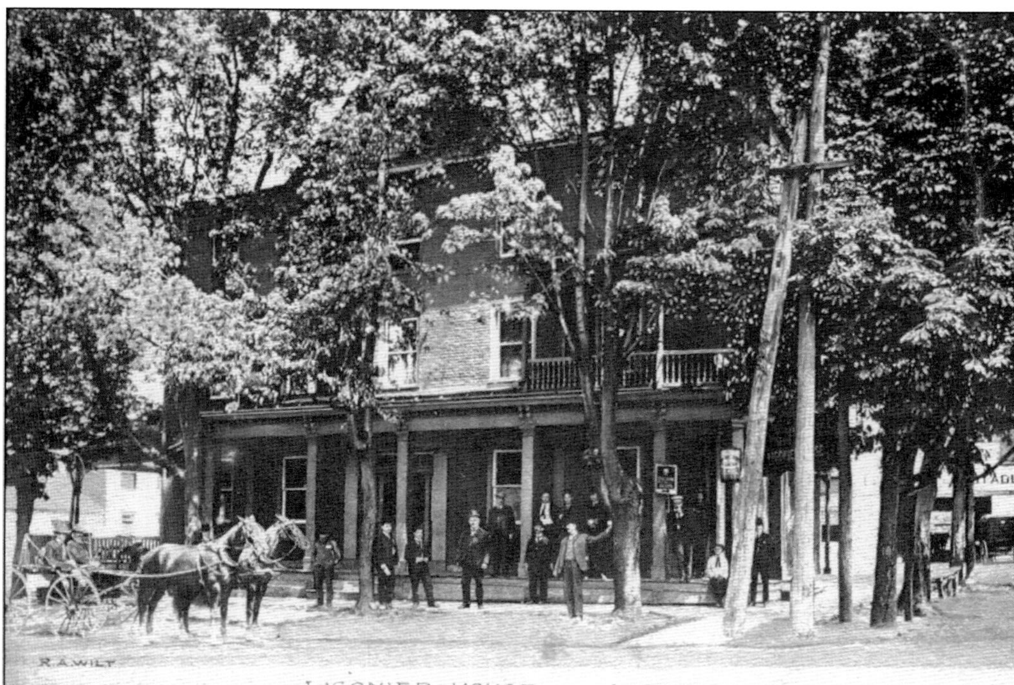

Built in 1824 by Thomas Seaton, the Ligonier House offered rooms for 25¢ a night or 35¢ if the guests wanted clean sheets. A third story was added to the front of the hotel in 1900. Eventually the Ligonier House was torn down to make way for the Ligonier Valley Library.

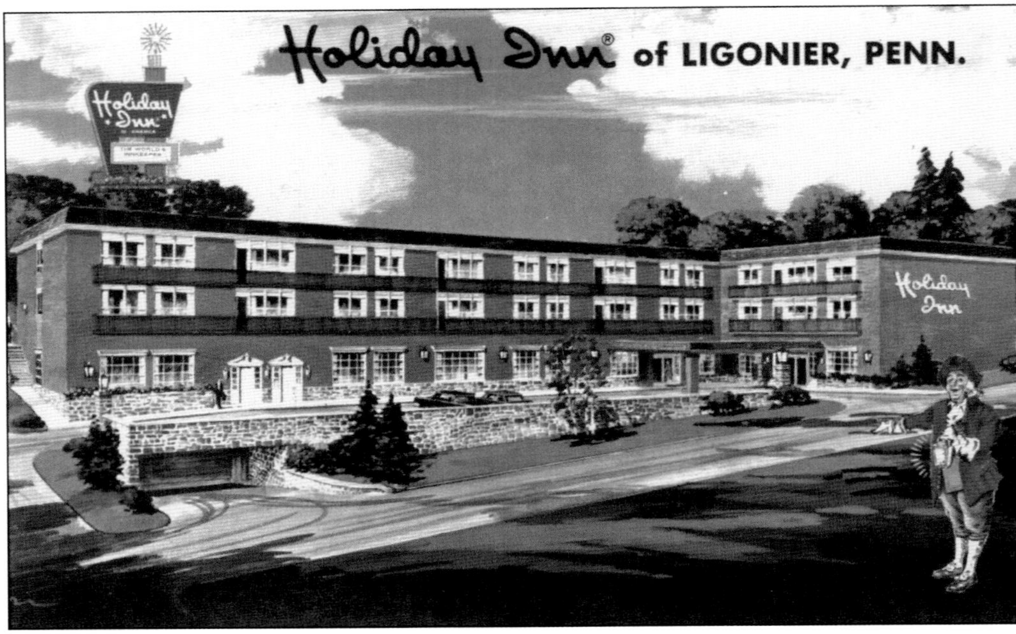

In the 1960s, the modern Holiday Inn was built on the site of the former resort hotels.

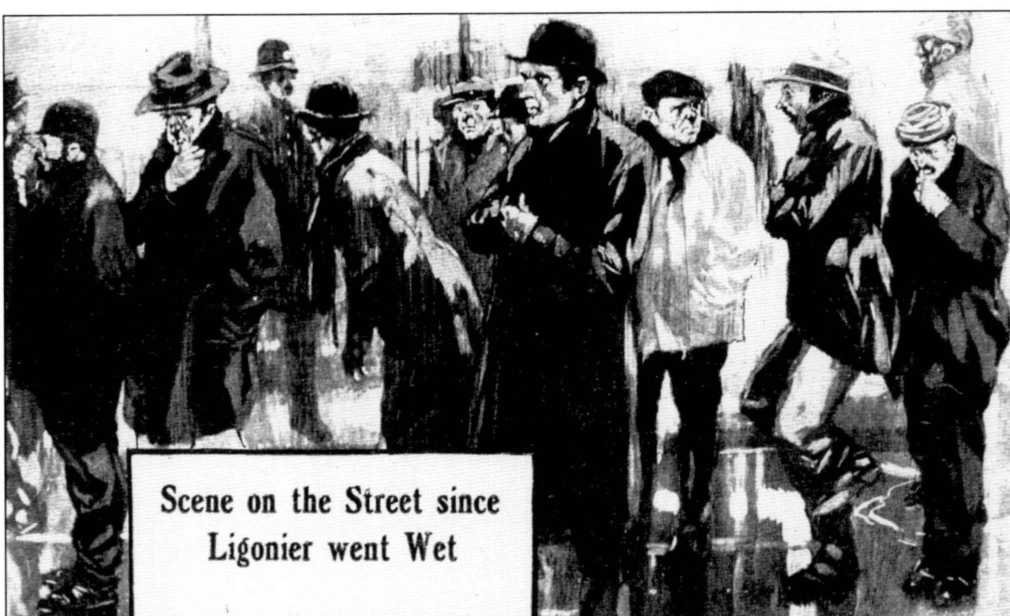

This generic card from Ligonier was published after Prohibition was repealed. It was reported that during the beginning of the century there was a very high level of wealthy alcoholism in Ligonier.

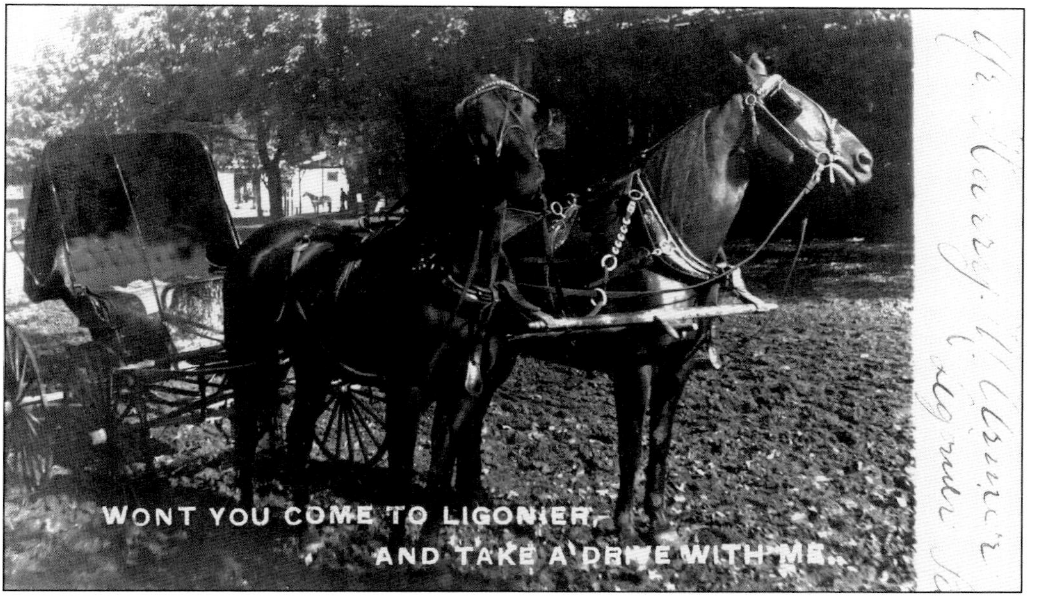

These are two generic cards from Ligonier. Publishers often published these generic cards featuring scenes of locations that could not be conclusively placed at any one location. The names of various towns could then be printed on the card.

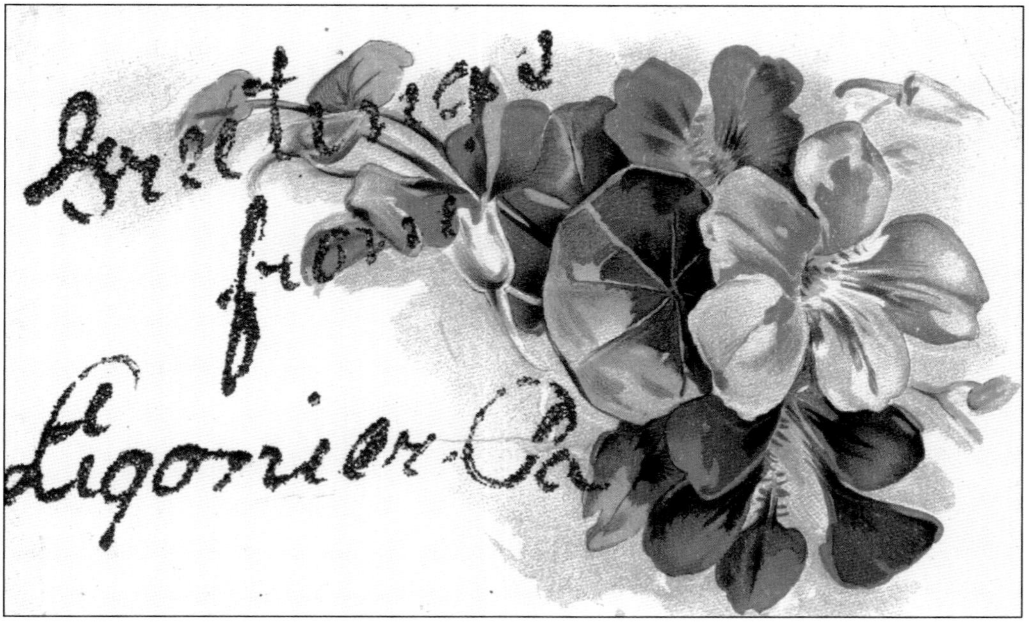

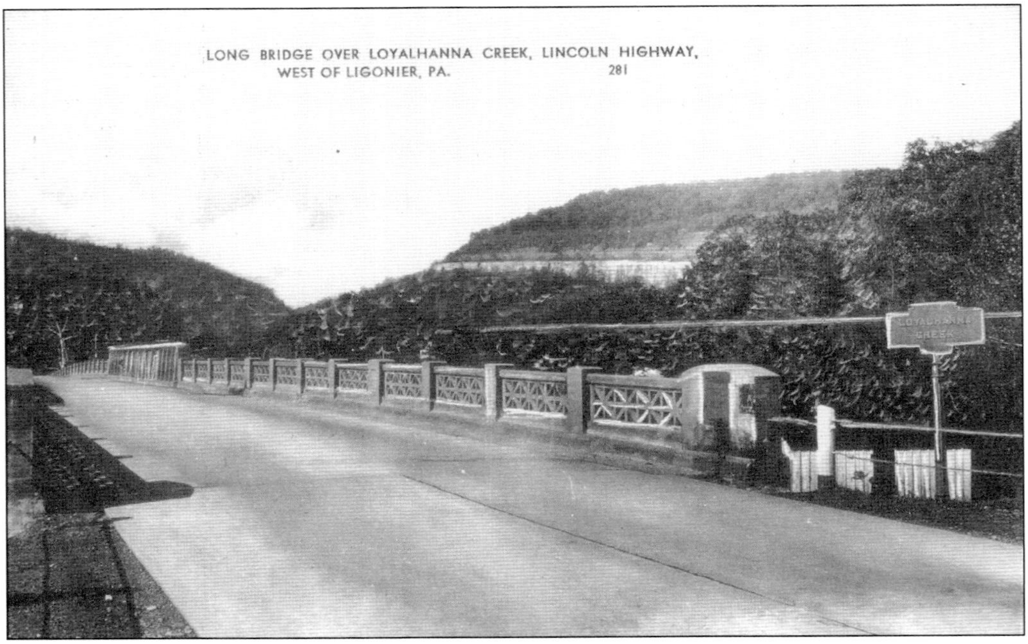

Built in 1925 by Pitt Construction, the Loyalhanna Viaduct was known locally as Longbridge. The Ligonier Valley Railroad ran underneath the viaduct, accounting for a slight hump in the center. After serving the region for over 60 years, the bridge was dismantled in 1986 and a new bridge was constructed.

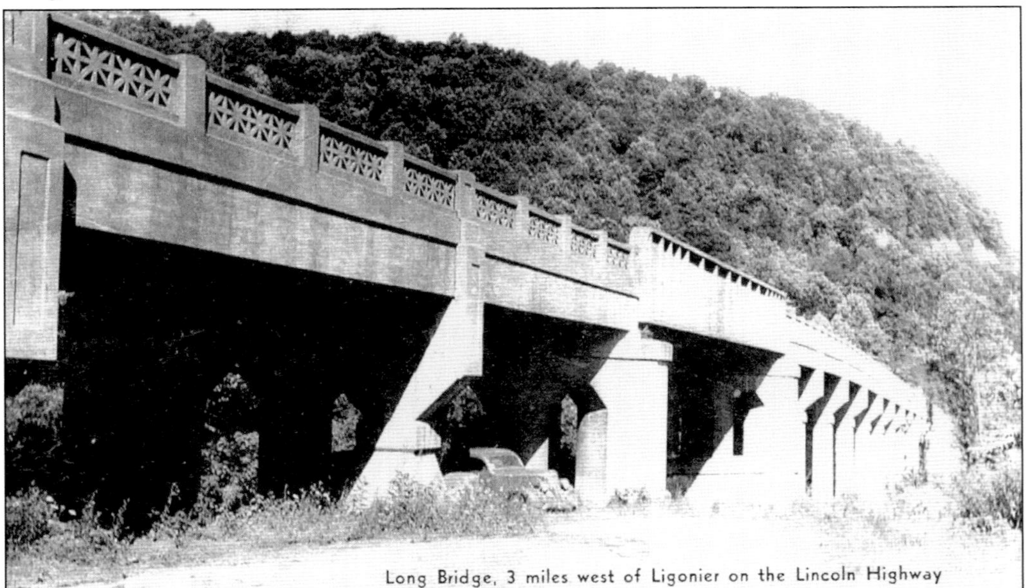

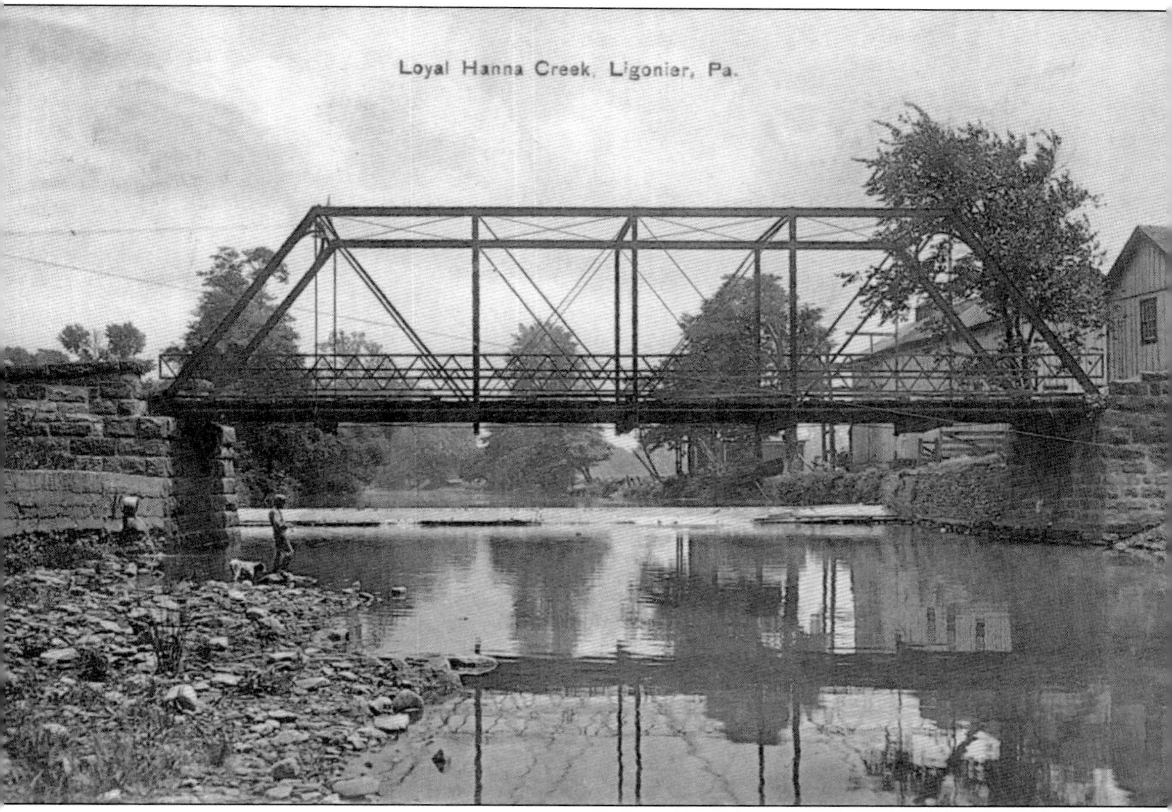

Flowing along the northeastern side of Chestnut Ridge, the Loyalhanna Creek flows through Ligonier and Chestnut Ridge before reaching Latrobe. The creek is a popular destination for canoeing and recreational trout fishing.

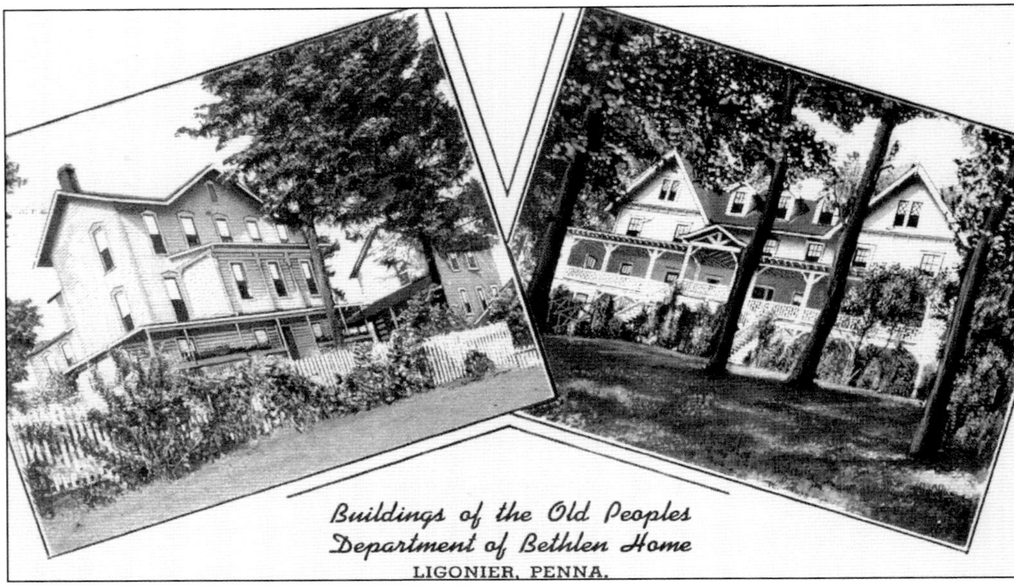

In 1921, the Ligonier Park Cottage, suffering from lack of business, became the Bethlen Home. The home was established by the Hungarian Reformed Federation of America and was named for Gabriel Bethlen, a prince from Hungary who had been an orphan. The charitable home took in orphans, dependents, and the elderly.

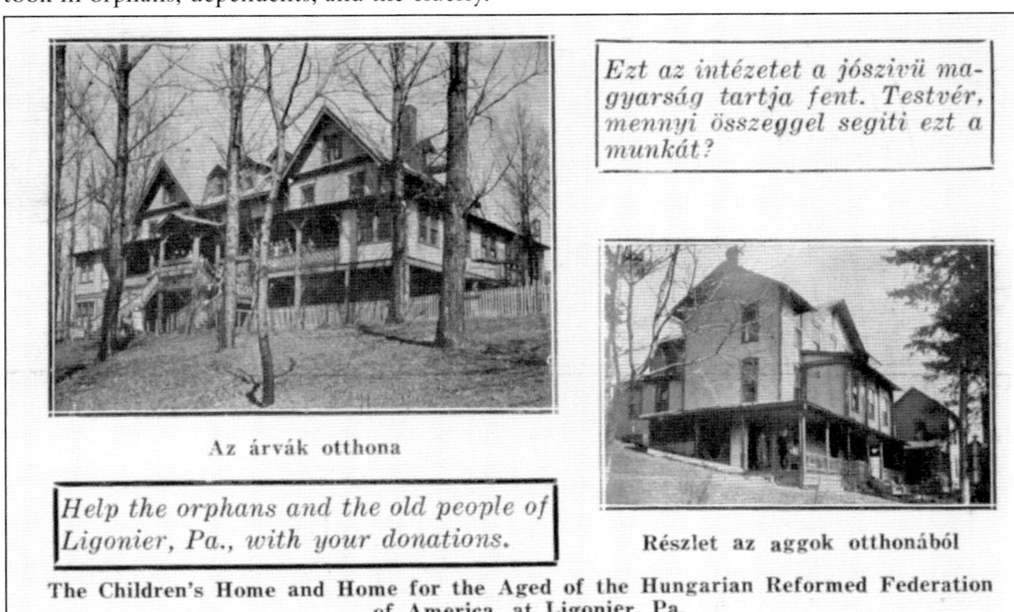

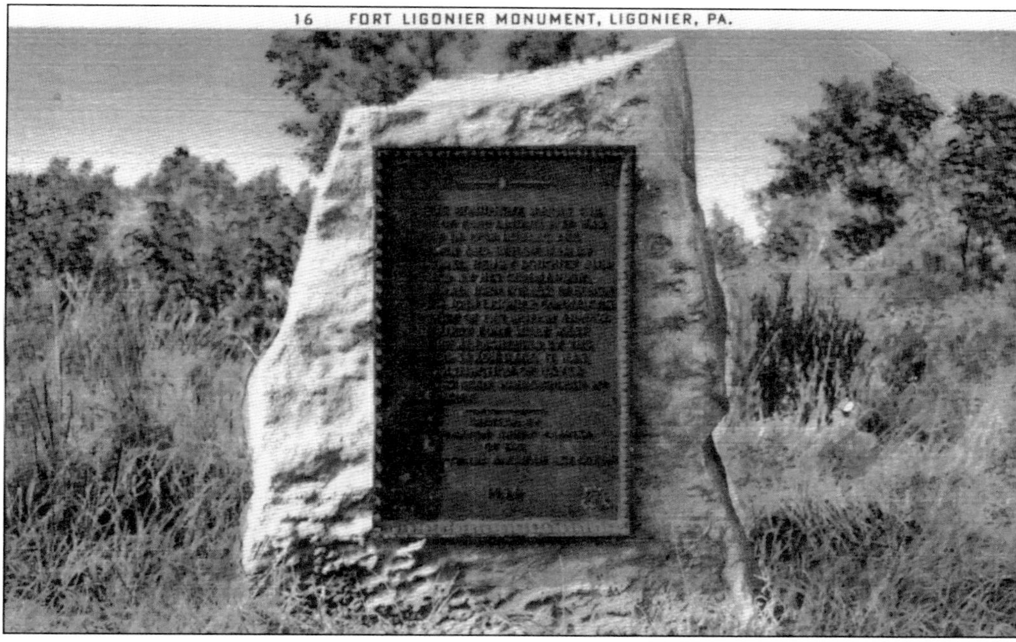

The inscription on the Fort Ligonier marker reads, "This monument marks the site of Fort Ligonier. It was built in 1758 during the French and Indian War by Colonel Henry Bouquet and named by his commander General John Forbes in honor of Sir John Ligonier, Commander-in-Chief of the British Armies. The first fort built west of the Alleghenies by the Anglo-Saxon race, it has the distinction of never having been surrendered to an enemy. Erected by the William Kenly Chapter of the Daughters of the American Revolution. 1934."

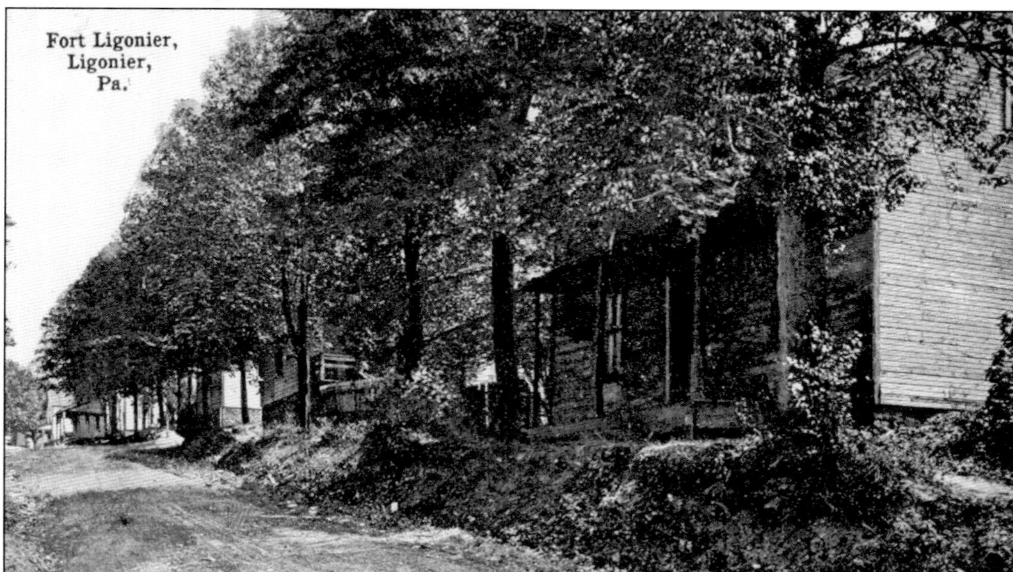

In 1927, John Jacob Hughes purchased the lot on which the center of Fort Ligonier had once been located, and he presented the deed to the Daughters of the American Revolution (DAR). In 1931, the DAR purchased the adjoining lot. The Fort Ligonier commemorative marker was erected in 1934 to mark the site of the fort.

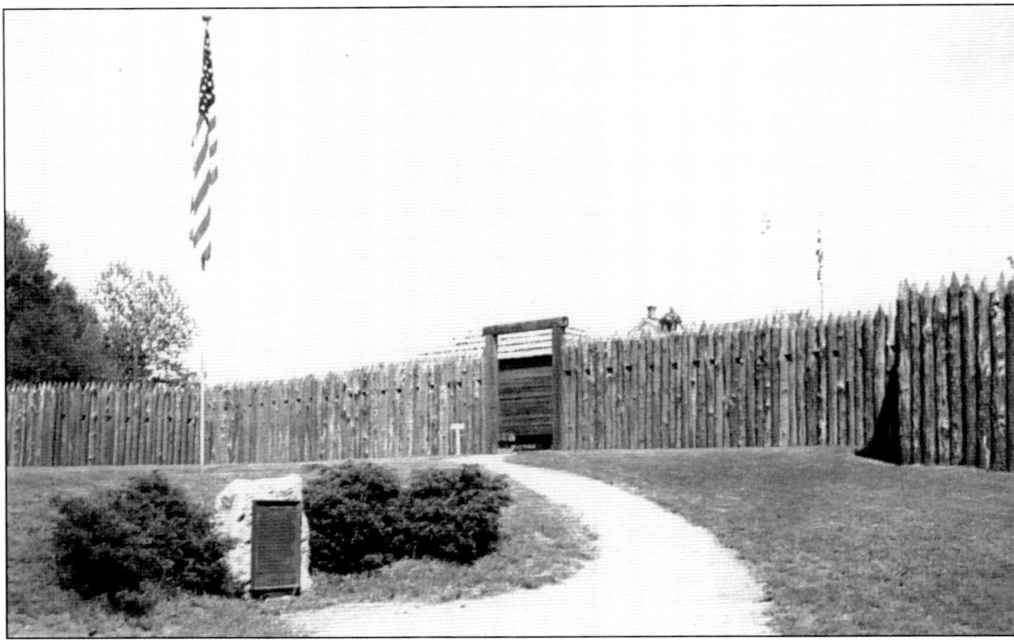

Part of the reconstruction of Fort Ligonier included the rebuilding of over 400 feet of heavy-pillared stockade wall. The 14-foot pickets were set side by side and three and a half feet deep. Using 18th-century construction techniques, this first phase of reconstruction took over three and a half months to complete. Inside the walls, the officers' quarters were rebuilt. Additional work to be completed on the fort as funds allow includes the reconstruction of the remaining outer retrenchments and the construction of additional buildings.

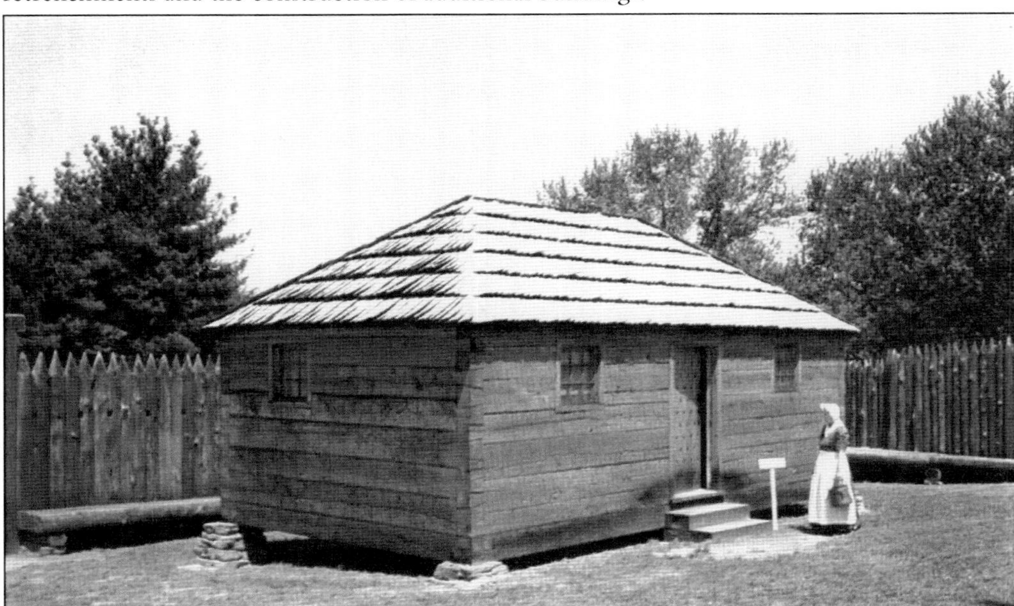

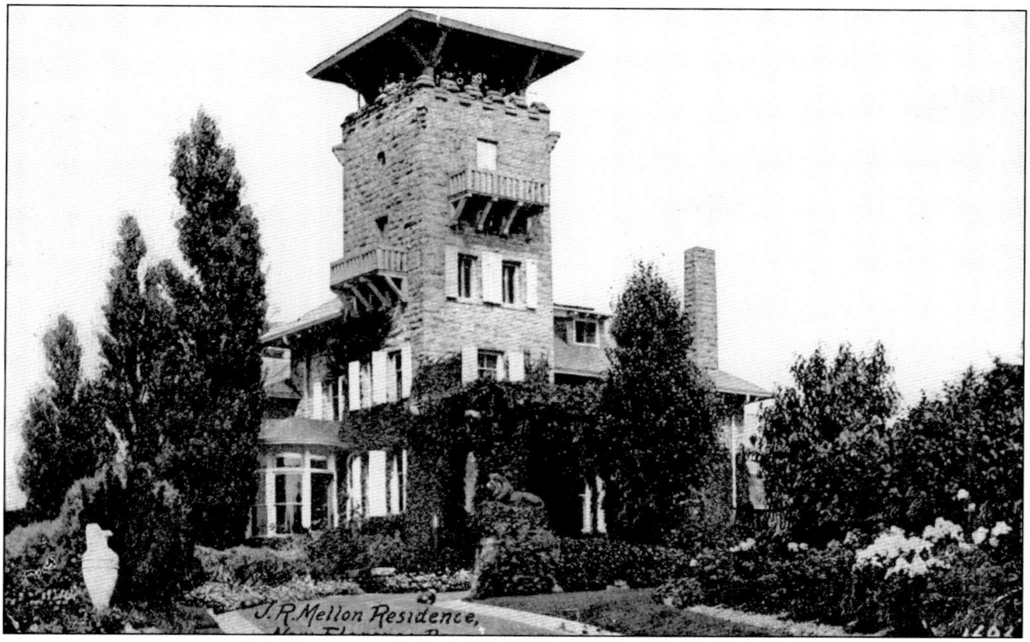

James Ross Mellon, a Pittsburgh financier and chairman, owned this home in New Florance. J. R. Mellon was the older brother of Andrew William Mellon. J. R. Mellon died in 1934 at age 88 of old age.

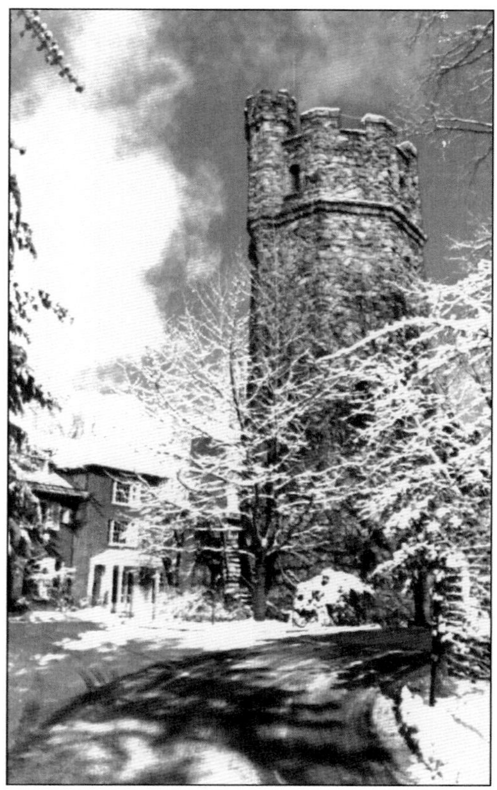

The Rolling Rock Club is an 18-hole tree-lined golf course. The club was originally a nine-hole course designed by Donald Ross. In May 1997, an additional nine holes were opened.

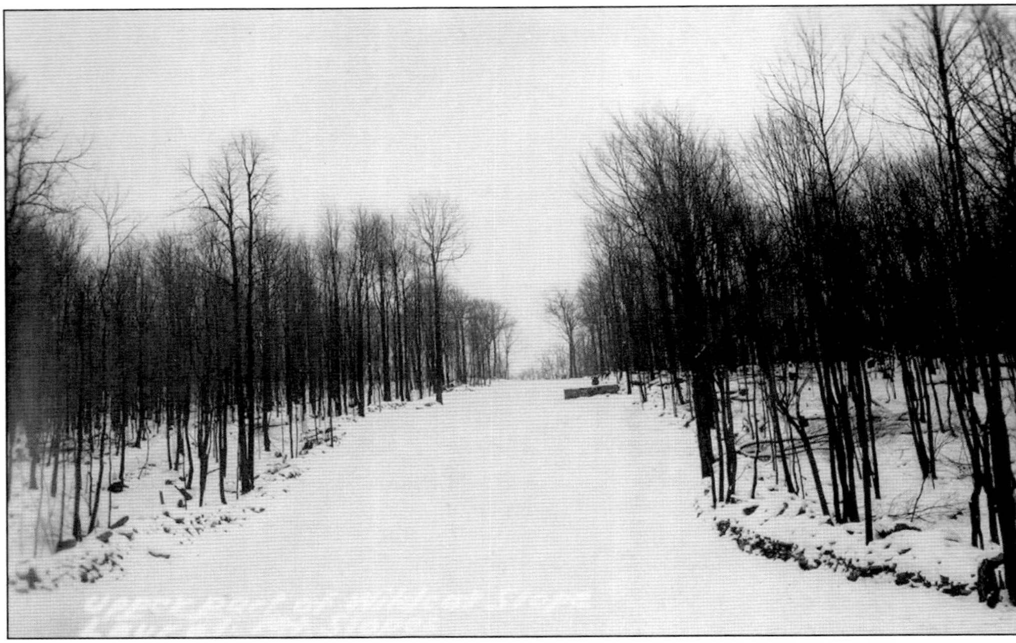

In 1939, Richard King Mellon realized that the steep terrain of the valley would be ideal for a ski resort. He hired Hannes Schneider to design one, and in the winter of 1940, Laurel Mountain Ski Resort opened.

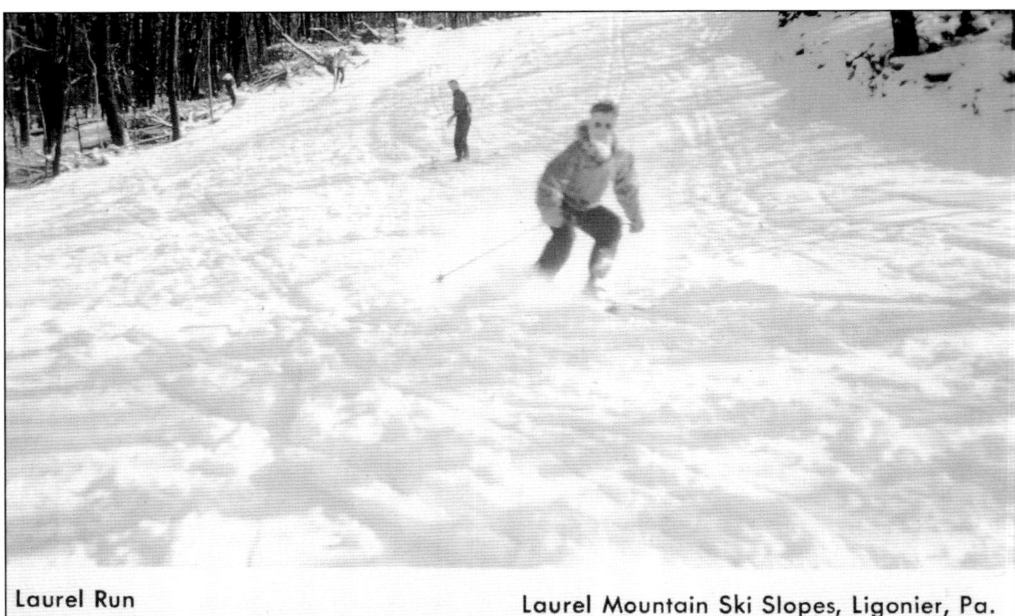

Mellon gave the ski resort to the Commonwealth of Pennsylvania in 1963 on the condition that it is used for recreation. In 1990, the state was forced to close the resort after various private lessees and the state attempted to operate the resort but failed.

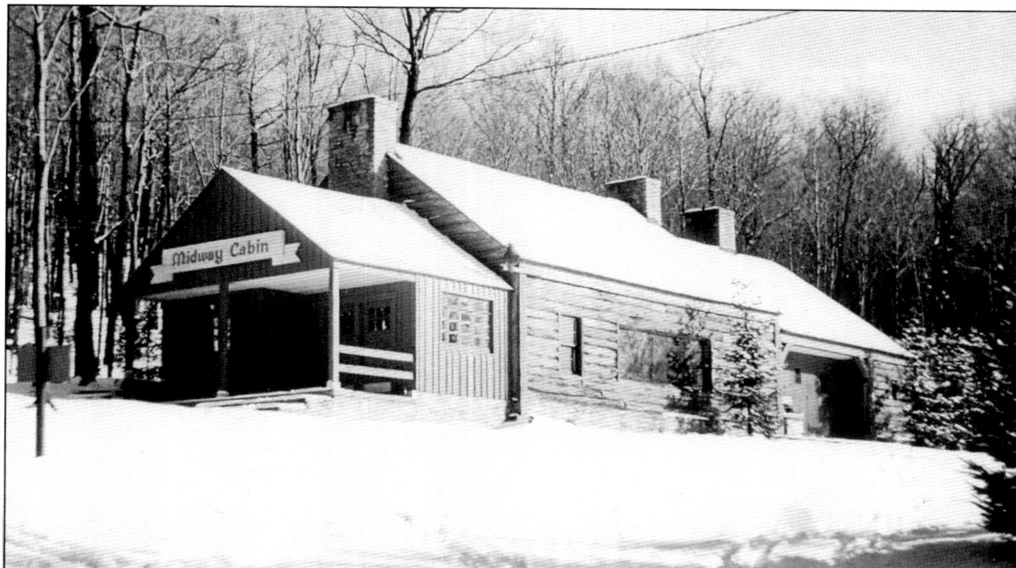

Laurel Mountain Ski Slopes, Ligonier, Pa.

Midway cabin was the original ski lodge built at Laurel Mountain Ski Resort. Travelers reached the cabin by way of Locust Camp Trail. The single lane did not hinder busses bringing skiers to the resort. Midway cabin is still in existence today—it just waits for the resort to find a new owner in order to reopen.

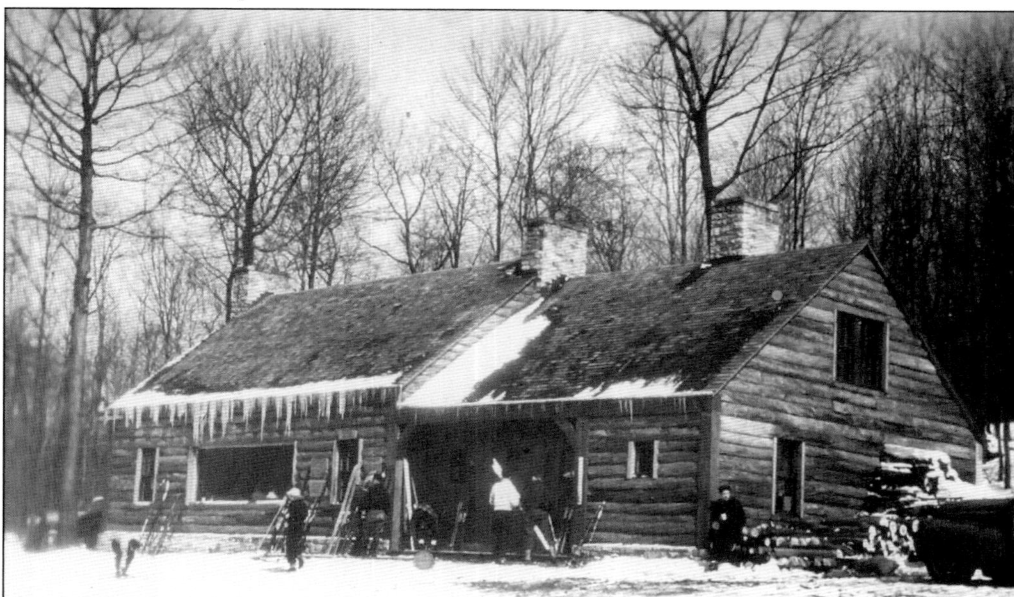

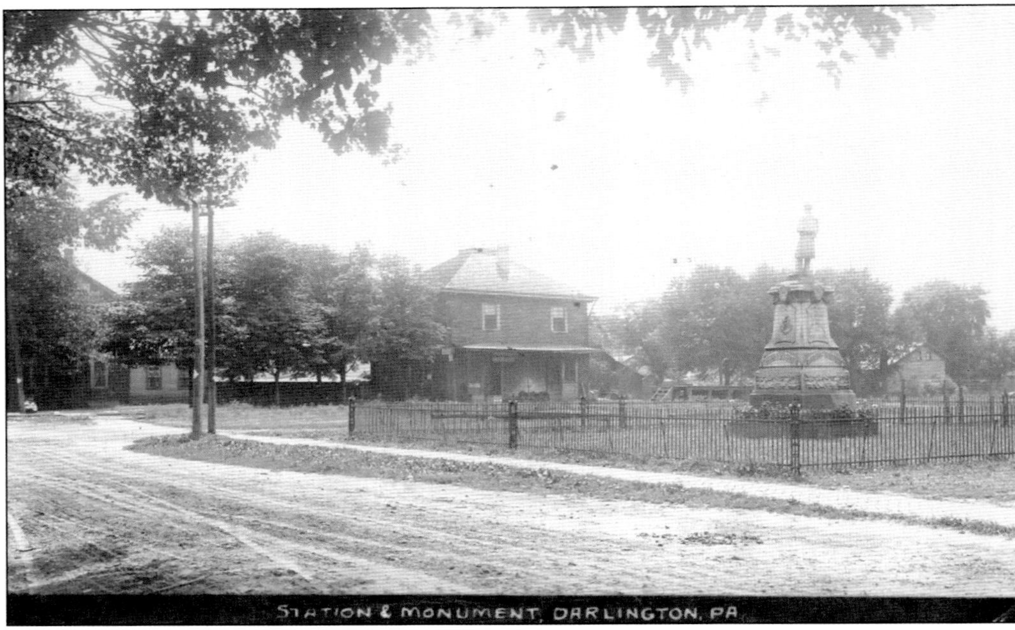

Built in 1900, the Darlington station was one stop from the Idlewild depot. The Darlington station served as both a workplace for the agent, who served as passenger agent, freight agent, and block operator, and as the residence for the agent and his family. The front room served as the ticket office, waiting room, and convenience store. The resident family had a living room behind the waiting room, two upstairs bedrooms, and a kitchen in the basement. Eventually Idlewild bought the property that the Darlington station sat on and the station fell into disrepair. Idlewild donated the building to the Ligonier Valley Railroad Association in 2006, and the association is working to restore the station to its former glory.

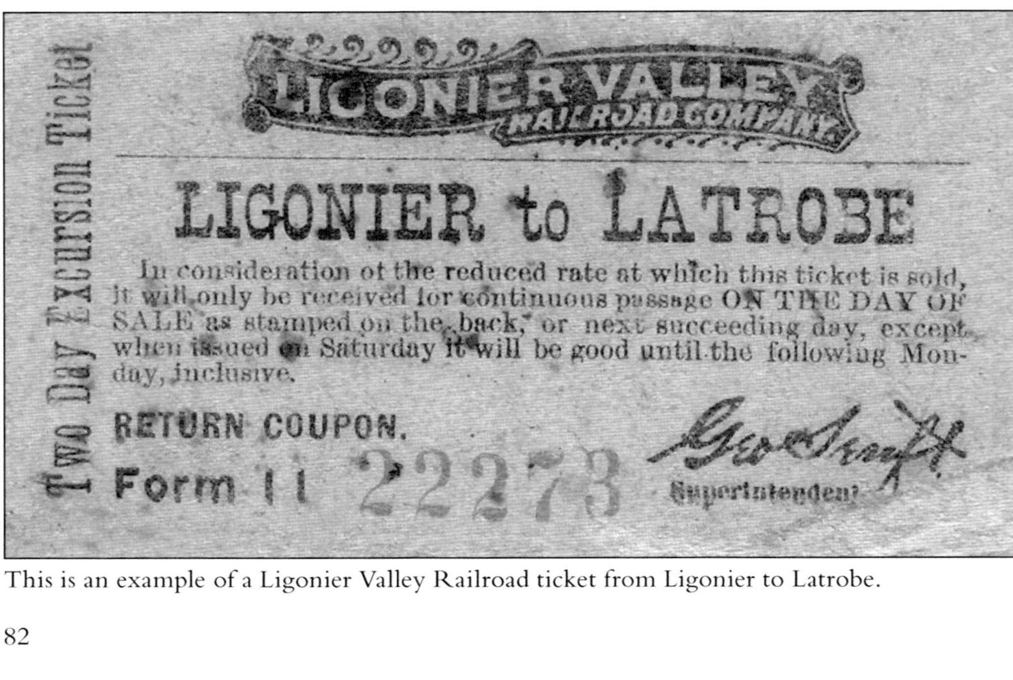

This is an example of a Ligonier Valley Railroad ticket from Ligonier to Latrobe.

Three

Idlewild Park

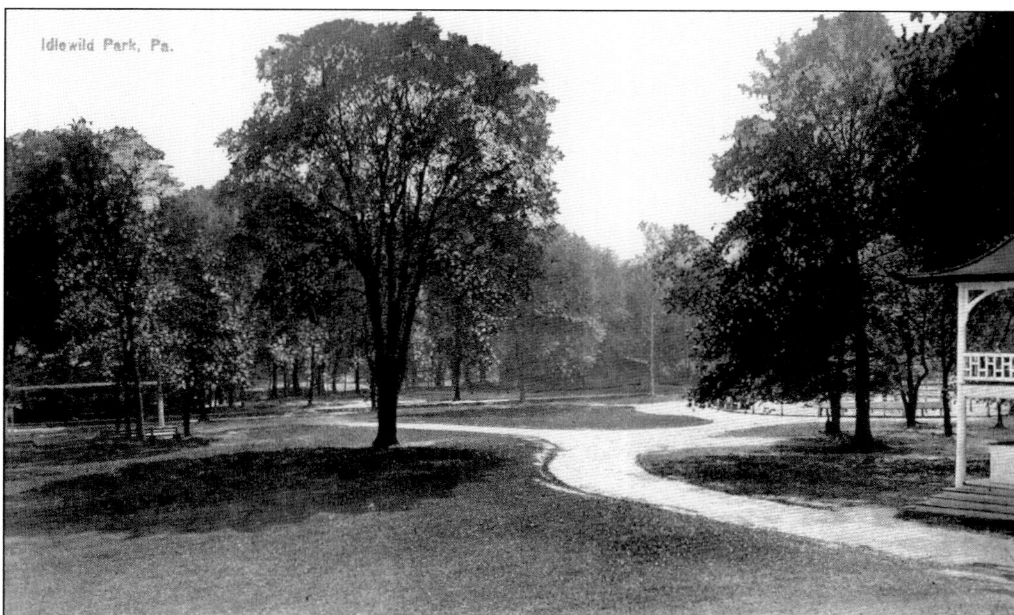

One of Idlewild's hallmarks was its grassy lawns, and winding promenades were popular among its visitors. This postcard shows the central area of the park, which almost a century later would become home to the Hillside Theater.

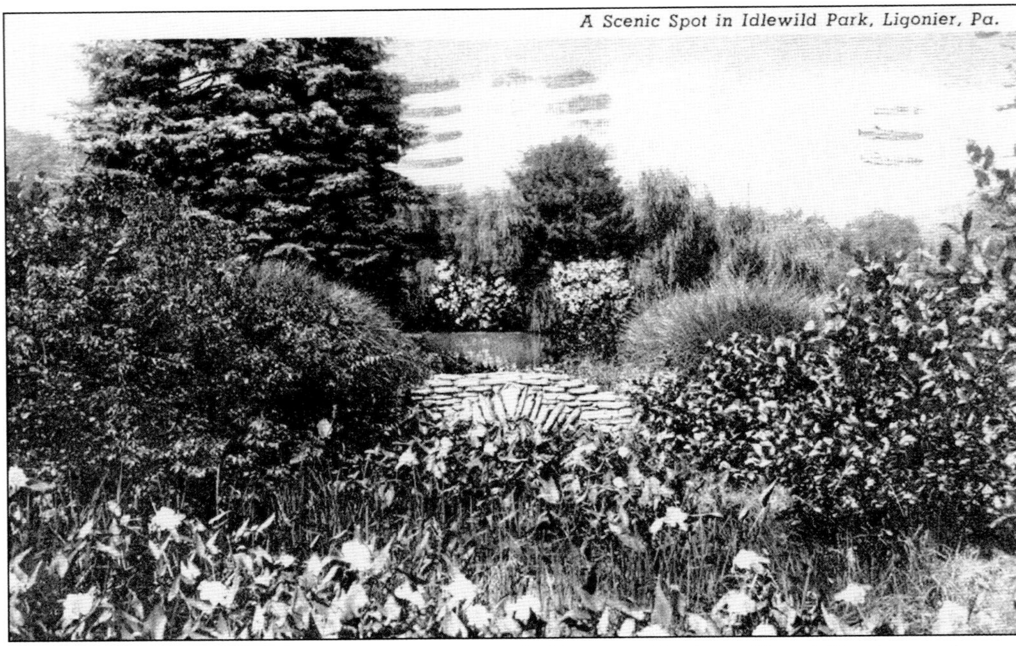

Idlewild Park was known as a "mountain park," known for its rolling hills, heavy forests, flowers, and shrubs.

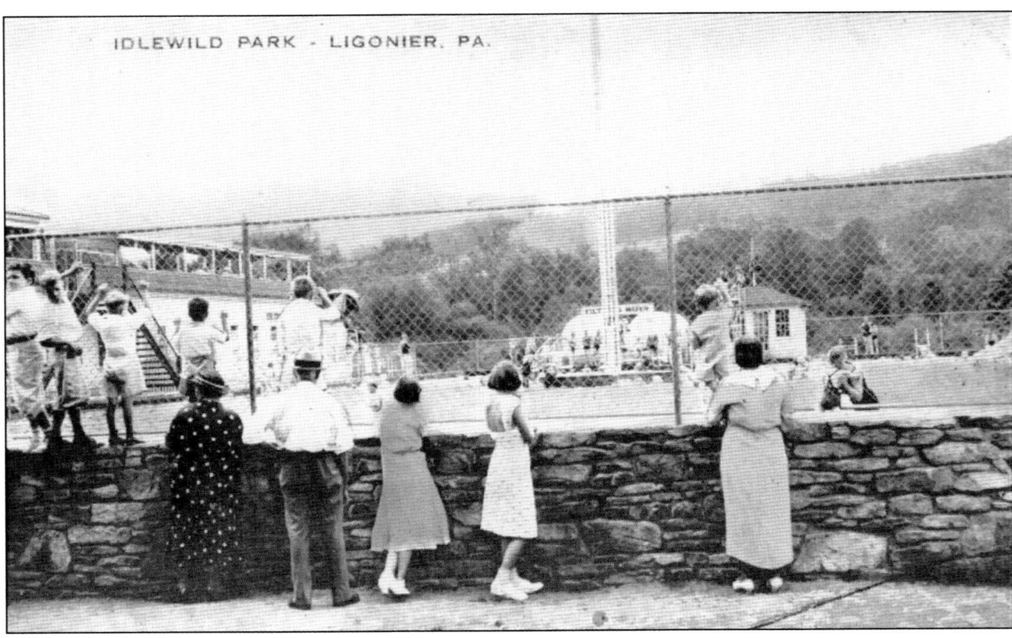

In 1932, Idlewild opened a large modern swimming pool on the island in the middle of Lake Bouquet. The pool measured 80 feet by 100 feet and was equipped with the finest sand filtration system for the time. The pool also included a bathhouse and a sand beach.

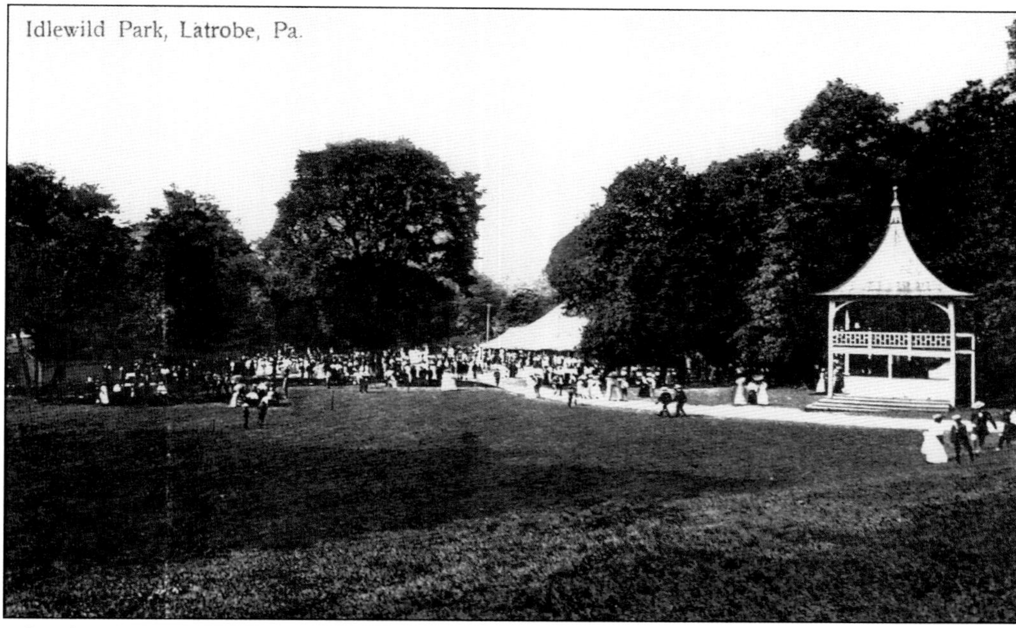

School and company picnics have always brought crowds to the park. This crowd is enjoying a sunny day at the park.

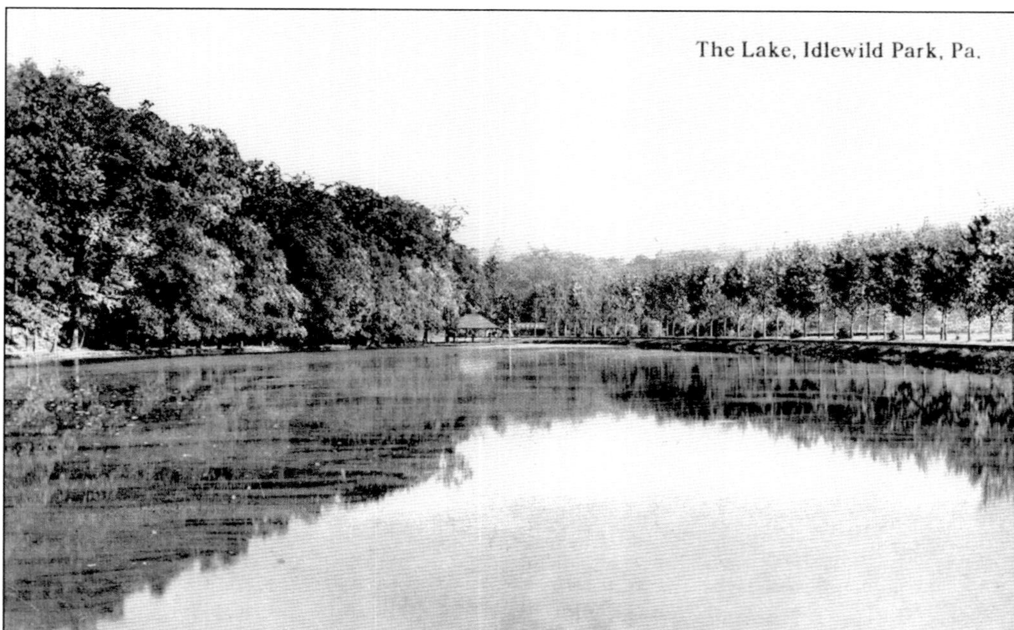

Idlewild's man-made lake, Lake Bouquet was named for Col. Henry Bouquet, from the French and Indian War. Four times the size of Idlewild's other man-made lake, Lake St. Clair, Lake Bouquet featured many canals and tributaries.

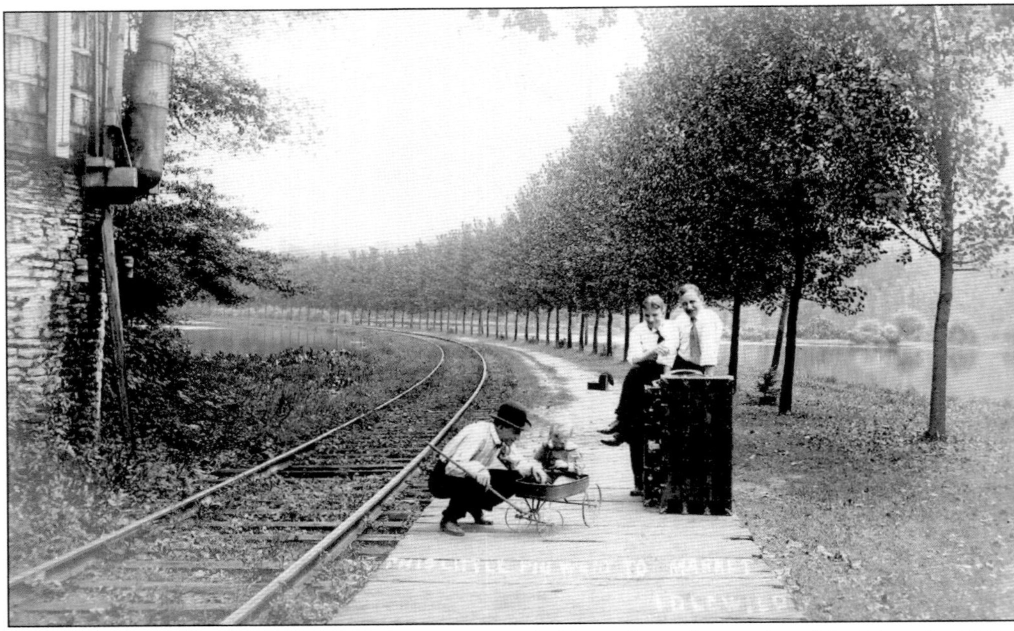

This postcard is a humorous card showing some children along the tracks of the Ligonier Valley Railroad that ran alongside Lake Bouquet. The card was sent to let friends and family know that the sender had been to Idlewild Park.

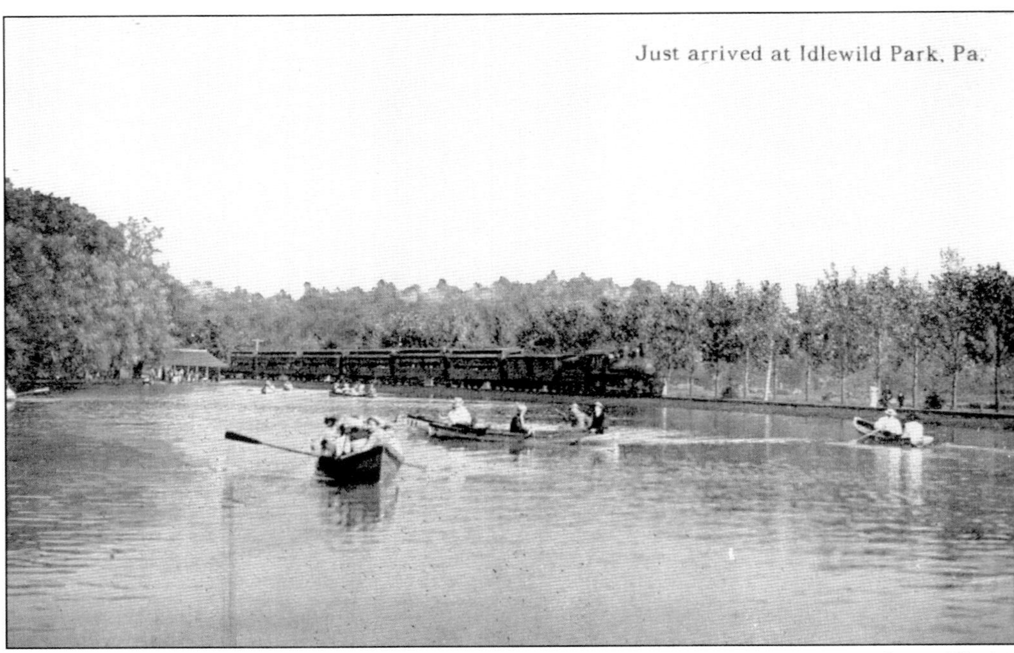

Rowboats were a popular attraction on Lake Bouquet. Much of this portion was later filled in when Idlewild expanded its water park facilities in 2000.

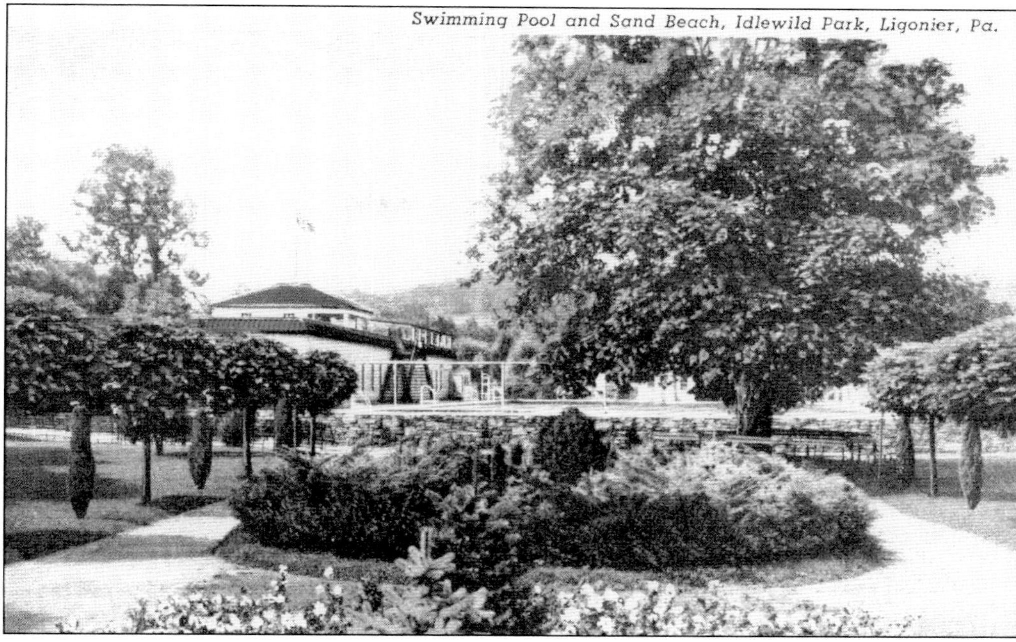

Eventually the pool's sand beach was removed and replaced with a lawn beach. Clogged drains and filters led management to make the decision.

The boathouse served as the boarding location for the park's vapor launch and swan boats. Later the Idlewild showboat also docked there. Through the years the appearance of the boathouse has changed, but it remains in the park serving as a dining pavilion.

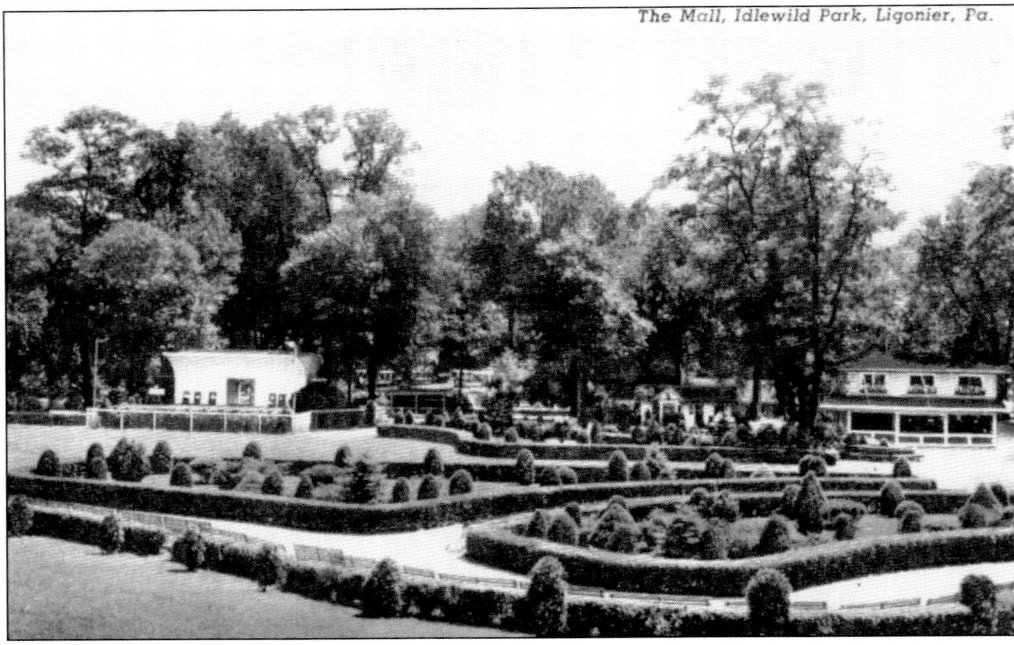

During the 1950s, the geometric displays of the hedges and shrubs made for fascinating displays amid the Idlewild Park midway, as well as adding to the beauty of the park.

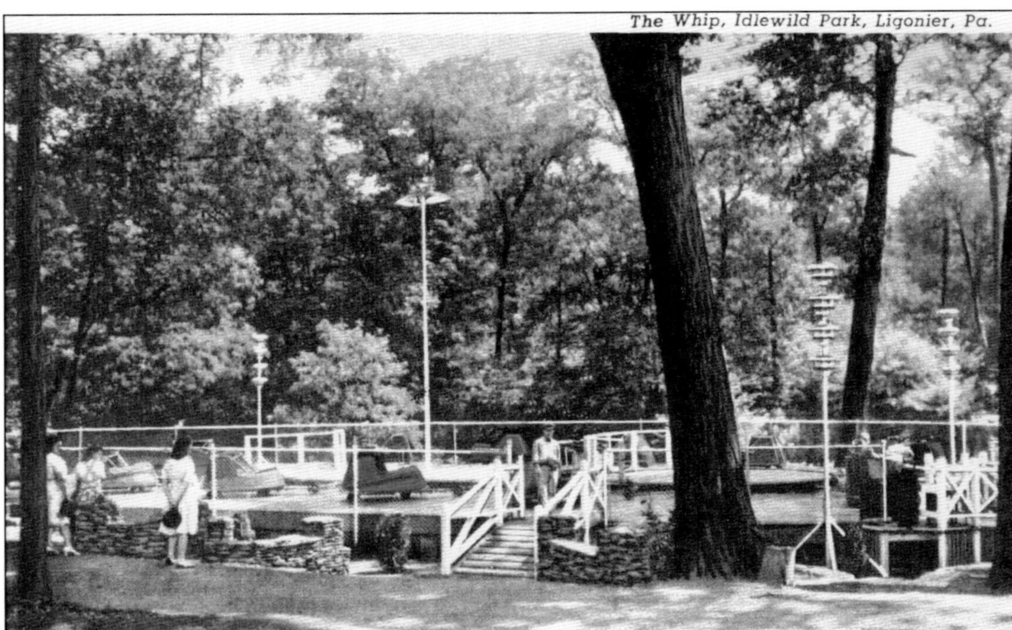

The park's current Whip was installed in 1939, replacing a smaller portable version that had stood since 1934. The ride's location next to the Loyalhanna Creek has lead to the creek being flooded several times. One such flood led to the replacement of the ride's original 12 cars.

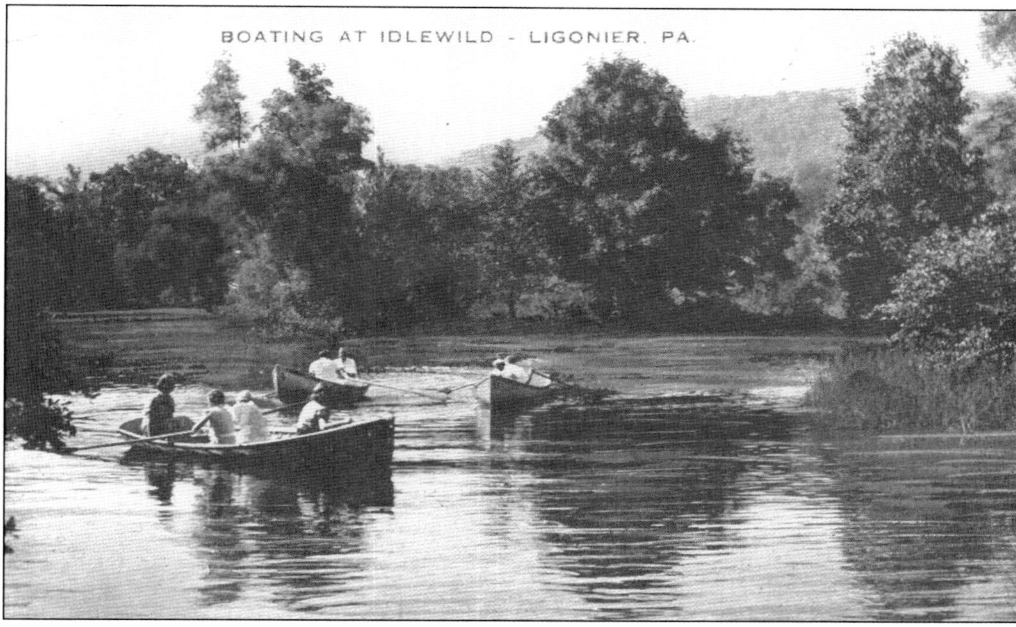

Often picnickers enjoyed the rowboats offered at the lake. For others not wanting to go into the water, a bicycle course circled the lake.

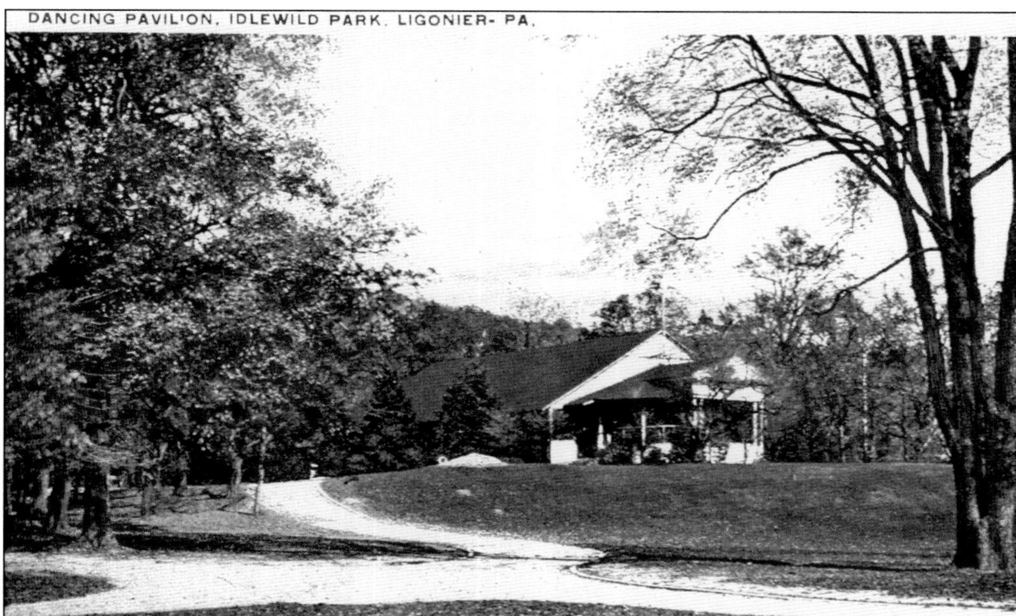

One of the early additions to the park was the auditorium, the park's dance hall, which sits on top of the hillside in the center of the park. The new dance hall featured a dance floor to accommodate 200, and it was surrounded by three rows of seating on either side. In the center was a raised music stand, and underneath was a room for coats and wraps. The auditorium now serves as a picnic pavilion and a pavilion for special events.

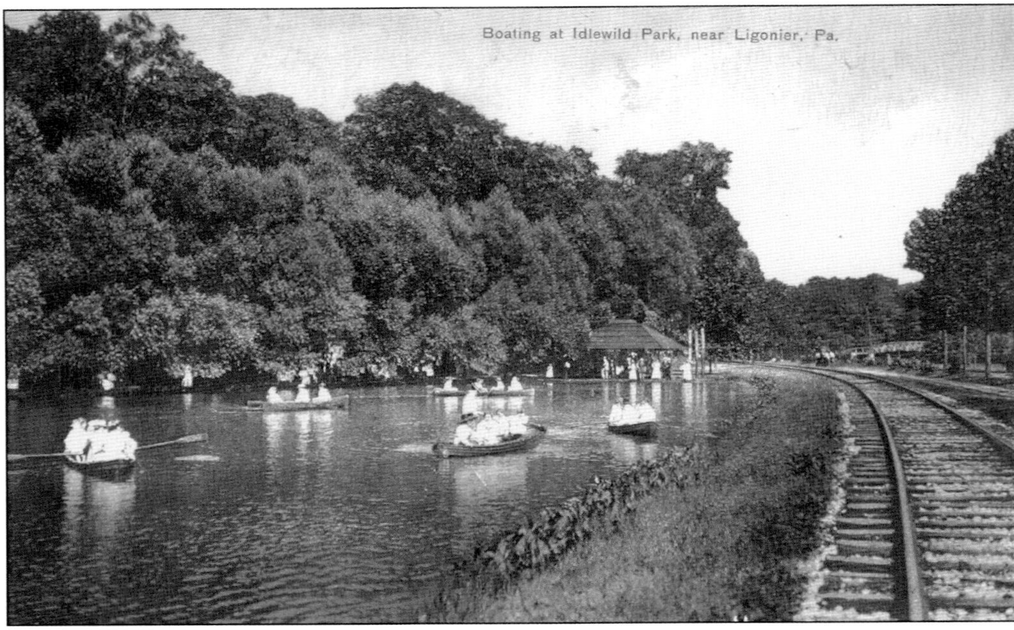

After leaving the Darlington station, the Ligonier Valley Railroad traveled along the edge of Lake St. Clair in Idlewild Park before traveling on to the Idlewild depot. Lake St. Clair covered four acres and was named in honor of Arthur St. Clair.

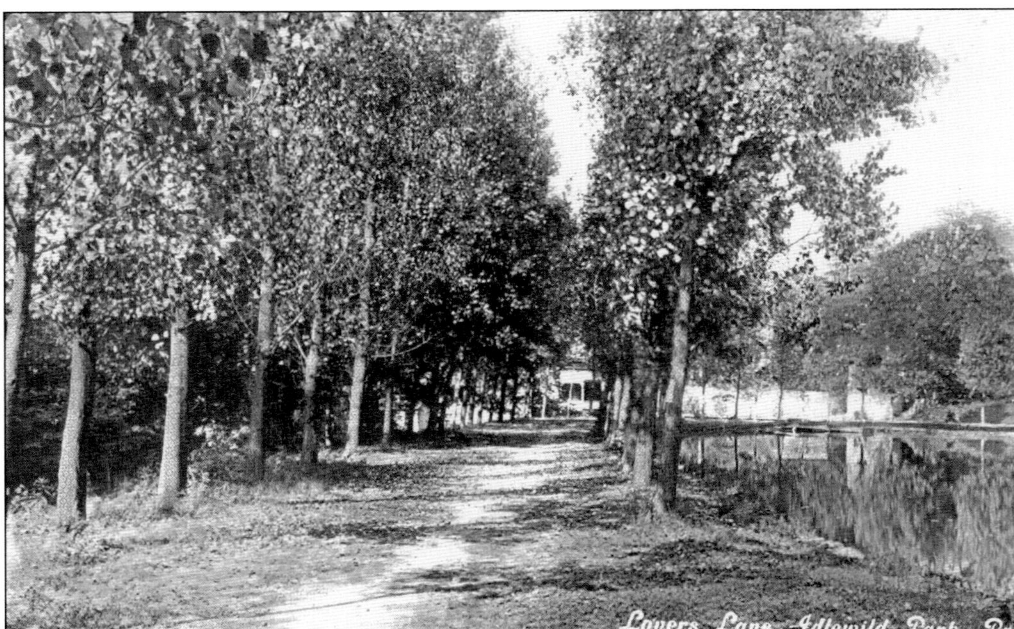

Shady walks surrounding Lake Bouquet offered a romantic setting for couples visiting the park. Referred to as "Lovers Lane," the scenic pathways have often been depicted in postcards.

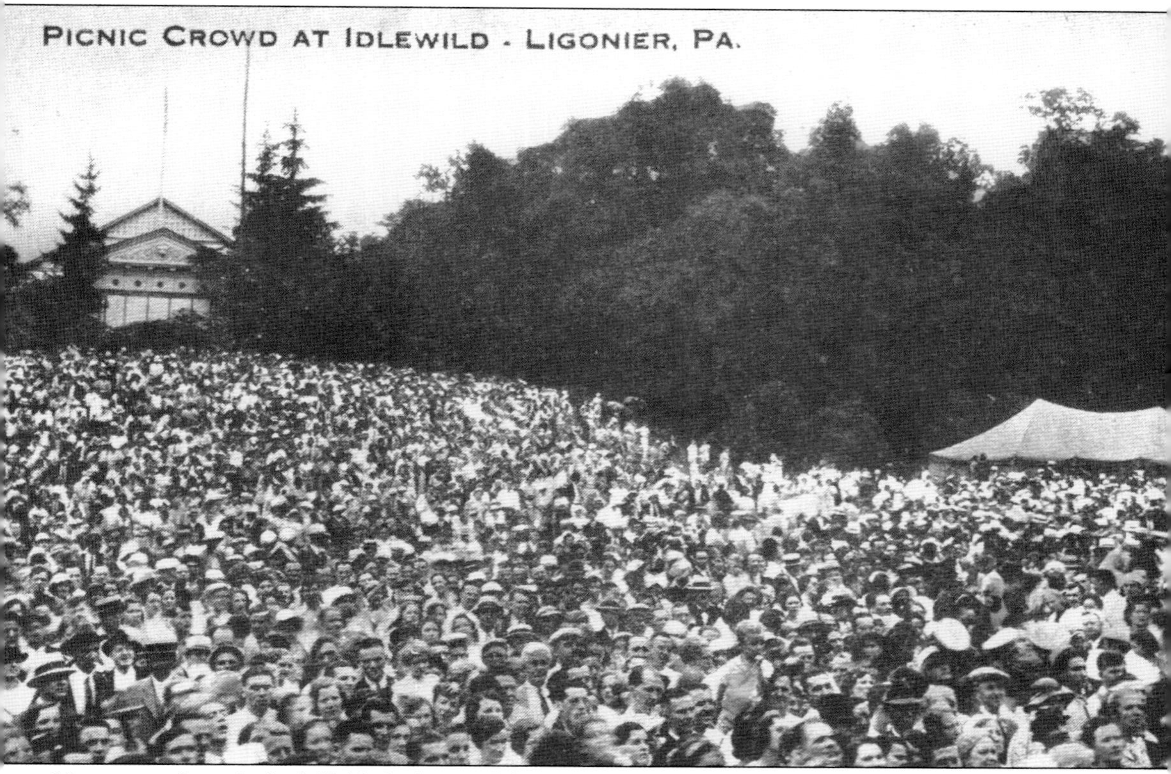

Huge crowds pack the hillside in front of the auditorium, as can be seen in this 1930s postcard. Aerial acts were commonly held at this location. Prize drawings for company and community picnics also took place at this location. These drawings often attracted thousands of hopefuls waiting to hear if their ticket would be called.

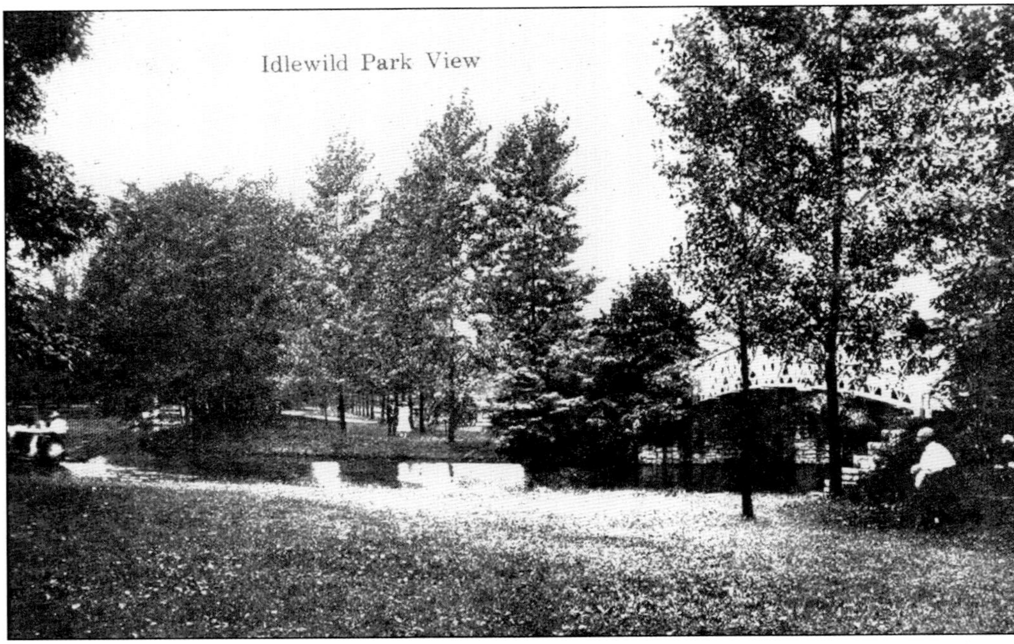

The bridge featured in this card spans the eastern edge of Lake Bouquet, leading to Flower Island. Just beyond the bridge are the tracks to the Ligonier Valley Railroad.

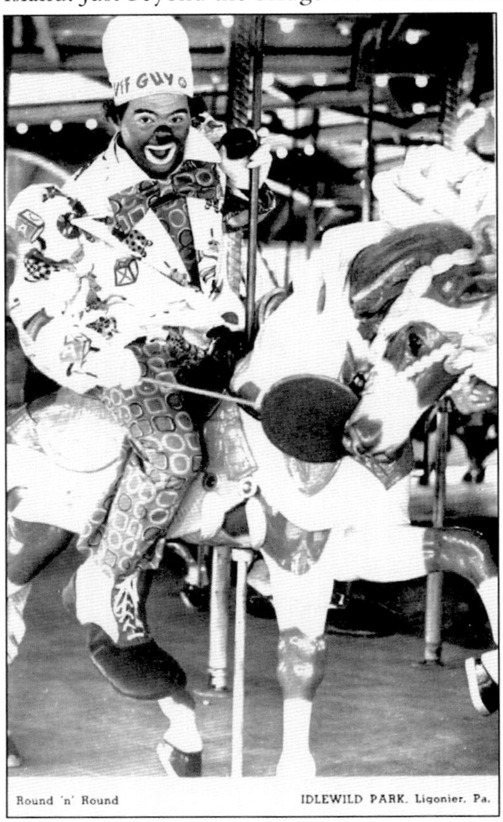

"You Can't Beat Fun" was Idlewild Park's slogan during the 1950s. This postcard showing a clown on the merry-go-round was meant to be a fun card, reflecting that theme.

The automobile entrance to Story Book Forest was modeled after a castle tower. Still visible from the road, Story Book Forest remains one of the Lincoln Highway's most popular roadside attractions.

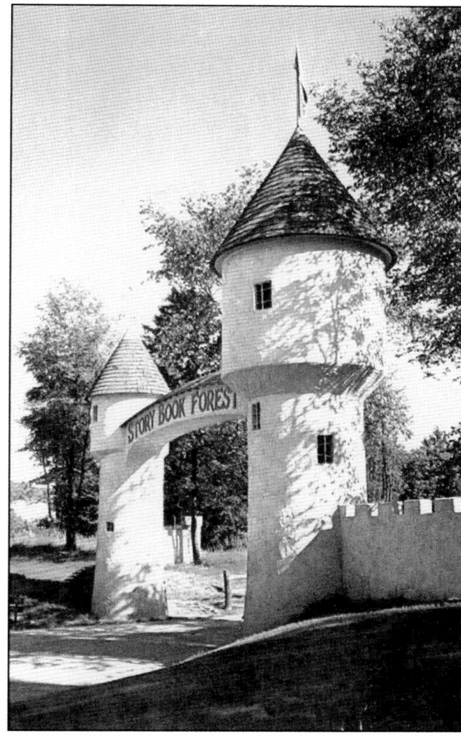

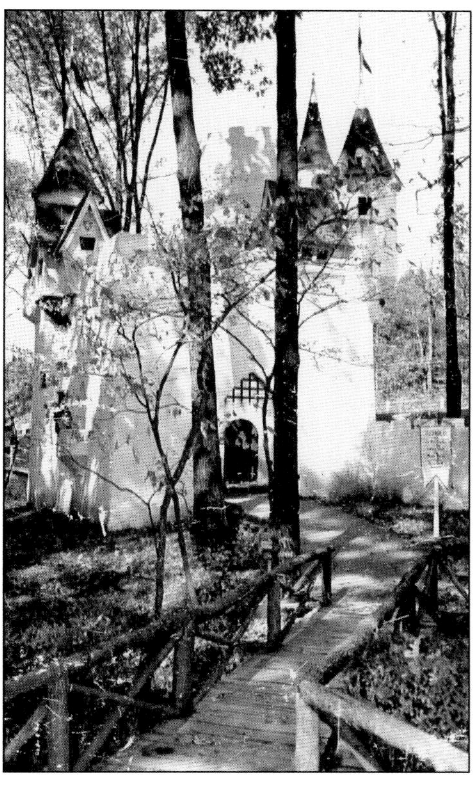

Greeting visitors for more than 40 years, King Arthur's Castle was built in 1956. Initially a walk-through attraction, the castle was converted to a tunnel in 1986 when an automobile entrance was added to Storybook Forest. In order to expand the entrance road to accommodate two-lane traffic, park management made the decision to remove the castle in 1997.

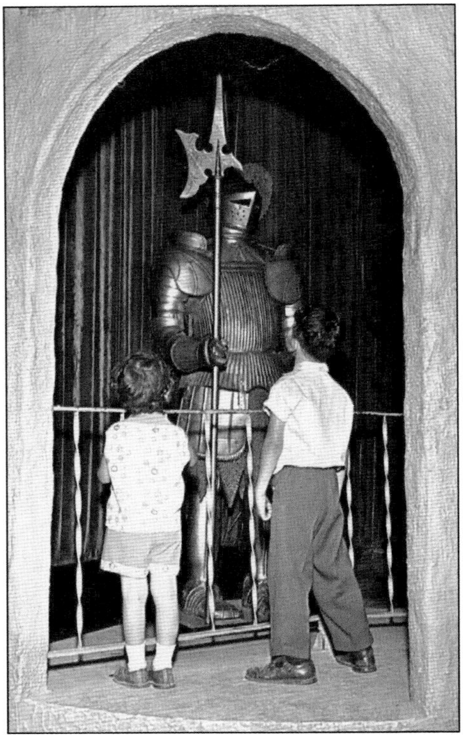

The Golden Knight stood within the castle walls. He would speak to visitors from his alcove within the tower. The knight had once been part of a Chicago restaurant, but once the restaurant closed the statue was brought to Story Book Forest.

Live characters are used in order to enhance the charm of Story Book Forest. One of the most beloved storybook actors is the Old Lady in the Shoe. Some of her children can be seen climbing all over the shoe. The "children" are actually figurines created by local artist Tony Diminno. Very detailed and lifelike, his works can be seen throughout the forest.

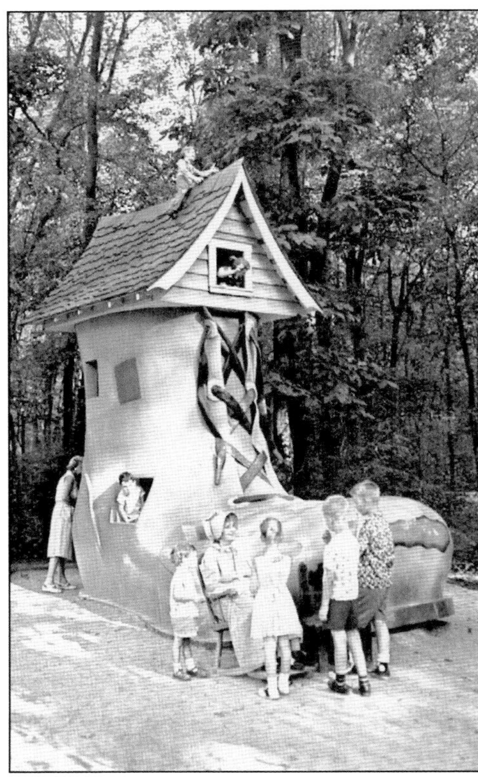

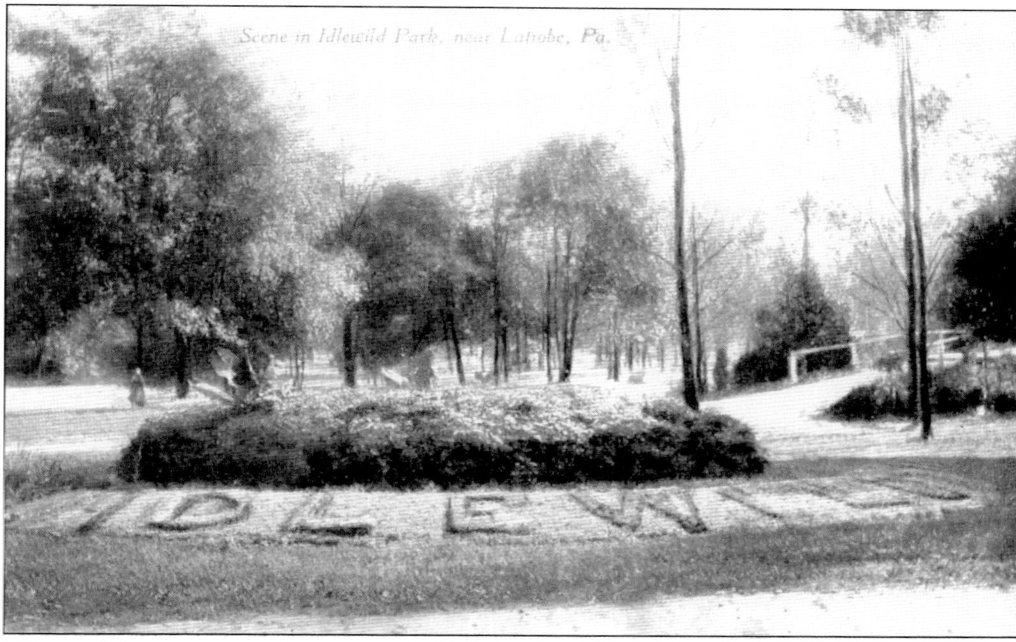

This card shows some of the meticulous grounds keeping that took place at Idlewild Park.

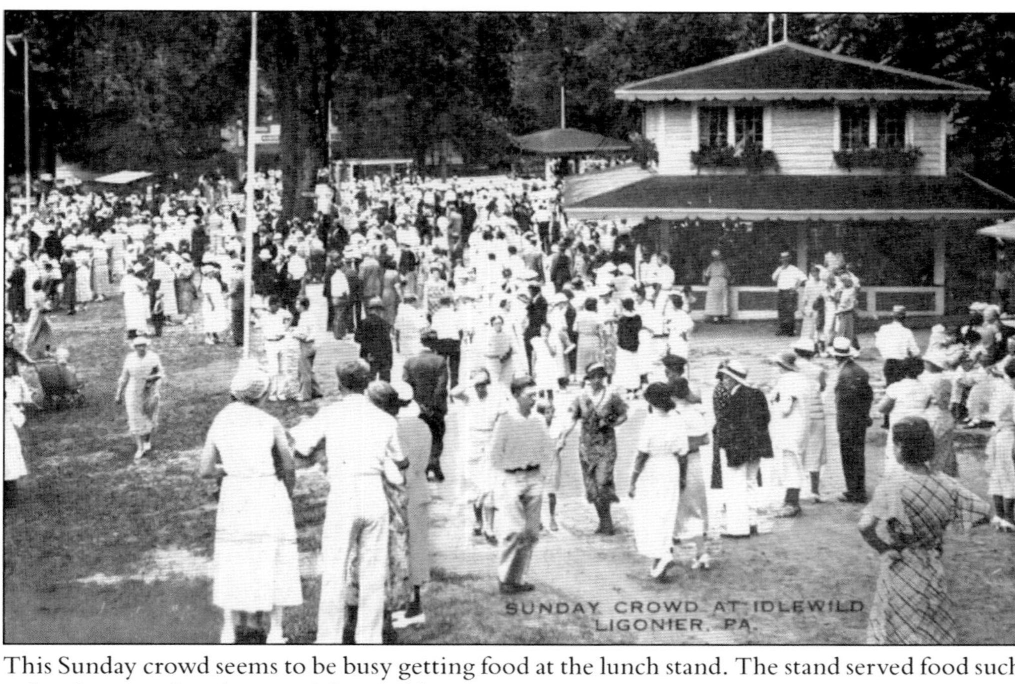

This Sunday crowd seems to be busy getting food at the lunch stand. The stand served food such as hamburgers, hot dogs, and french fries.

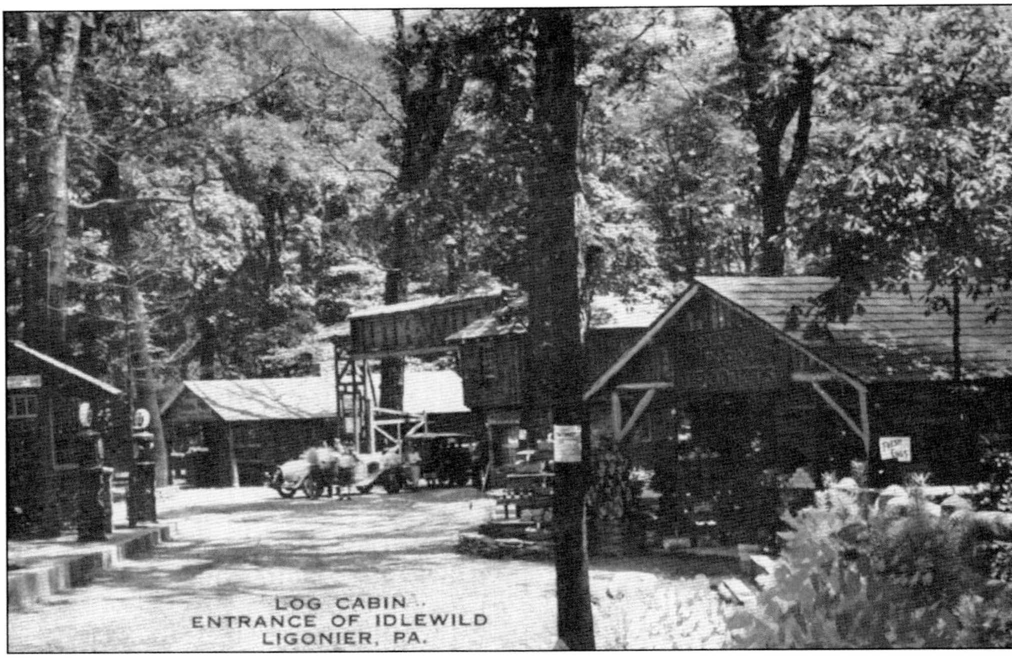

The 1930s Idlewild Park log entrance featured several businesses, including a Gulf Oil station, the Trading Post gift shop, the Roundhouse, and the Ligonier Valley produce market. The log structures were made of logs shipped from Canada.

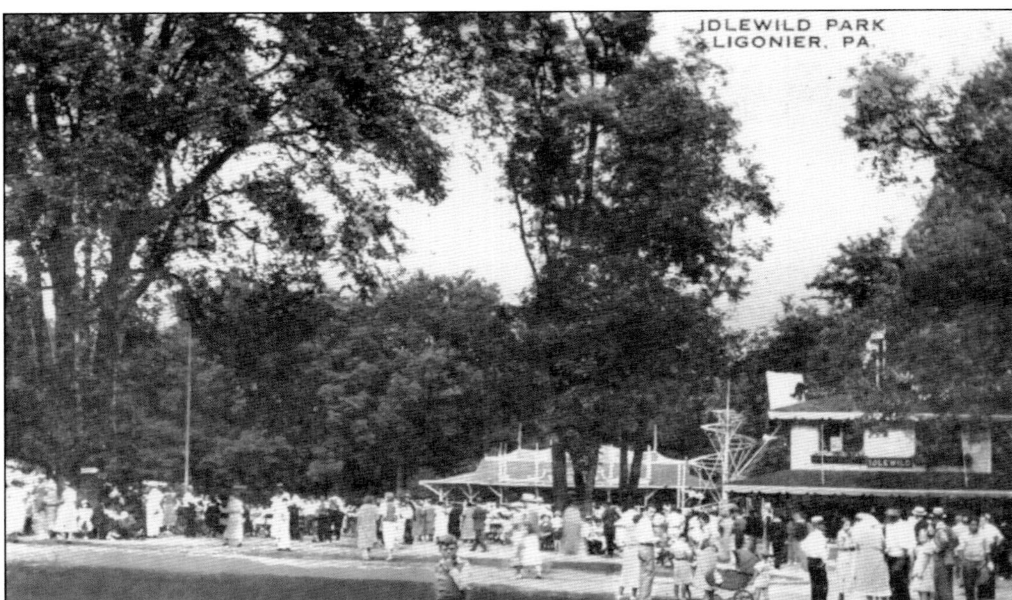

Built in 1931, the new two-story Idlewild Park depot can be seen to the right of this picture. On the second floor were the park offices and a souvenir stand, while a refreshment stand and waiting room were located on the first floor. Also visible in the center of the card, behind the tree, is the Skooter building. The building was also home to 20 electrically operated Lusse bumper cars.

Four

Surroundings

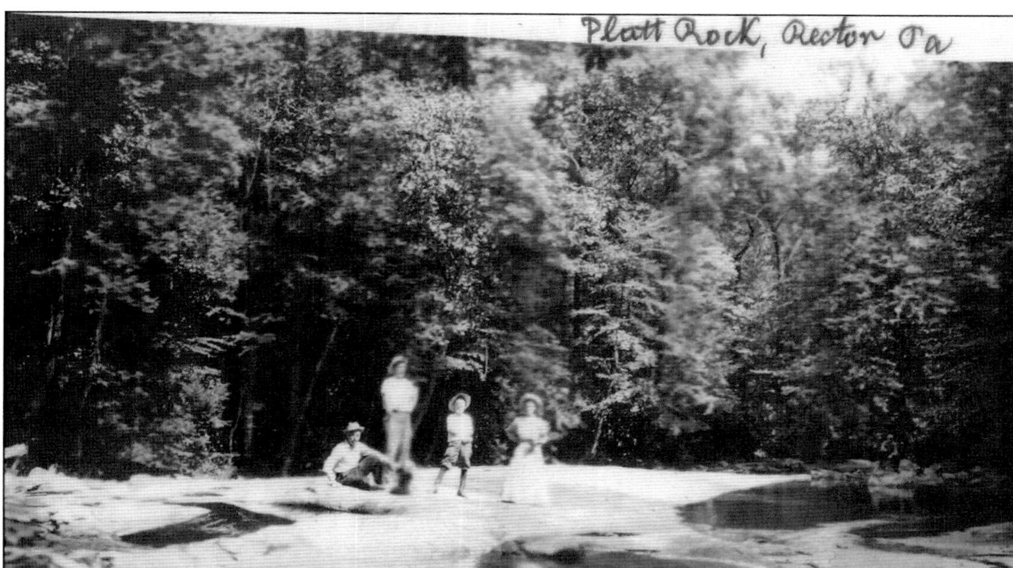

Flatt Rock Trail, located in Linn Run State Park, is a half-mile trail that concludes at a large flat rock in Linn Run Stream. The individuals in this postcard are enjoying a relaxing day at the river.

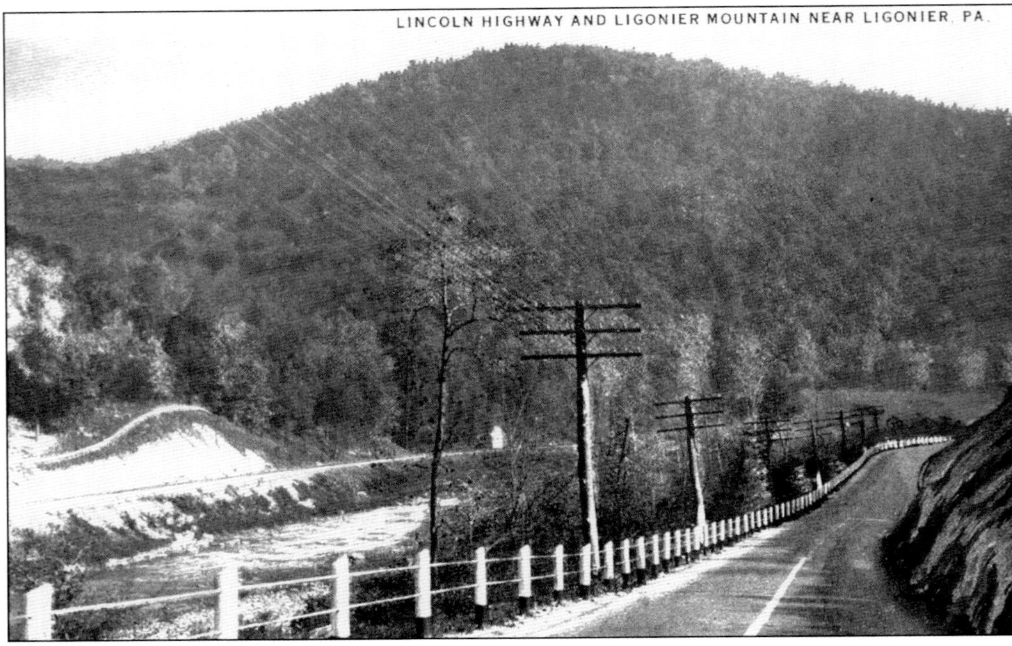

The Lincoln Highway was a vital part of life in Ligonier and Latrobe. The highway, which supplied the economy and transported goods and services, brought visitors to town.

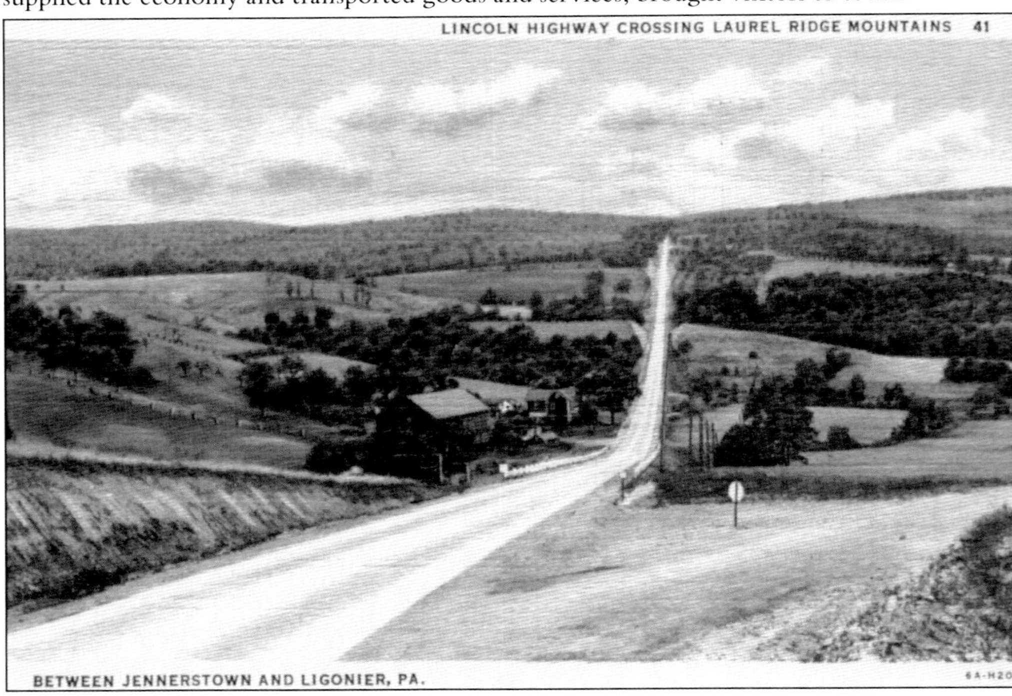

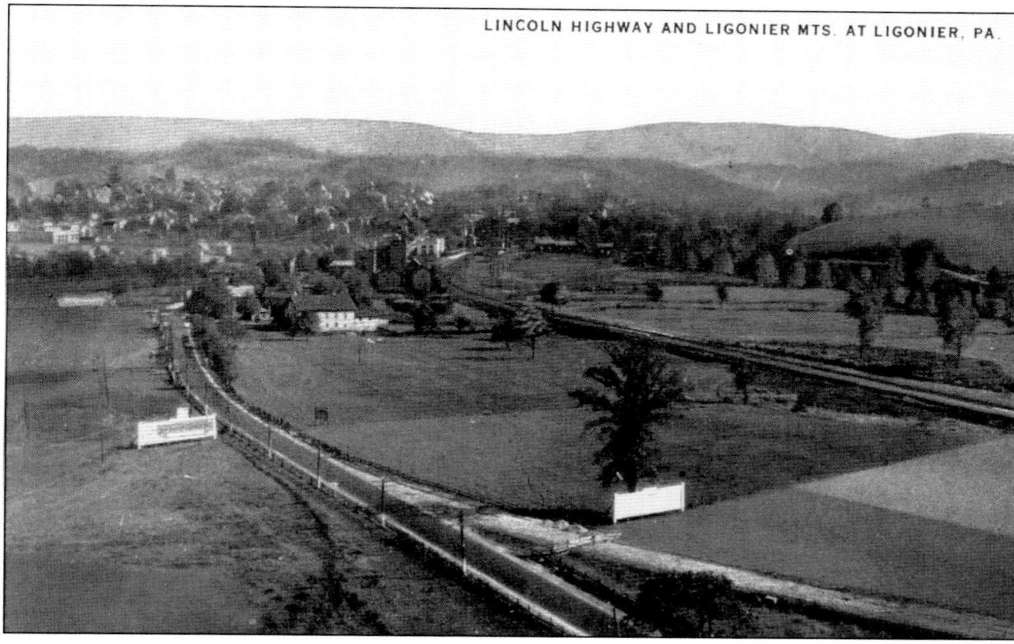

This postcard shows a much-less-developed Ligonier. Route 30 east- and westbound lanes are visible in this card, as is the Ligonier Valley Railroad station in the center of the card.

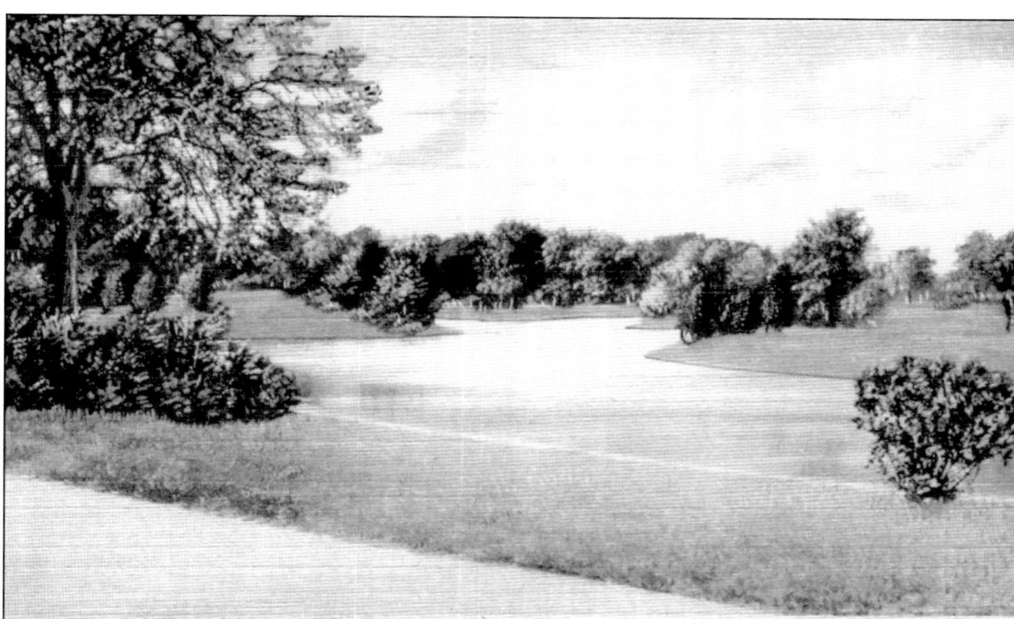

This generic card shows a beautiful scene in Ligonier.

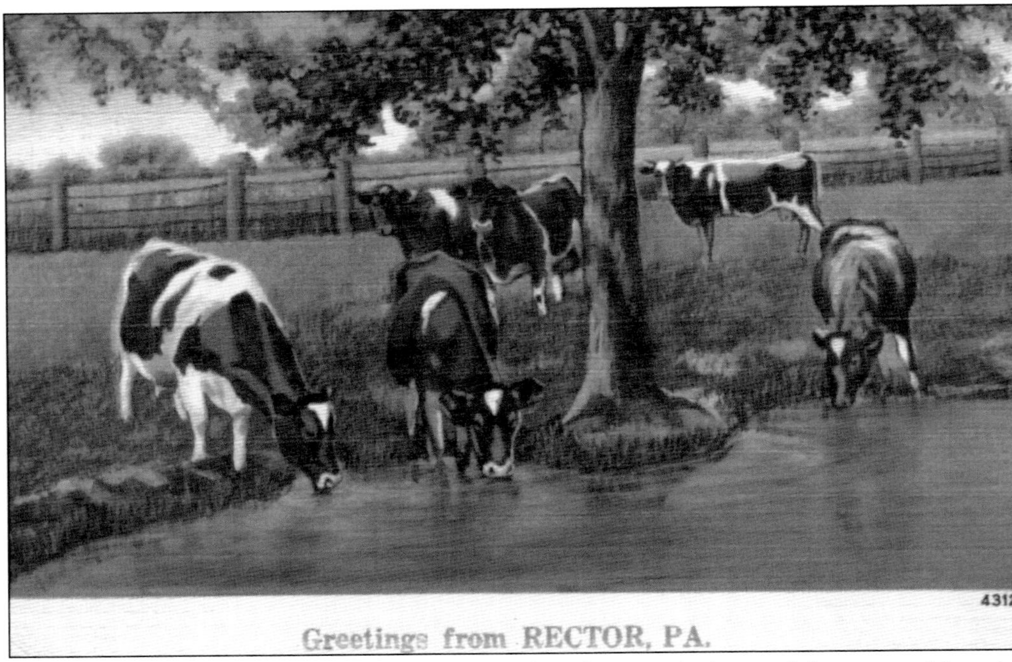

Located five miles southwest from Ligonier, Rector is located between Ligonier and Laughlintown.

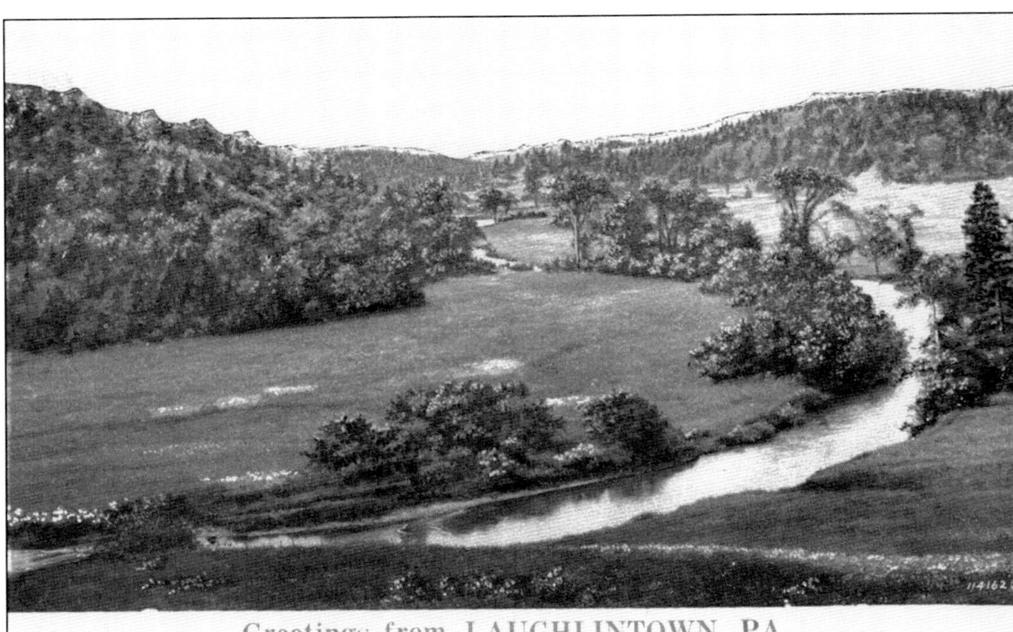

Home of the Compass Inn and the Forbes State Forest, Laughlintown is located four miles from Ligonier.

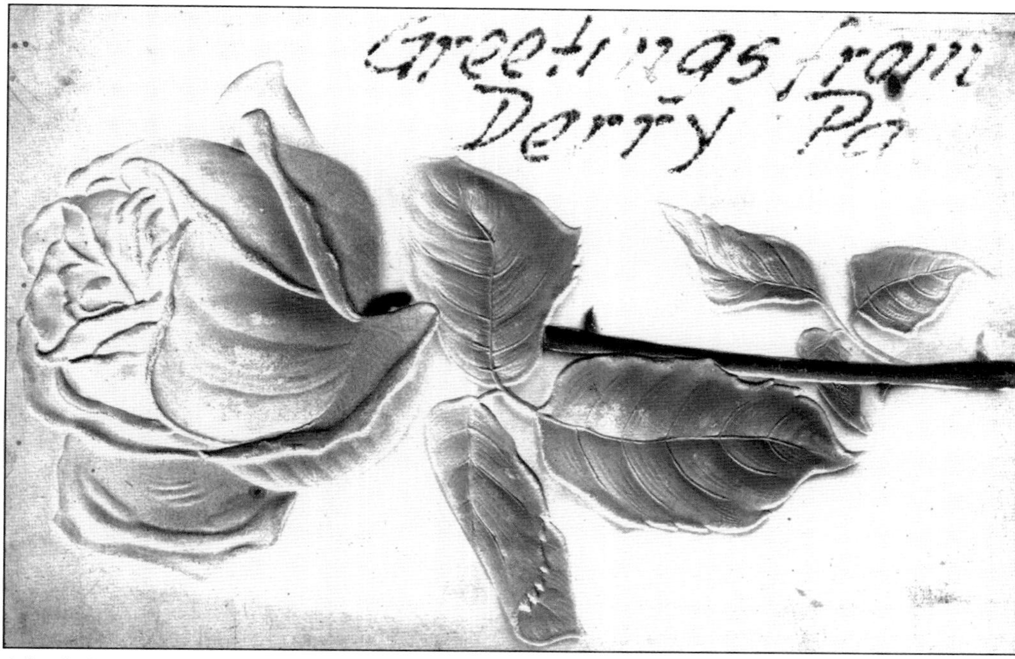

After being incorporated as a stop on the railroad, Derry's main industry changed from agriculture to the transportation of goods, services, and ideas.

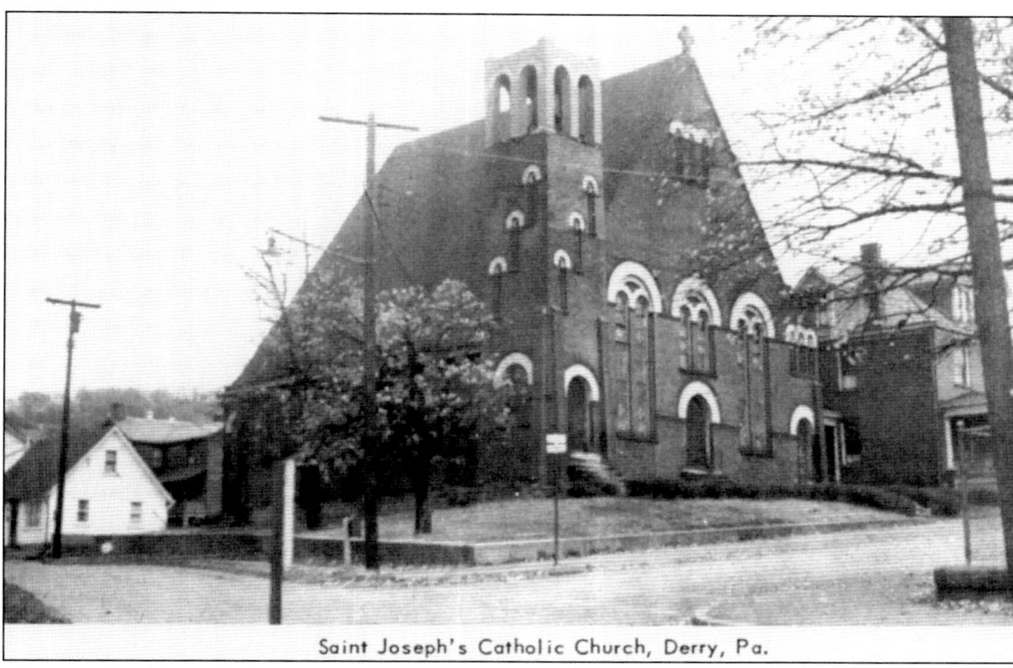

Saint Joseph's Catholic Church, Derry, Pa.

The St. Joseph's Catholic Church was replaced with a newer facility in 1959.

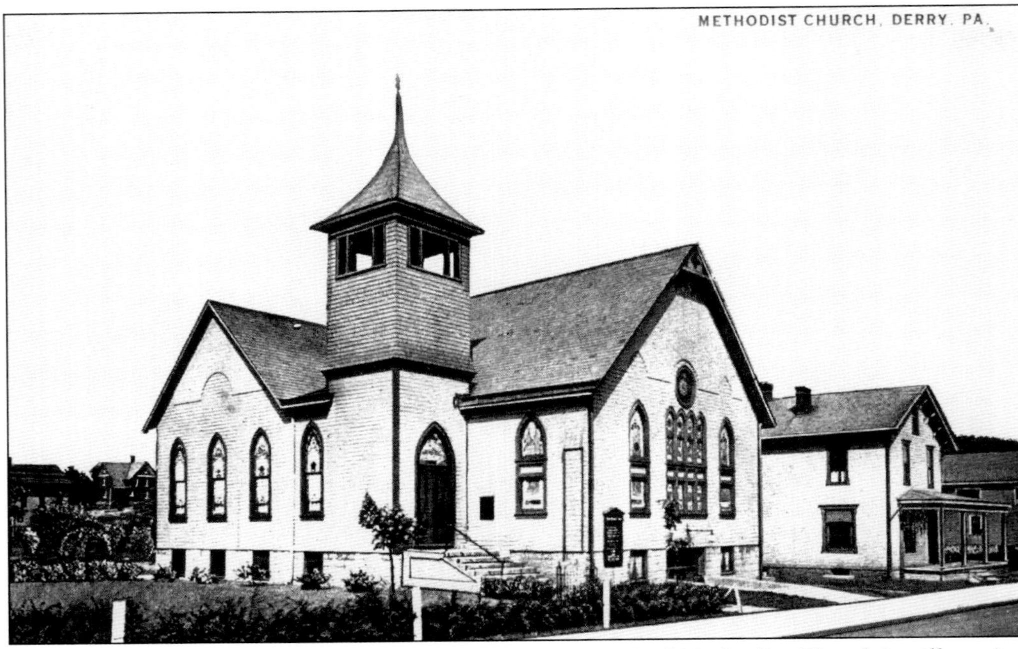

Located on Third and Ligonier Streets, the Derry First United Methodist Church is still serving the Derry community. Although minor renovations have been done to the building, the exterior remains largely unchanged.

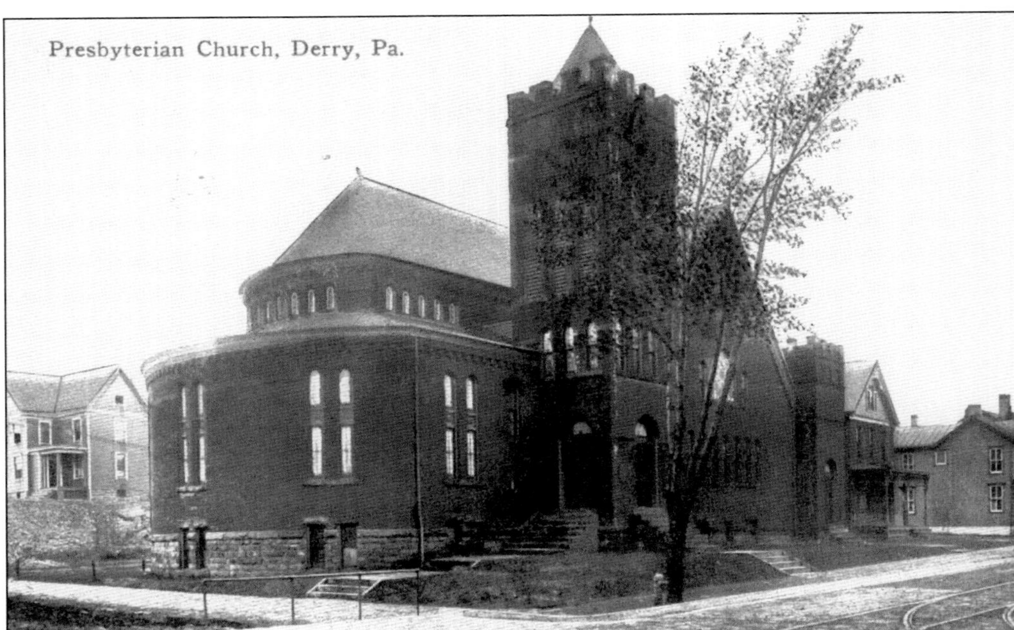

Located on North Chestnut Street, the Derry Presbyterian Church was built in 1894 and added onto in 1986.

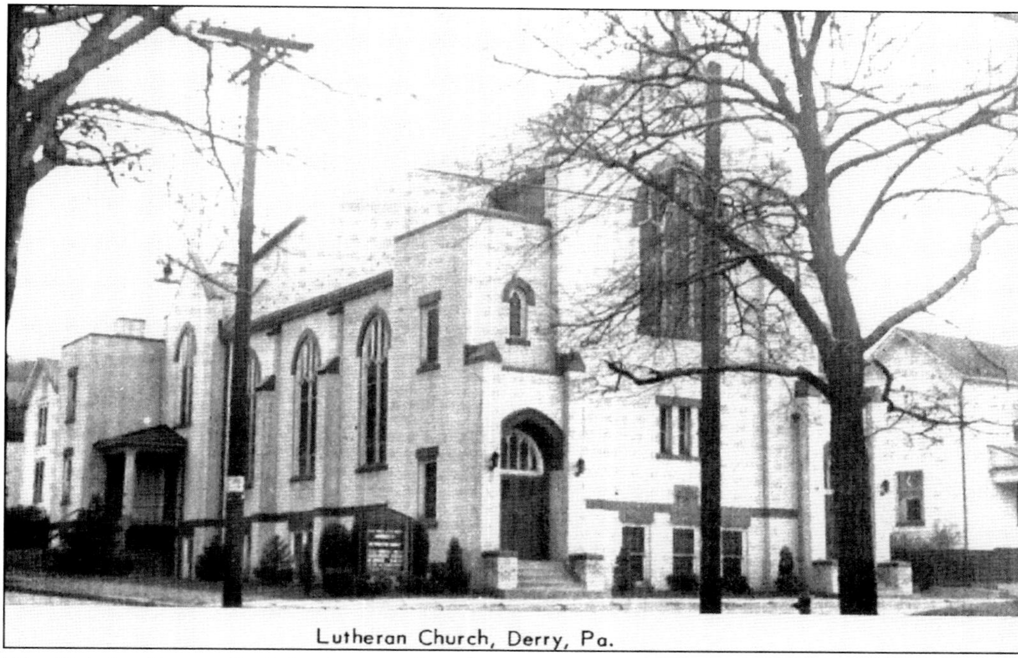

The Trinity Evangelical Lutheran Church, located on West Fourth and Chestnut Streets, has been serving the Derry community for over 80 years. The outside facade remains largely unchanged.

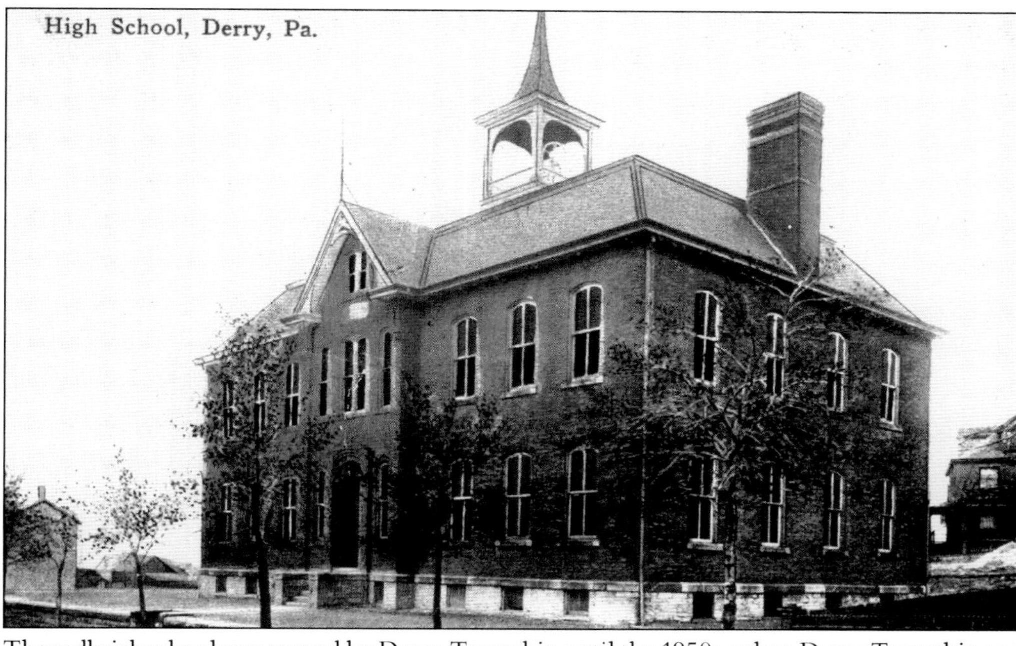

The redbrick school was owned by Derry Township until the 1950s, when Derry Township and Derry Borough school districts merged. The Derry Township School still exists, located near the present high school, although through extensive renovations it is barely recognizable.

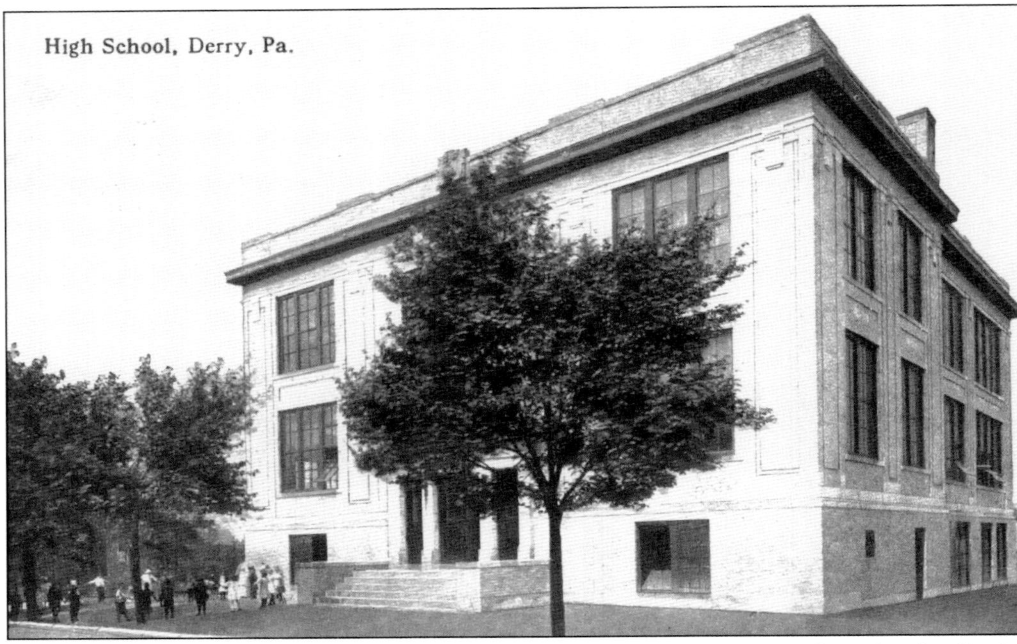

Located along Route 217, the school was originally owned by Derry Borough, and as the district grew, a wing was added to the school. The original school building was eventually torn down, and the additional wing is now used as private offices.

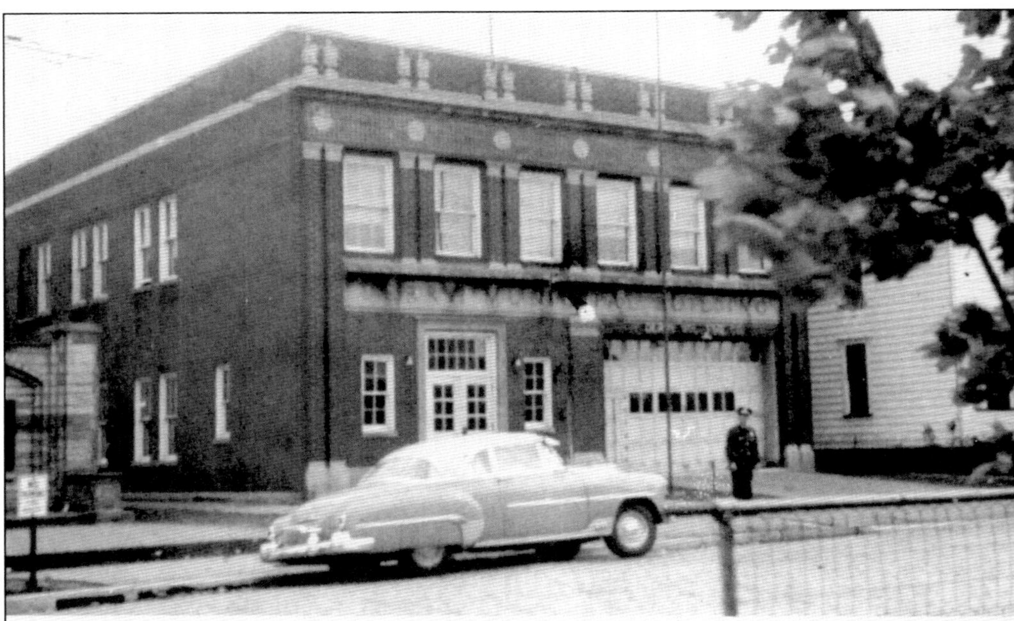

Built to house the Derry Fire and Police Department, the Derry Municipal Building is located on East Second Avenue.

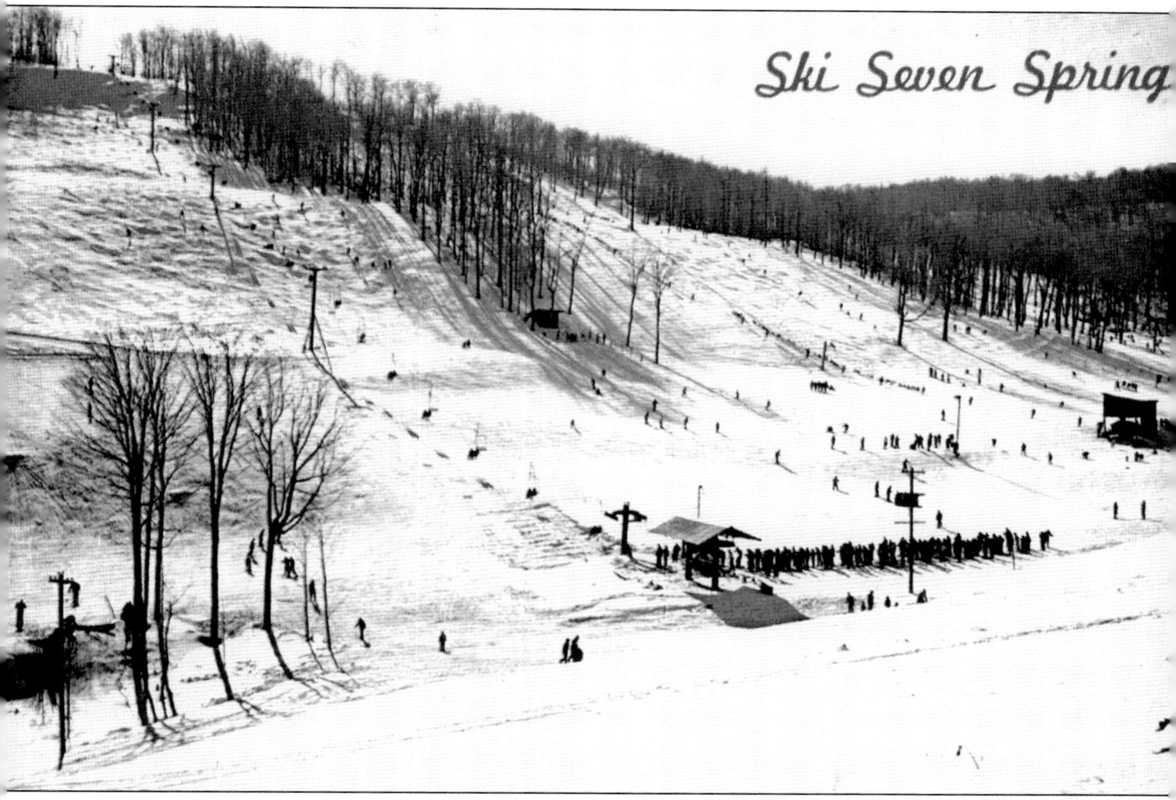

Seven Springs Mountain Resort, located in Champion, offers a wide variety of activities, including fishing, hiking, and golfing in the summer and skiing and snowboarding in the winter. The resort was originally opened in 1932 by German-born forester Adolph Dupre. The Dupre family ran the resort until 2006, when the Dupre family sold the resort to the Nutting family.

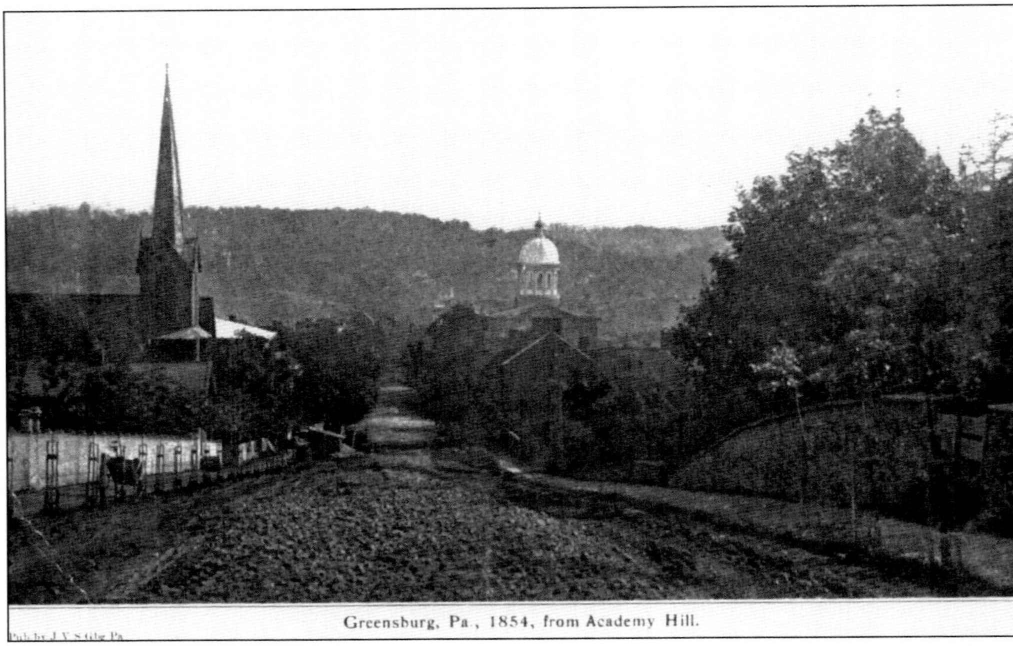

This postcard from 1854 taken from North Main Street at Academy Hill shows a much different view of Main Street than many later cards would. Noticeably absent are any carriages or pedestrian traffic, and the dome of the city's third courthouse on the right and the spire of the Episcopal church on the left dominate the skyline. In later years, many of the trees on the tree-lined sidewalks would also be removed, as would the railroad tunnel under Main Street.

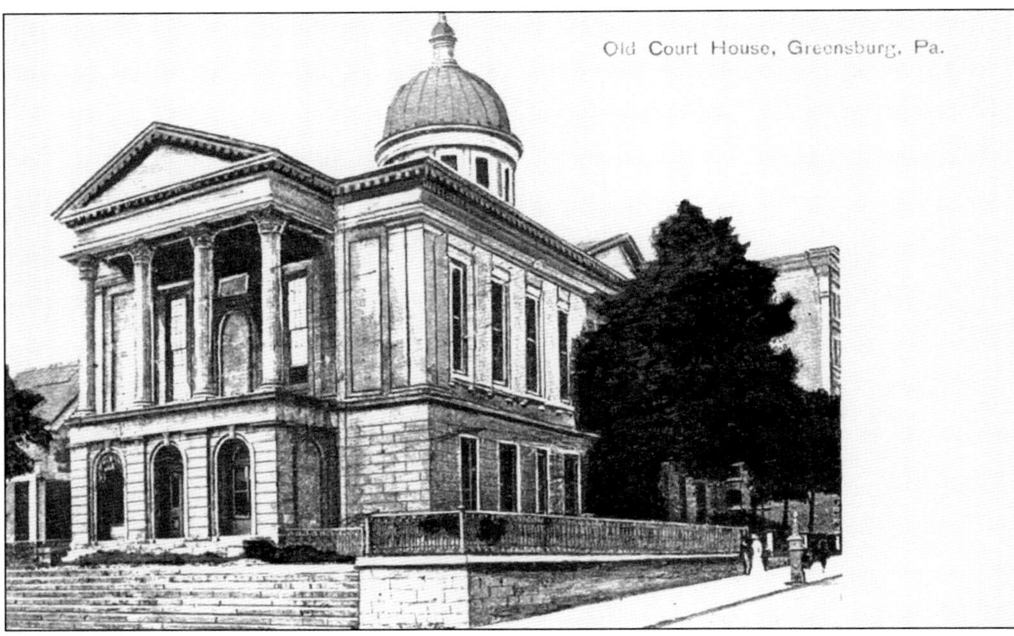

The county's third courthouse, which was built in 1856, served the county for 50 years, but by 1900 more space was needed, and the building was demolished in 1901 to make way for the county's fourth courthouse, which is still in use today.

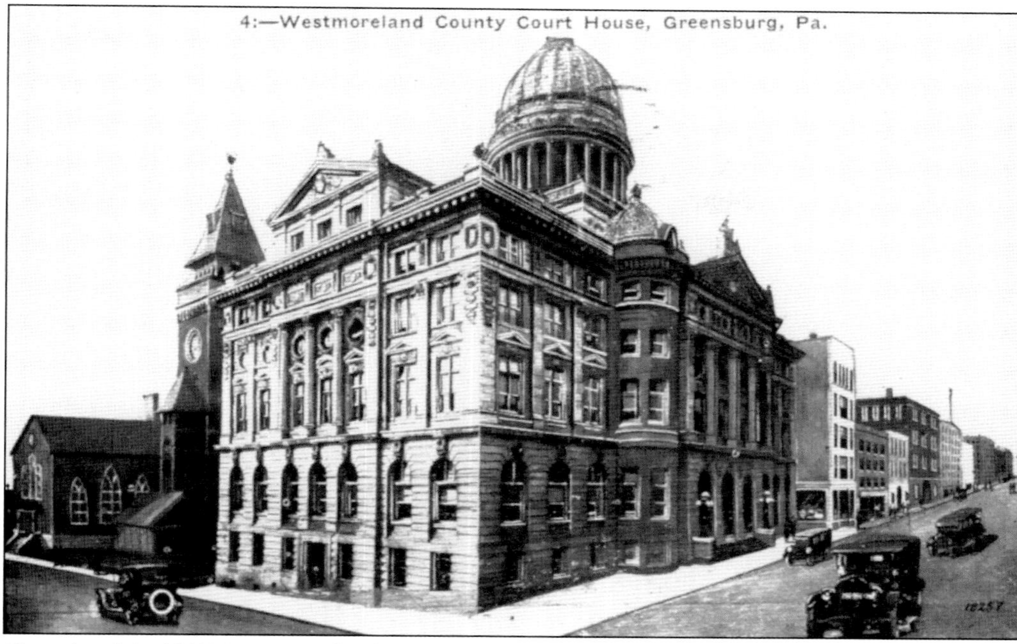

Completed in 1907, Westmoreland County's fourth courthouse stands on the corner of North Main and West Pittsburgh Streets in Greensburg. The original Westmoreland County Jail, erected in 1883, was located directly behind the courthouse. With 72 cells, the jail functioned until 1963, when it was torn down, having outlived its usefulness. The very visible clock tower served as a town landmark for many years.

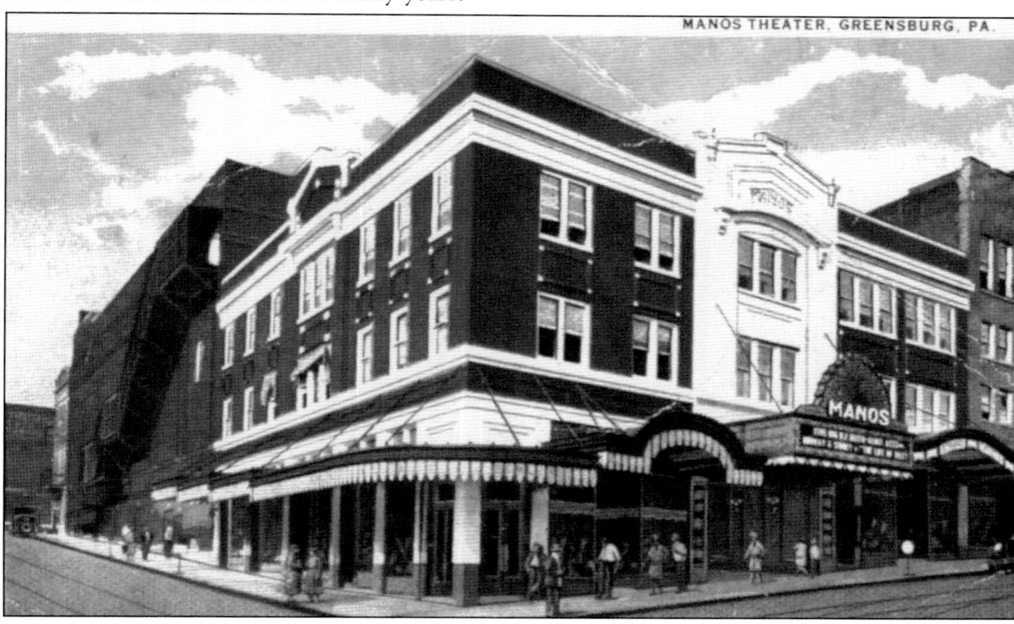

In 1920, the Manos family purchased the Rialto Theater on Otterman Street. The family expanded the theater and renamed it the Manos Theater. The theater was reopened in 1926 and had a seating capacity of over 2,100. Now the theater operates under the name the Palace Theater and is operated by the Westmoreland Trust.

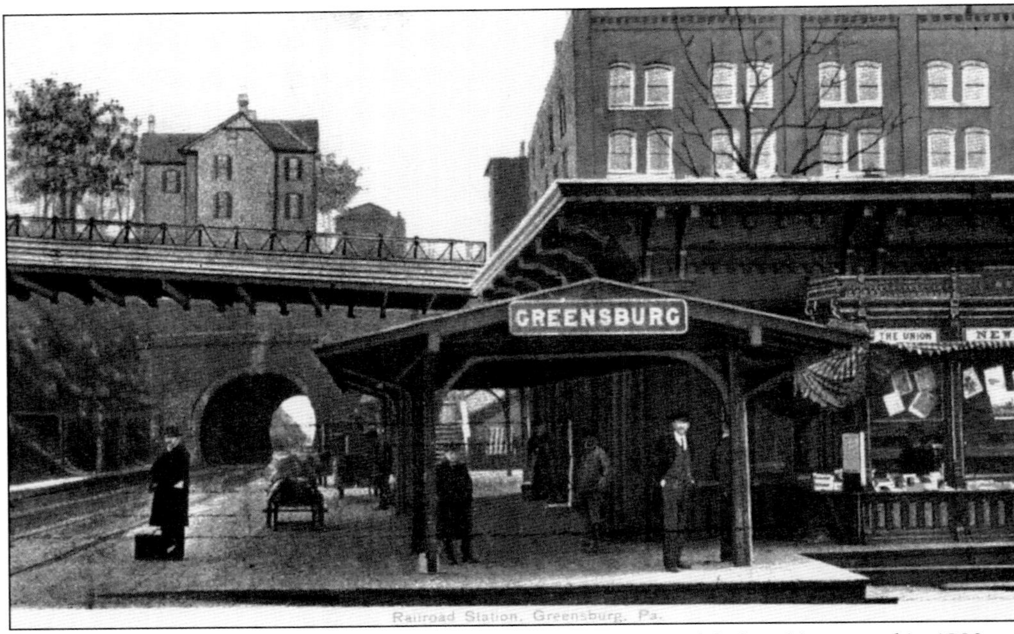

The first Pennsylvania Railroad station in Greensburg was remodeled and improved in 1893 and stood until 1909. The tunnel, which can be seen in the background, was used until the tracks were raised in 1910. This eliminated the grade crossing at Harrison Avenue. The station was eventually torn down in 1911 to make way for a new station.

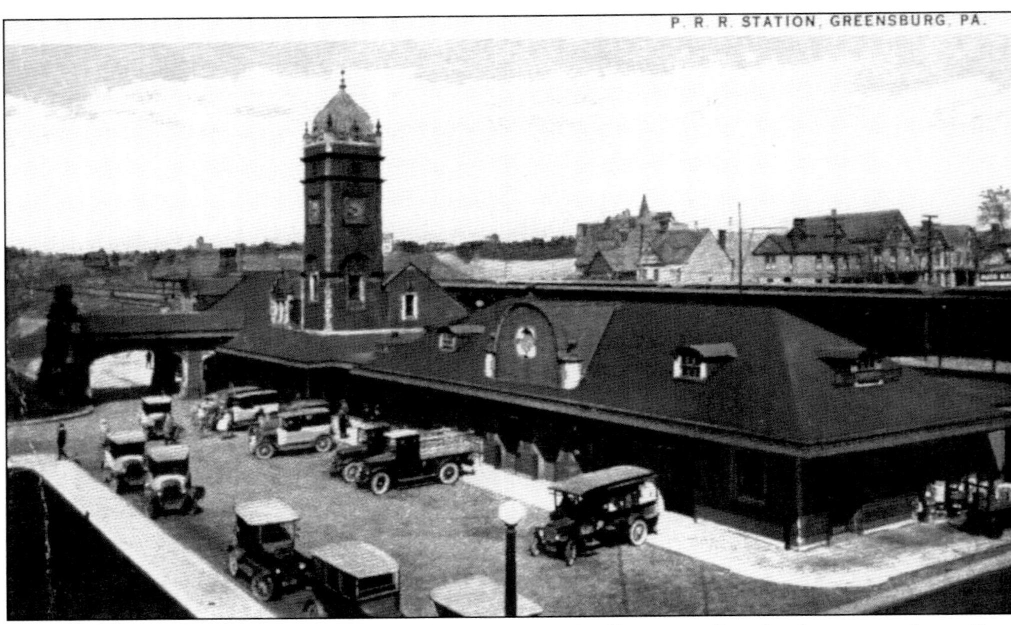

In 1911, a new Pennsylvania Railroad station was built to service the large number of rail passengers that were passing through Greensburg on a daily basis. For many years, it was the fourth-busiest station on the main line. In the 1950s, the Greensburg railroad station closed due to decline in rail travel and the rise of automobile use. The station was remodeled and reopened in 1997 by the Westmoreland Trust.

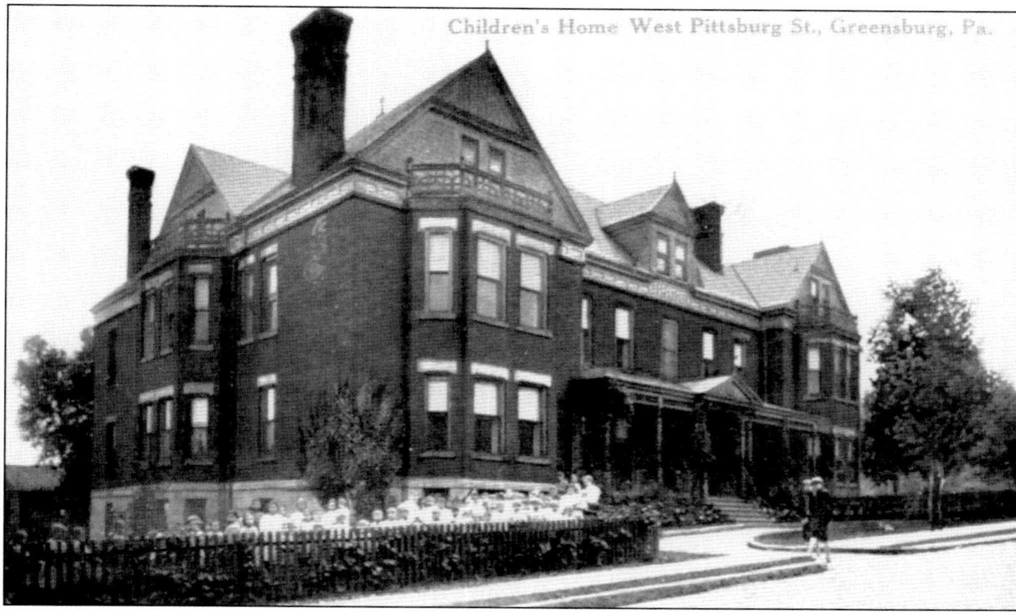

Founded in 1886, the Westmoreland County Children's Aid Society acquired the Frank Scherer mansion in 1897 at 514 West Pittsburgh Street. After 85 years of operation, rising costs eventually forced the society's closing in 1971. The closing of the Westmoreland Society marked the closing of the last county children's home in the state. Although several thousand children were cared for during the society's existence, only 13 children were left at the end. The building was demolished in 1972 and is now a hospital parking lot.

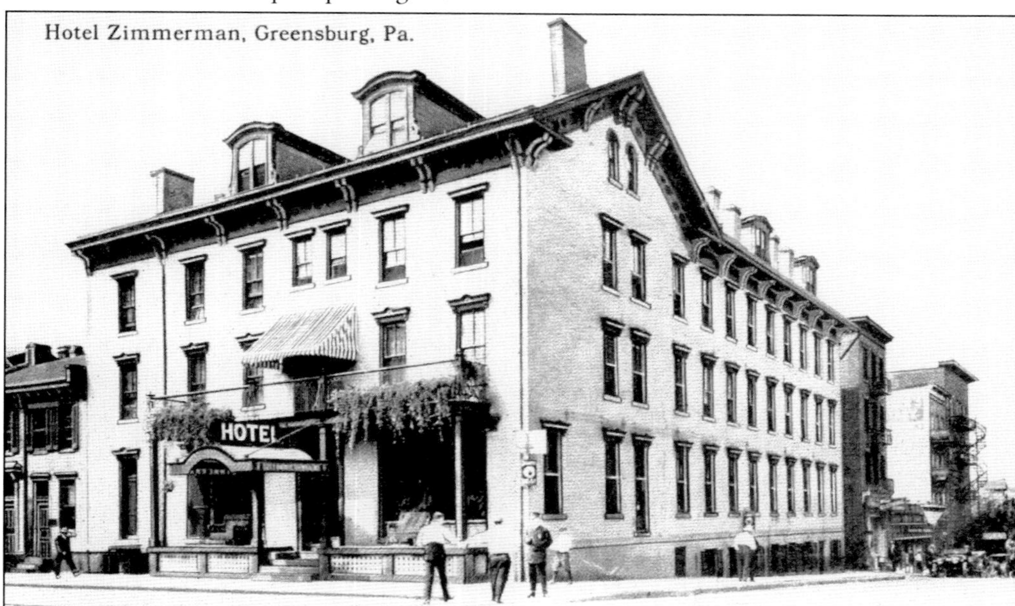

The Hotel Zimmerman, located at Second and South Main Streets, was an upscale dining and lodging spot as well as a local hub of activity. The Zimmerman closed its doors in 1921 with the beginning of Prohibition. Eventually Troutman's department store replaced the Zimmerman on the corner.

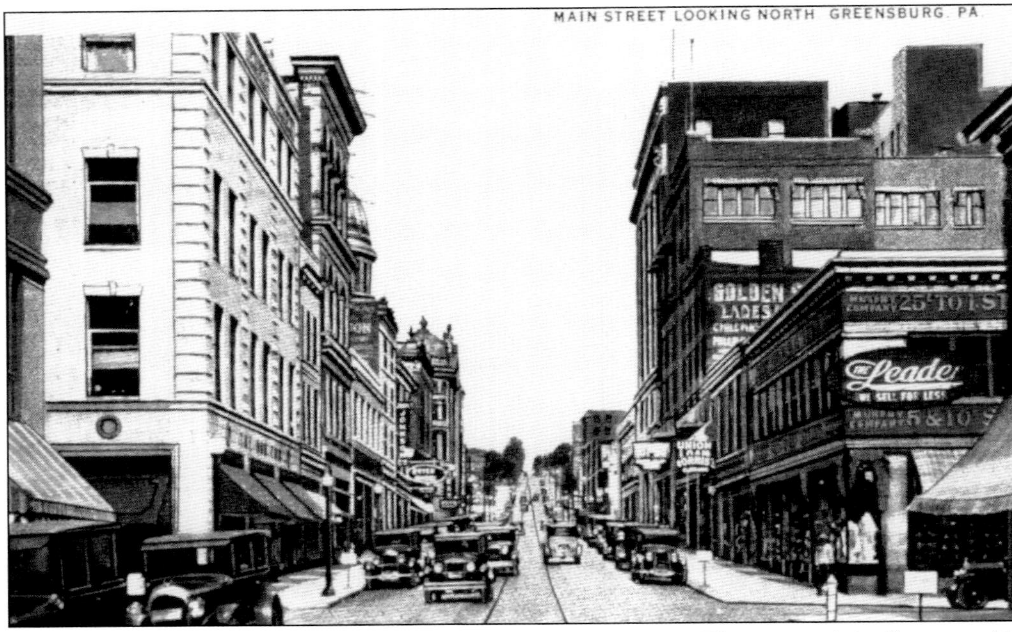

This postcard shows the G. C. Murphy 5 and 10 on Main Street. The store originally opened in 1911 but later relocated to South Main and Second Streets in 1939. The store eventually closed down on Christmas Eve in 1985.

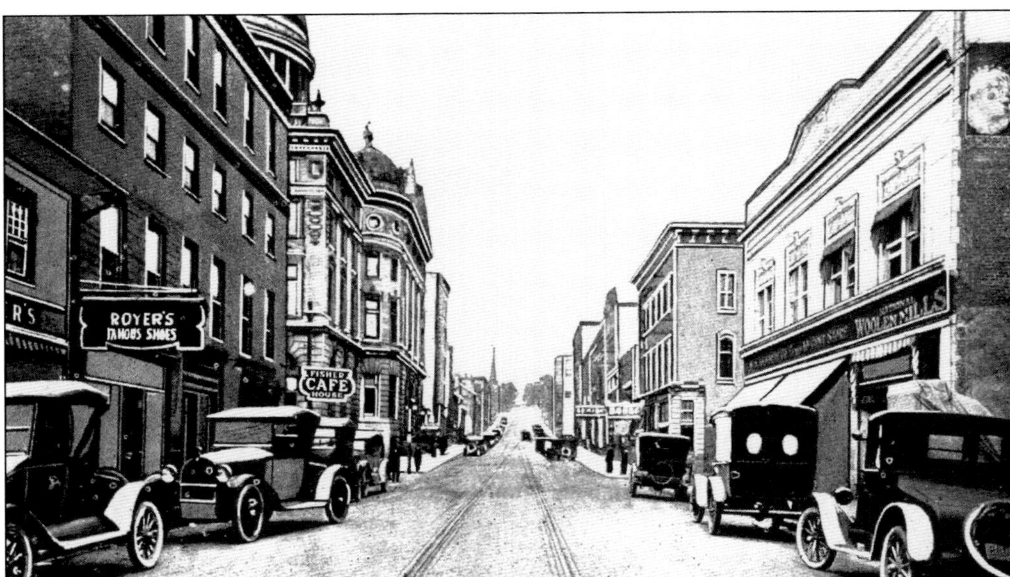

Royer's shoe store opened in 1914 and expanded to its location on South Main Street in 1923 after Arthur Smith had taken over the management from the store's founder, Frank Royer. Eventually the store added men's, women's, and children's clothing. In 1964, Royer's was one of the first companies to open a store at the new Greengate Mall. The downtown store was closed in 1979, when the company was bought out by Lang's Fashions. Farther down the street the Fisher House Café can be seen.

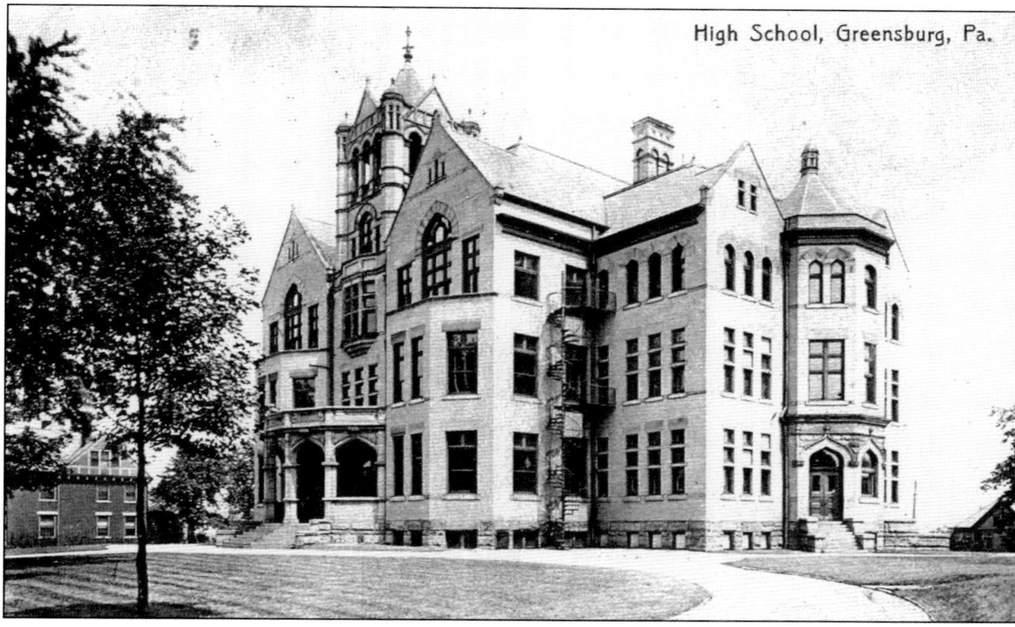

Ground was broken for a new high school in June 1896. Open for the 1897 school term, the yellow brick school featured a vast stairway and room to accommodate 150 senior high and 200 junior high students. The third floor featured a large auditorium, reportedly the largest in the county. In 1959, after years of heavy use, the high school was condemned, and the building was torn down in 1960.

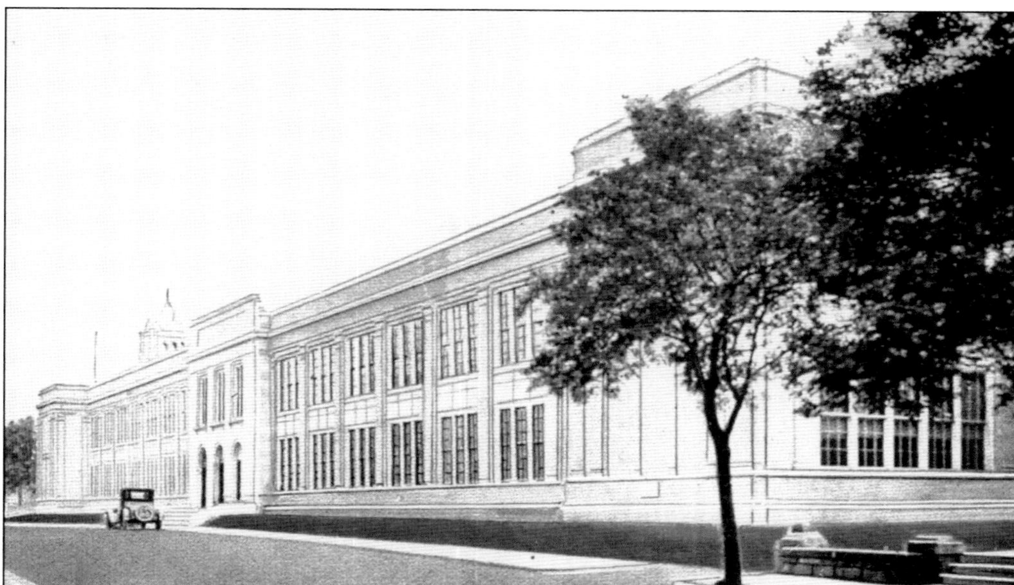

In 1924, work began on a massive new million-dollar high school to solve the district's problem of overcrowding. The new school featured 43 classrooms, shops, laboratories, a gymnasium, a swimming pool, and an auditorium, which was also used for other community functions. In 1978, the building was becoming run down from heavy use and the district took on a $7.2 million remodeling project, which was completed in November 1979.

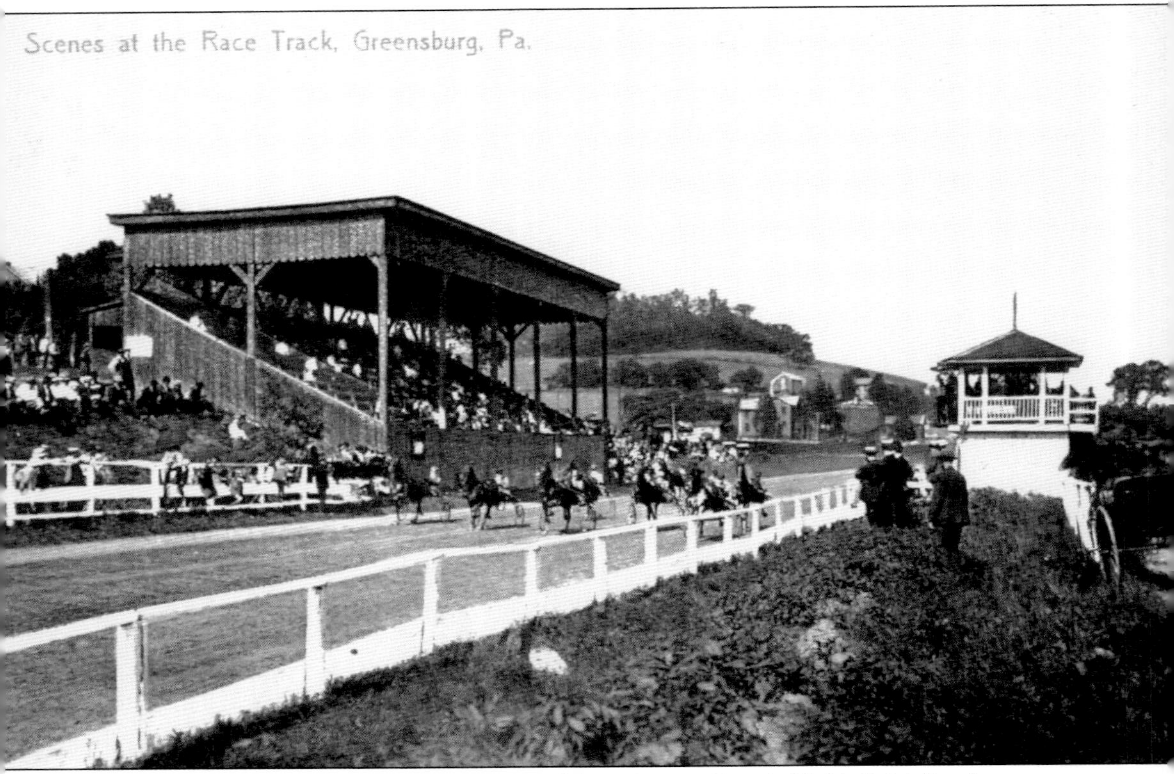

This 1913 postcard shows a horse race taking place at Lynch Field. Initially the races were amateur events, but later national races with professional drivers were scheduled. Racing at Lynch Field came to an end after the 1909 season when the Driving Club suspended operations. Thomas Lynch bought the property much later and donated it to the city to use for recreational purposes. The city, in turn, named the park after Lynch. The track facilities included the track, the grandstand, and a starter's stand for officials.

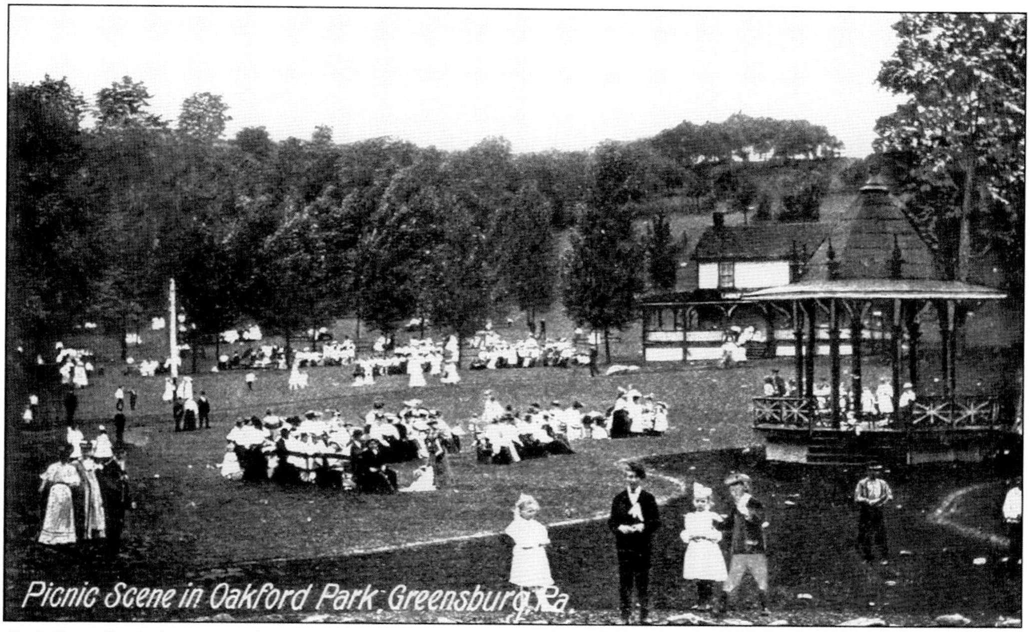

Oakford Park hosted school picnics for both the Jeannette and Penn Township School District school picnics. This postcard shows the Jeannette School District's school picnic in 1908. Schoolchildren, parents, grandparents, and other relatives would come out to the park to enjoy a day of fun.

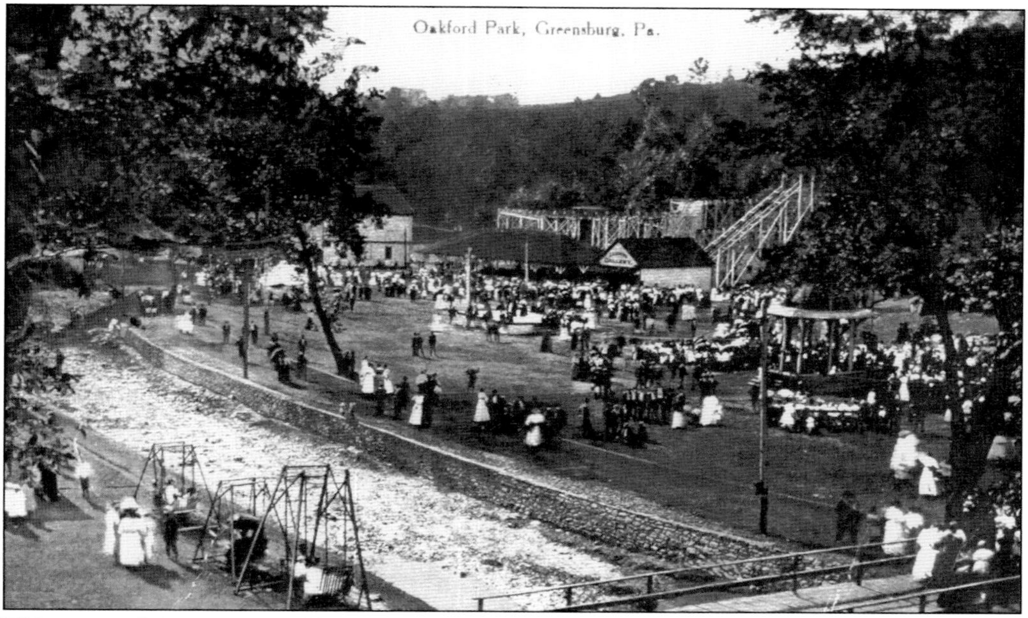

This postcard gives a view of the park from Oakford Park Road. The large building in the middle is the entrance to the roller coaster, which was a three-way, figure-eight coaster named the Leap Frog. It was the number one attraction at the park. Also visible are picnic areas and pavilions.

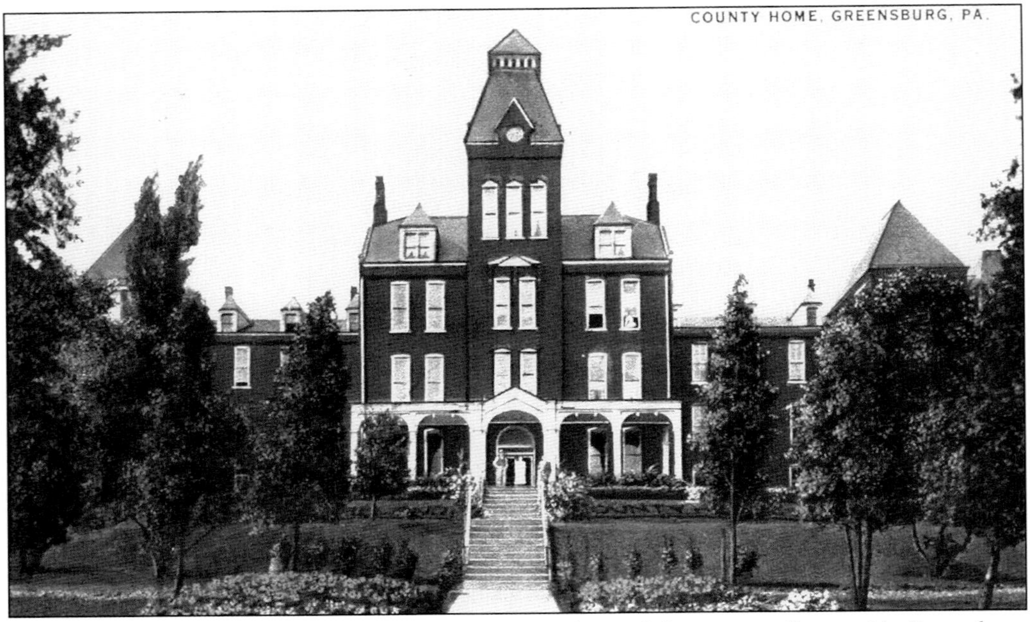

The Westmoreland County Home, or poorhouse, was located about two miles outside Greensburg in Hempfield Township. The home was situated on 180 acres purchased from William Snyder. To keep the home operating, its residents would help with the day-to-day activities of running the home, including harvesting the crops.

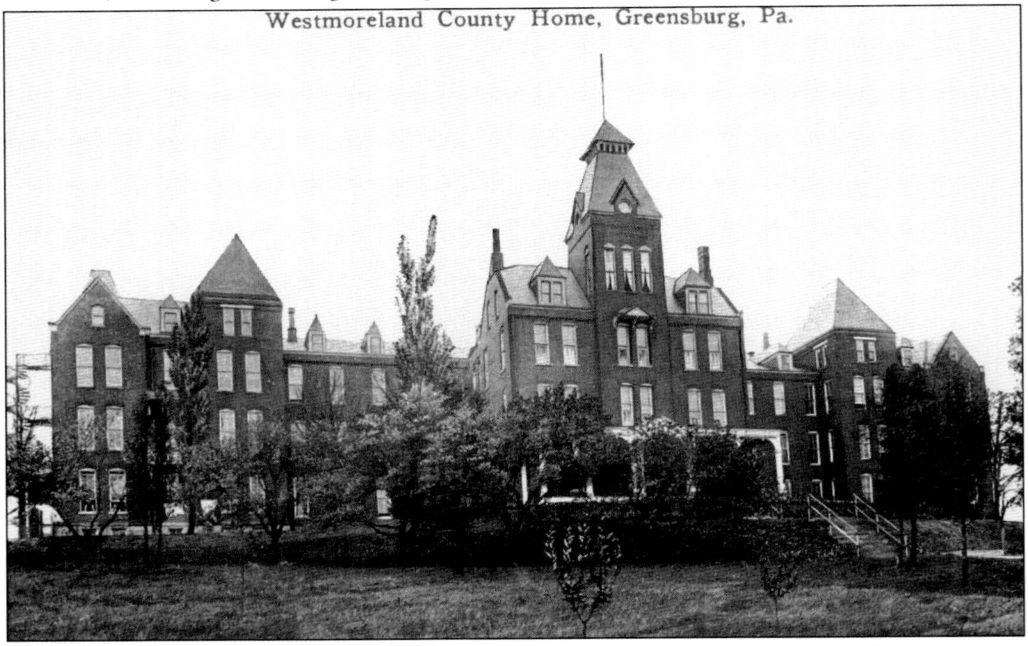

Three buildings occupied the site of the county home during its lifetime. The first home was destroyed by fire in 1862, but because the building's brick walls sustained little damage the building was able to be rebuilt at minimal cost. The second building was also destroyed by fire in 1878, and afterward a much larger and more modern building was built. Now the Westmoreland County Jail occupies the site of the county home.

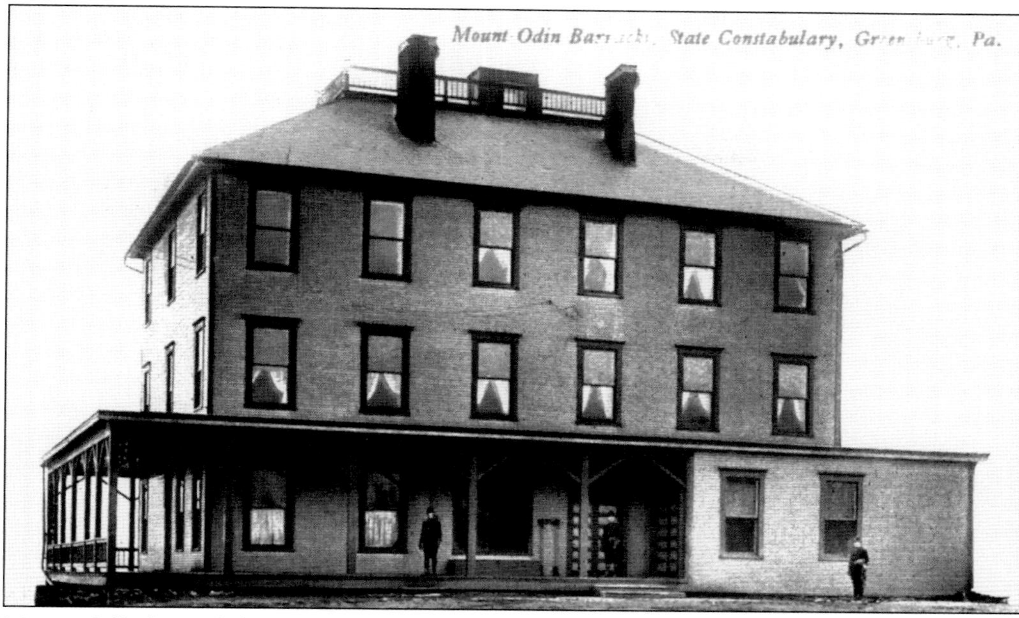

Mount Odin housed the Troop A Pennsylvania State Police, which was formed in May 1905. It was the first of four original troop locations and the only survivor of the first four. In 1913, the troop located to Point Lookout, where the police barracks are still located.

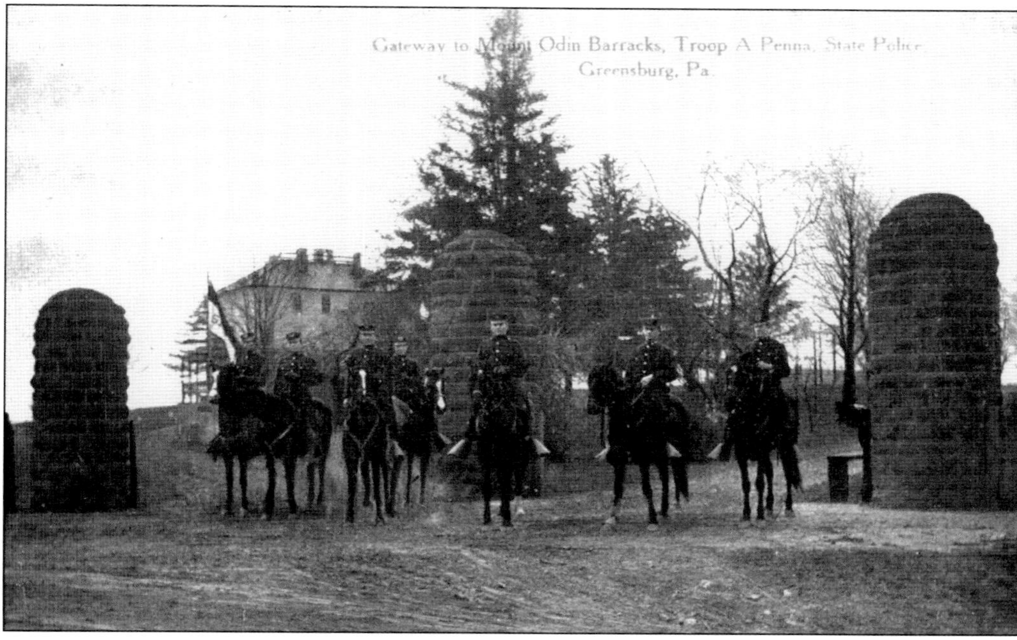

This postcard shows the gateway to the Mount Odin Barrack with the mounted state police. The primary purpose of the police force at that time was to offer police protection to the rural areas in the district where no organized police force existed. After the consolidation of the state police and the Pennsylvania Highway Patrol, the state was divided into four squadron districts with Troop A being part of the first squadron.

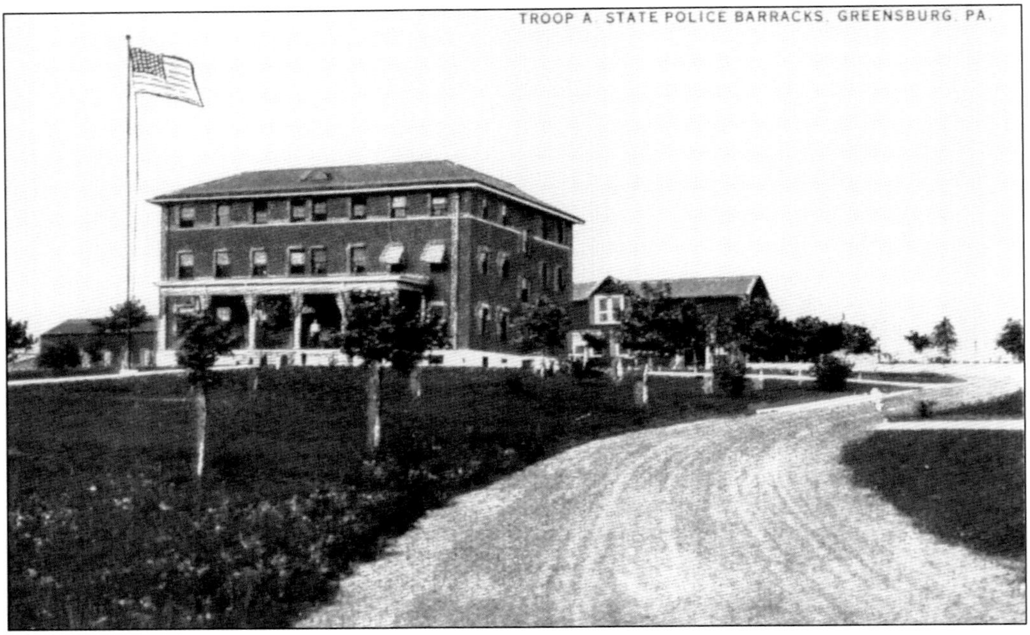

In 1913, Troop A moved to Point Lookout as keeping the barracks at Mount Odin proved inconvenient since the horses were stabled several miles away at what is now Lynch Field.

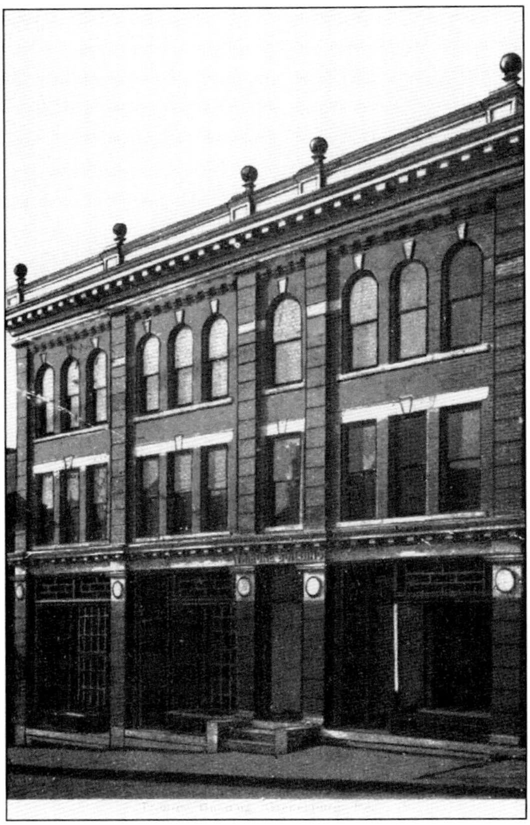

The *Tribune-Review* was located on North Main Street in this redbrick three-story building until 1960, when the newspaper moved to its current location on Cabin Hill Drive. After the paper's relocation, the old building was demolished along with other neighboring buildings to make room for a city parking lot.

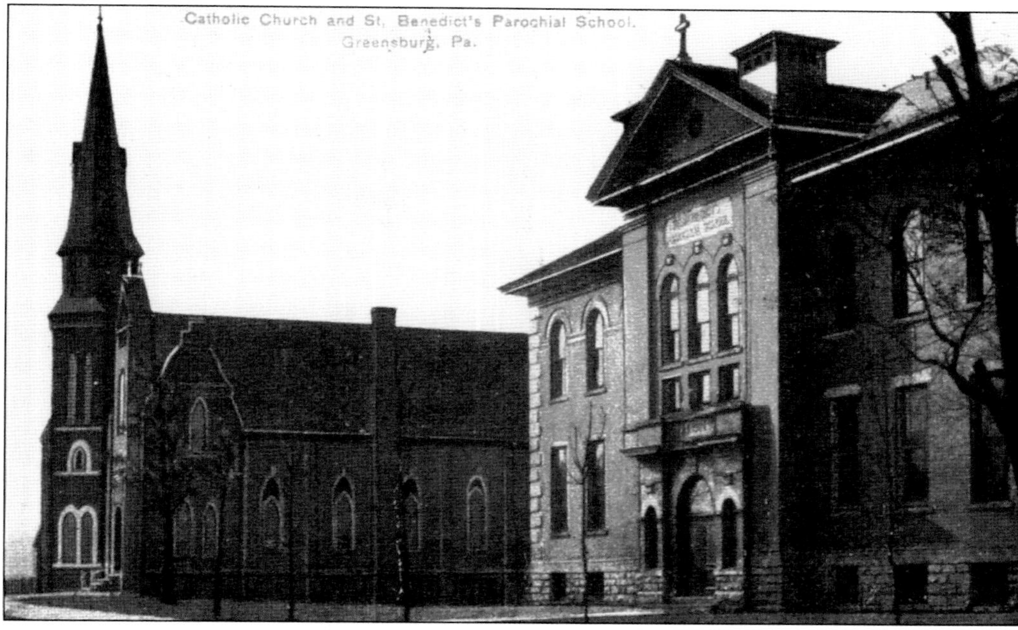

The first Holy Sacrament Catholic Church stood on Academy Hill from 1848 to 1925, when a replacement was built. Located beside the church was the St. Benedict's Parochial School, built in 1904 as part of the Most Holy Sacrament Parish. In 1951, with the formation of the Diocese of Greensburg, the school's name was changed to Blessed Sacrament Cathedral School, and most recently in 1995, the school became known as Aquinas Academy.

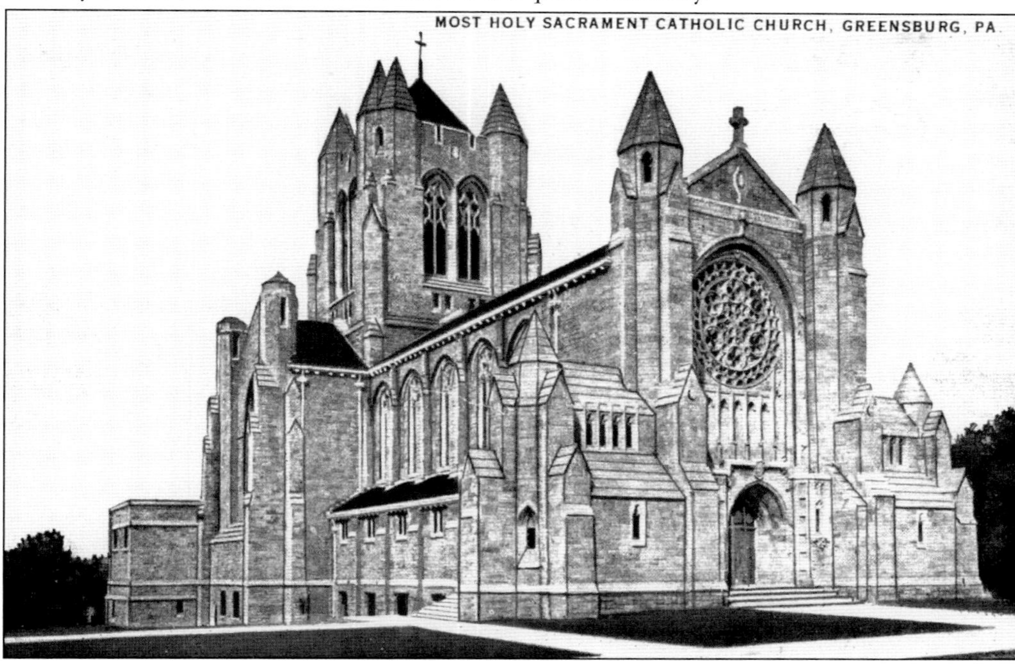

Dedicated in September 1928, the Holy Sacrament Catholic Church is today the largest church in the county and the second to stand on the site. It became the Blessed Sacrament Cathedral in 1952, when the Greensburg Diocese of the Roman Catholic Church was created.

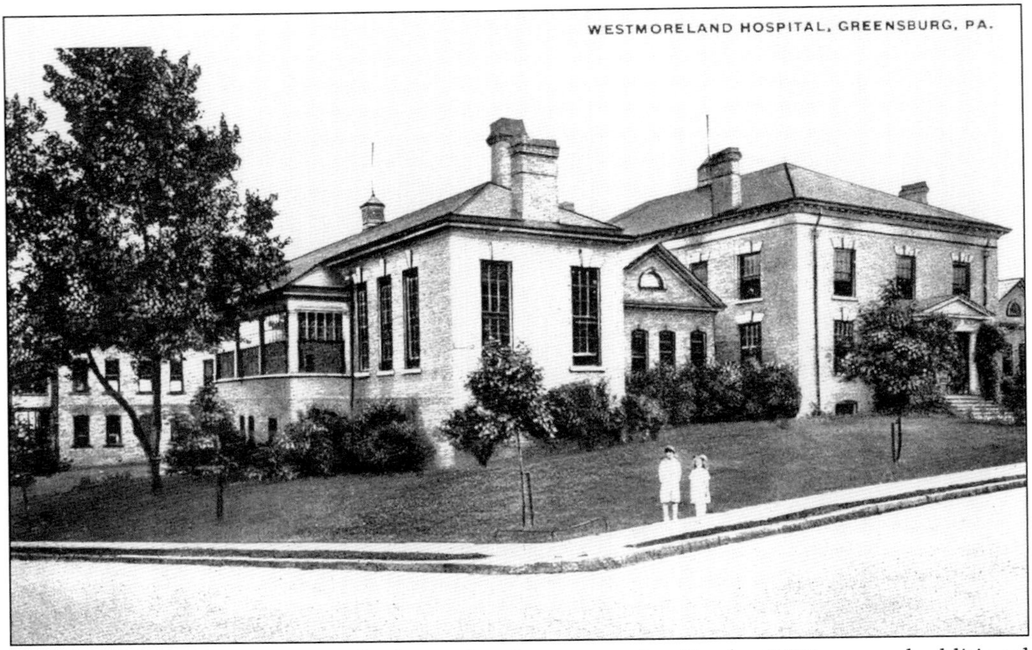

In 1898, Westmoreland Hospital relocated to its present site. By the 1930s, several additional buildings were added to the campus, including a nurses' home. Over the years, many changes would come to the hospital, and many of the buildings seen in the picture no longer exist.

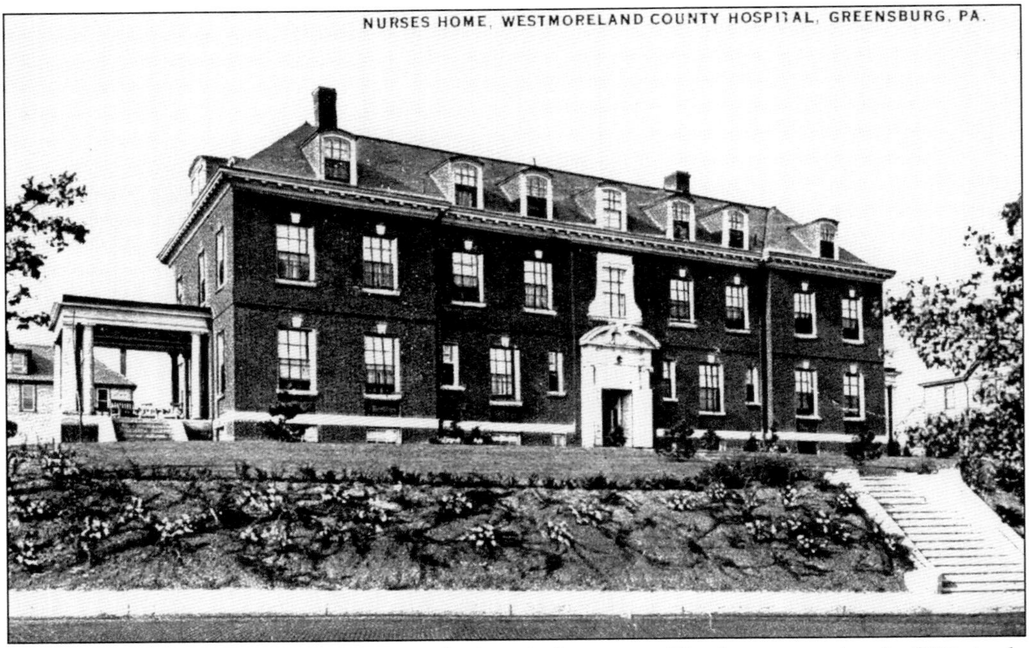

In 1920, a nurses' home was added to the hospital campus. The home consisted of 38 single rooms, a large living room, classrooms, and a laboratory. A boiler room and laundry room were also added, equipped with equipment considered state of the art for the time. The nurses' home still remains today, located on West Pittsburgh Street behind the hospital.

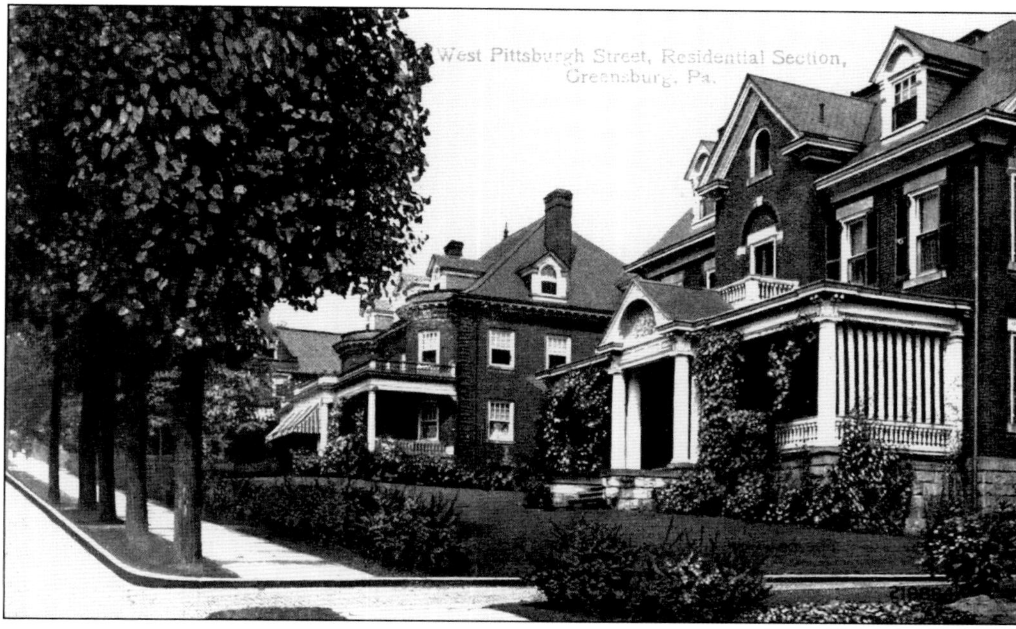

West Pittsburgh Street was also home to some of the city's elite, which is evident by the tree-lined sidewalks and the well-cared-for homes. To live on West Pittsburgh Street was a way of showing wealth and status in Greensburg. As the economy of Greensburg began to decline, however, many of the large West Pittsburgh Street homes could no longer survive as private residences. Almost all of them have now been converted into doctors' offices, funeral homes, or other places of business.

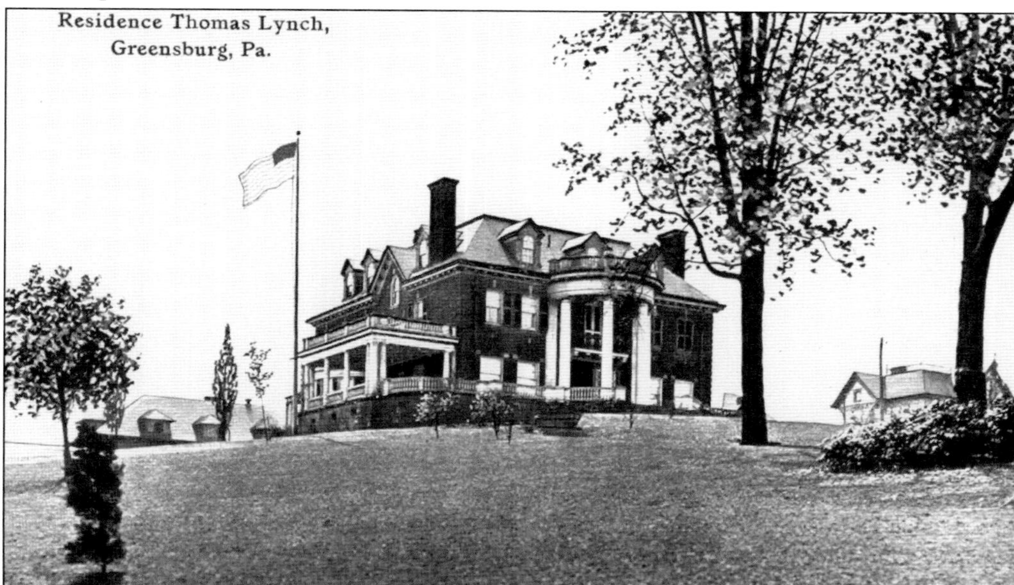

After the closing of the Greensburg Seminary, industrialist Thomas Lynch, president of H. C. Frick Coal and Coke Company and other mining interests, bought the West Pittsburgh Street property in 1905 to build an impressive stone mansion. The mansion later was bought by the Old Republic Insurance Company, which still has its offices there today.

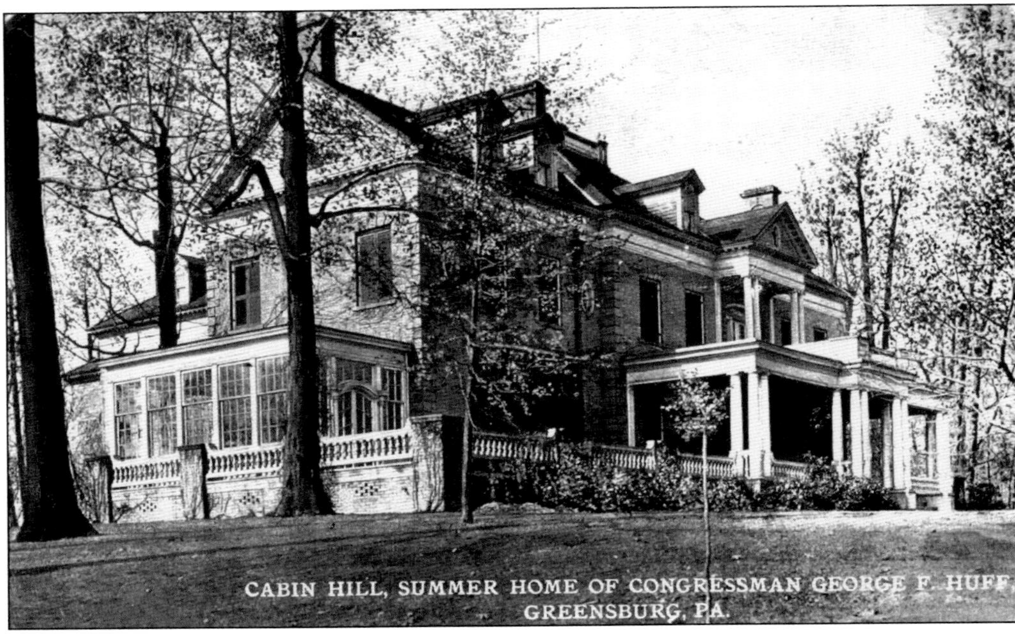

This postcard shows the home of Congressman George F. Huff's mansion, which sat atop 200 acres on Cabin Hill. The mansion stood from 1885 to 1953 when the home, which was owned by the R. H. Jamison family, was torn down to make way for Allegheny Power's headquarters. The house had several trails through the surrounding woods, which still remain today.

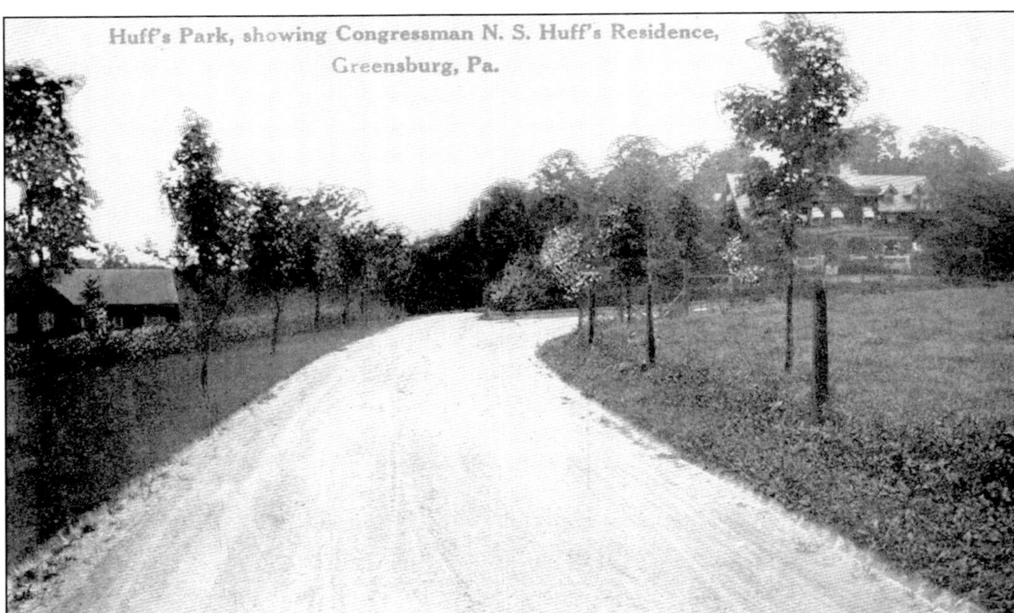

The Lloyd Huff home is located among the fine homes through the years at Rose Fountain Park at the upper end of North Maple Avenue. The house was rebuilt and enlarged in 1898.

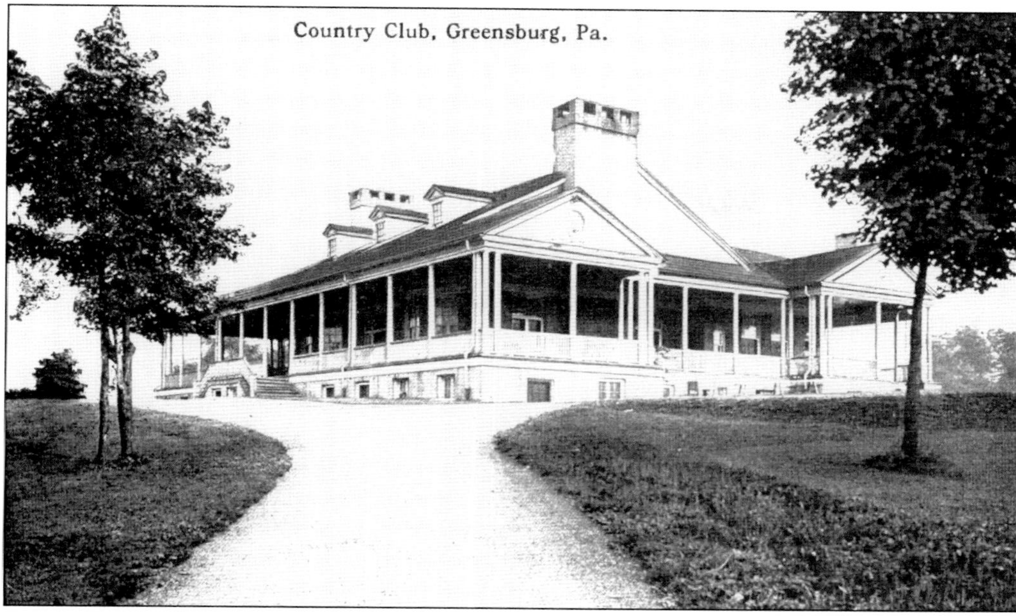

The Greensburg Country Club was founded in 1904 along the trolley line to Oakford Park. Plagued by fire, the original clubhouse was destroyed in 1906. During the 1918 influenza epidemic, the clubhouse served as an auxiliary area hospital with women from members' families helping in the emergency. In 1998, the club suffered another devastating fire, but the building was able to be salvaged and is still in use.

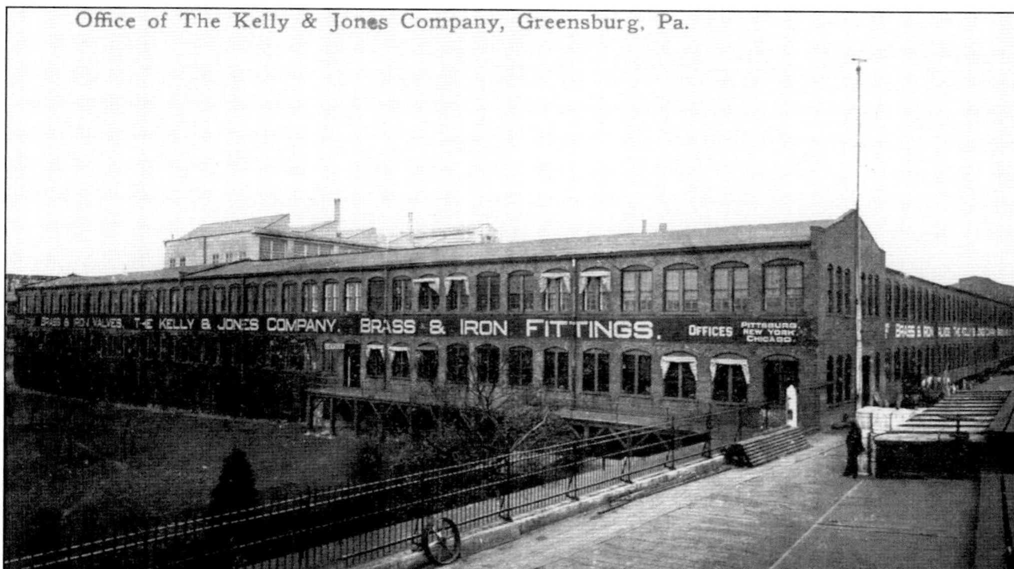

Kelly and Jones began in 1887 when John T. Kelly and George M. Jones brought their valve-fitting operations to Greensburg from Jersey City, New Jersey. The first melting for valve production took place on January 1, 1889. On September 29, 1925, the Kelly and Jones complex was sold to the Walworth Company. Building deterioration and rising costs of modernization eventually forced the plant to close in May 1980. The only reminder of the Kelly and Jones factory is the Wellington Square building, which now houses offices.

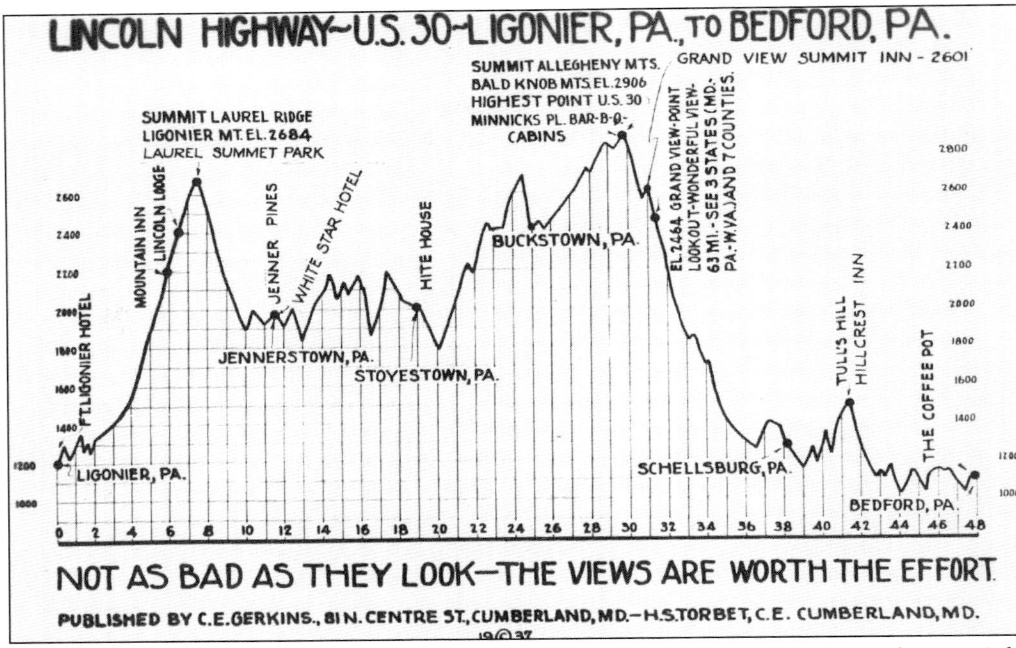

This postcard highlights some of the attractions that visitors on the Lincoln Highway might see. Some of the featured sights are the Fort Ligonier Hotel in Ligonier, the White Star Hotel in Jennerstown, the Grand View Point Lookout, and the Coffee Pot in Bedford.

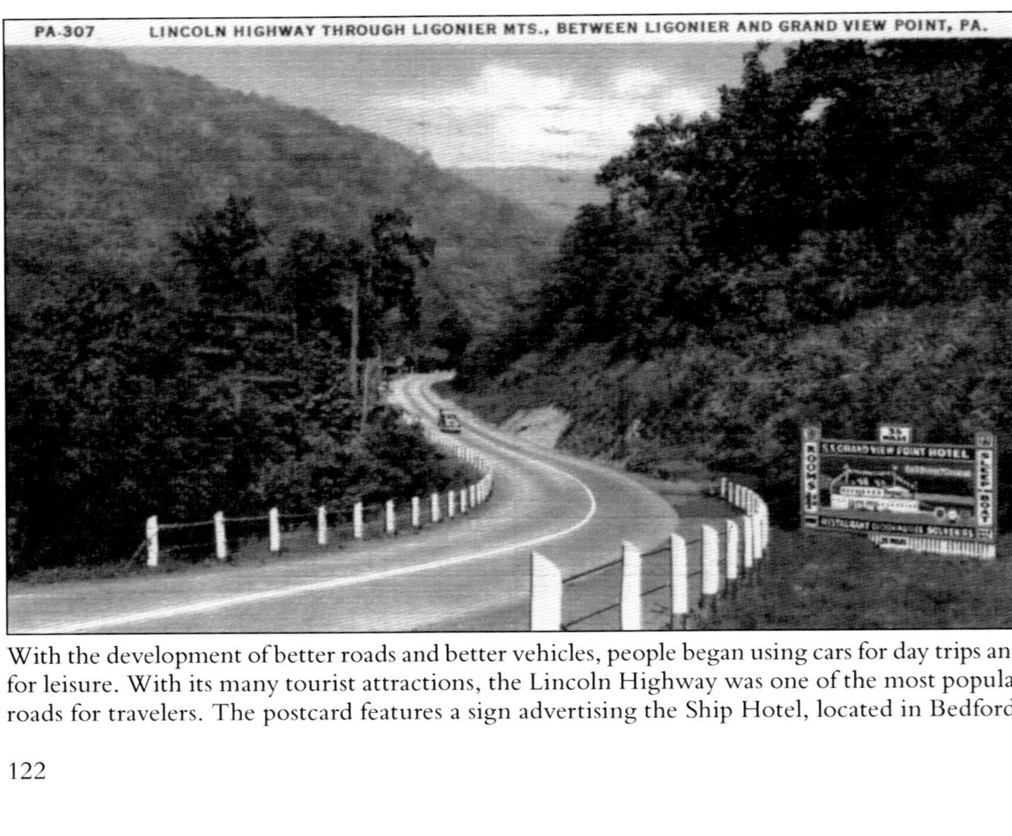

With the development of better roads and better vehicles, people began using cars for day trips and for leisure. With its many tourist attractions, the Lincoln Highway was one of the most popular roads for travelers. The postcard features a sign advertising the Ship Hotel, located in Bedford.

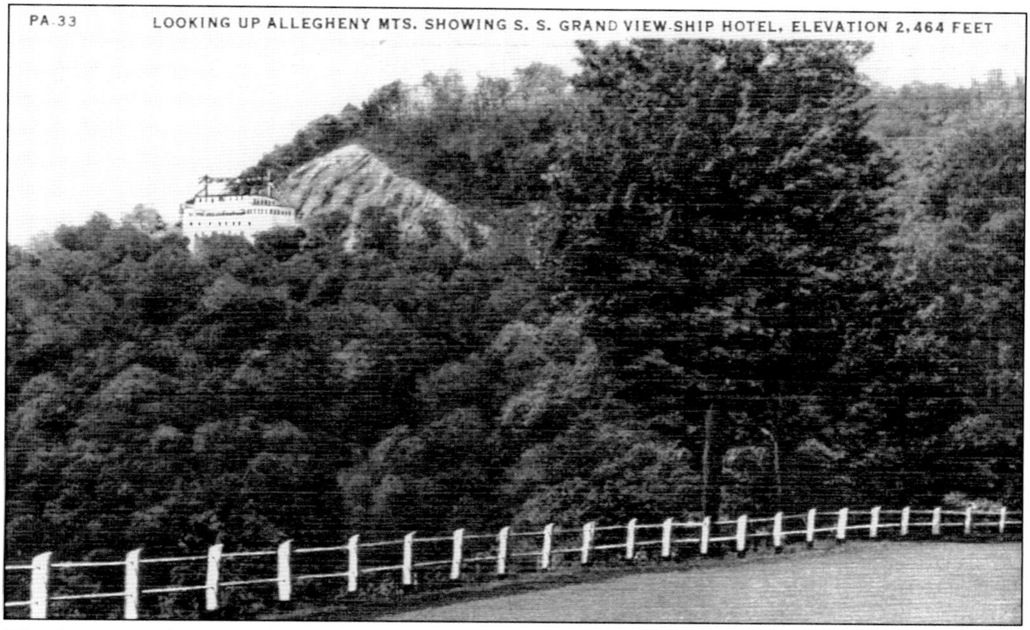

The S.S. Grand View Point Hotel, located outside of Bedford, was a favorite tourist attraction among Greensburg's citizens. Built in 1932, the hotel offered visitors a view of "3 States and 7 Counties." Often called the "Steamship of the Alleghenies," the ship offered lodging for 49 guests in its first-class, second-class, and steerage rooms.

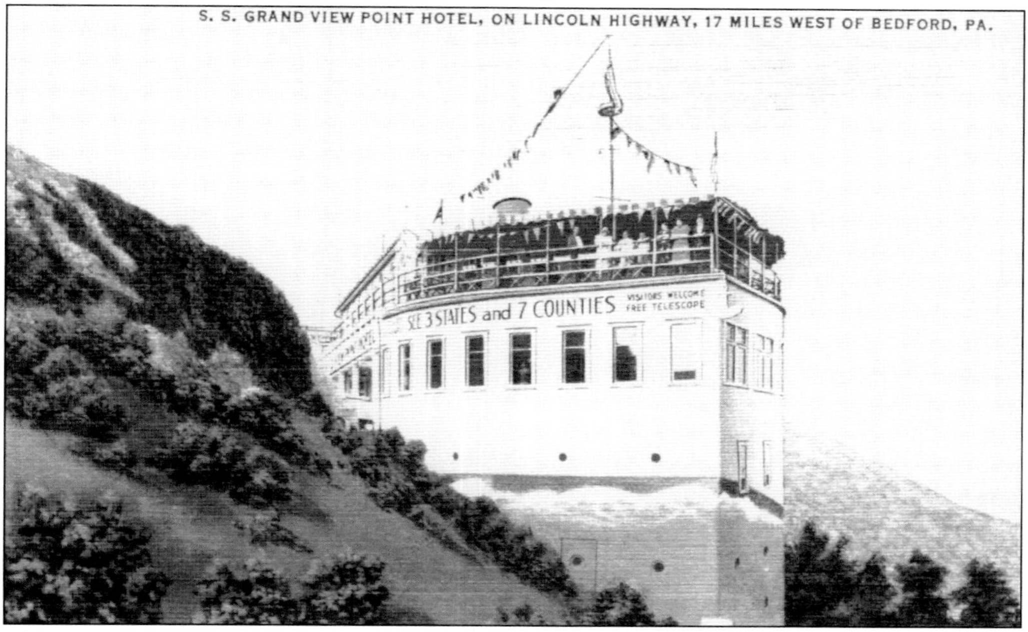

Although the completion of the Pennsylvania Turnpike hurt business, it still remained a popular tourist attraction. In 1973, following the death of the owner, Herbert Paulson, the ship was sold. The new owners covered the outside with wood and renamed the establishment Noah's Ark. The business failed, and eventually the building was abandoned. After years of deterioration, the ship burned to the ground in 2001.

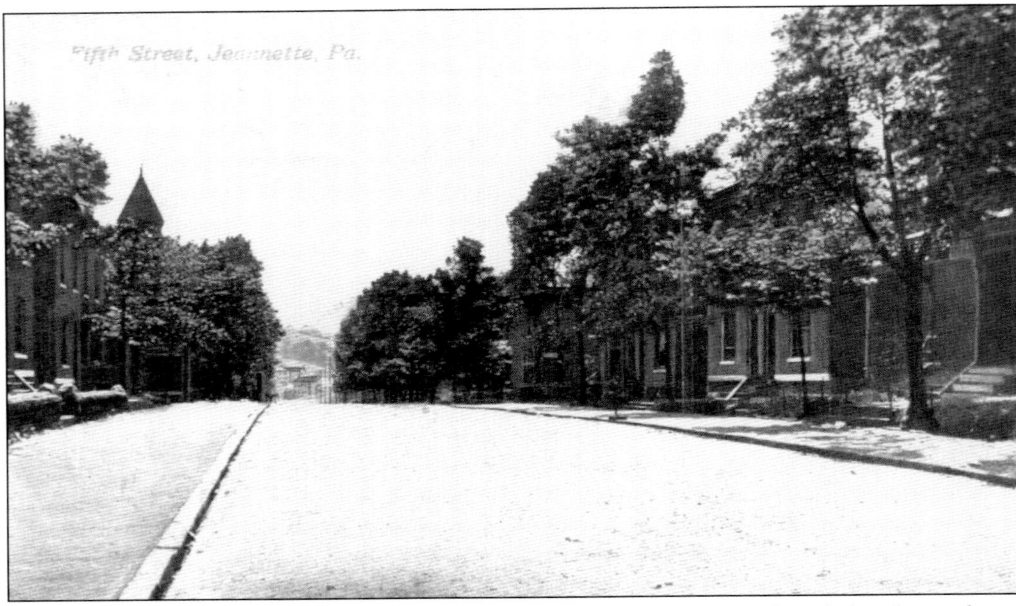

The row houses on Fifth Street were built in 1888 when Jeannette was founded and were home to workers of the glass factories and their families. This postcard shows how they were well taken care of by their owners.

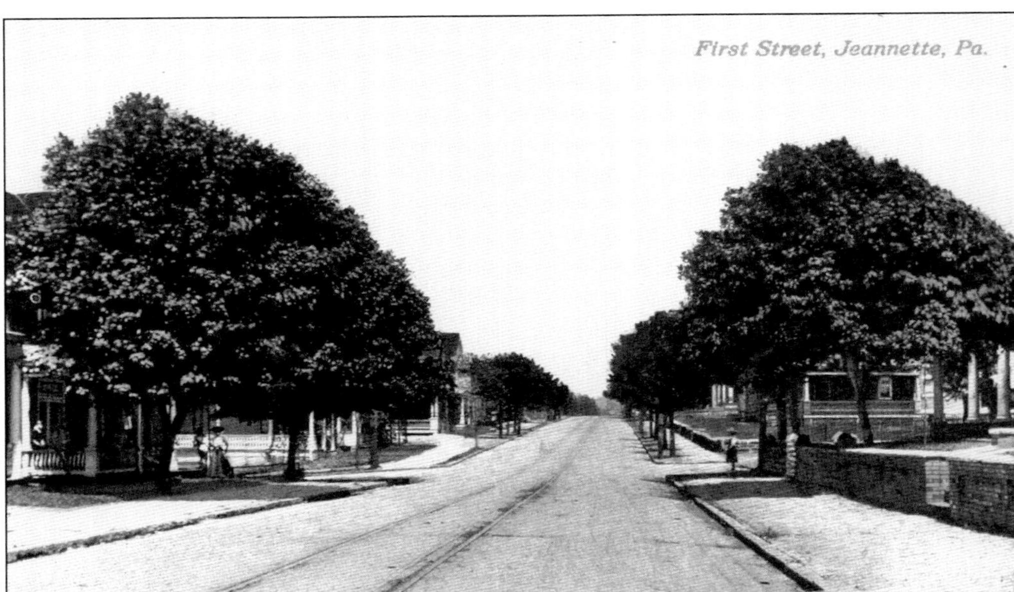

North First Street in Jeannette was home to some of the city's elite, which is evident by the tree-lined sidewalks and the well-cared-for homes. To live on either North First or North Second Street was a way of showing status in the community.

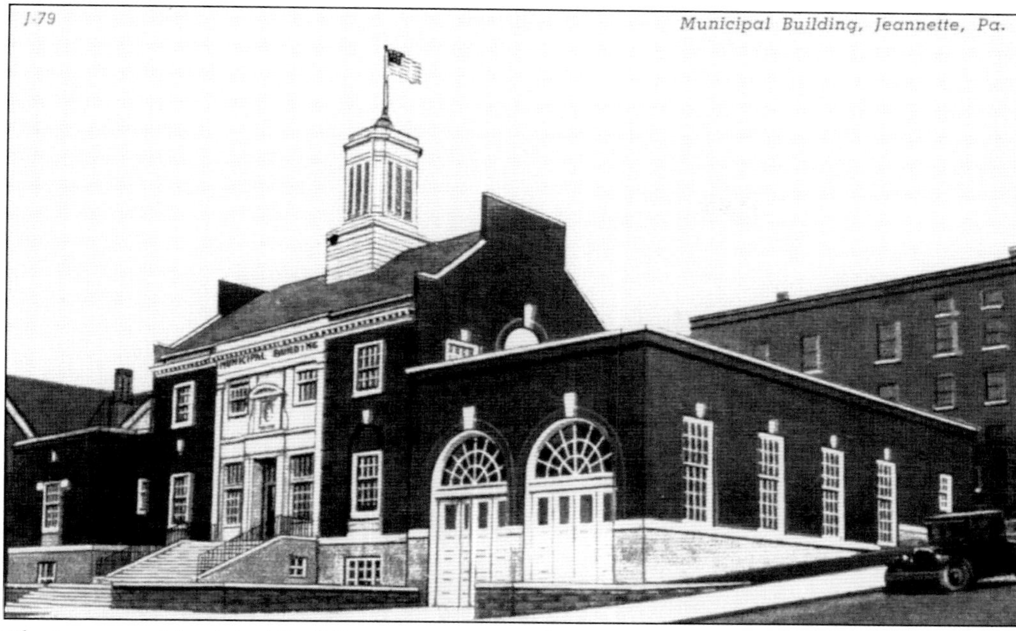

The Jeannette Municipal Building was constructed in 1927 on the site where the Hotel Marian once stood. Located at the top of Clay Avenue, it covered almost an entire block and was the most prominent location in Jeannette. The building then became home to the Jeannette Public Library, the police station and jail, and the Jeannette Fire Department, as well as the offices of the city council and the mayor.

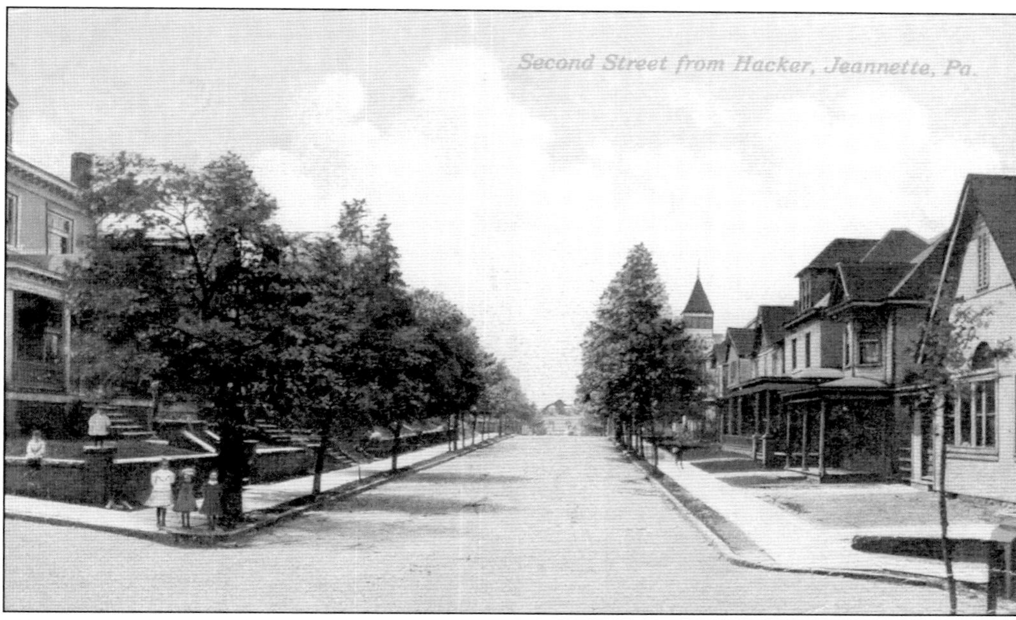

This postcard of North Second Street from Hacker Street shows large, well-kept homes and churches. The first building on the right is the Baptist church, which burned down in the 1920s and was replaced by a new brick building. The tower in the distance on the right belongs to the Lutheran church.

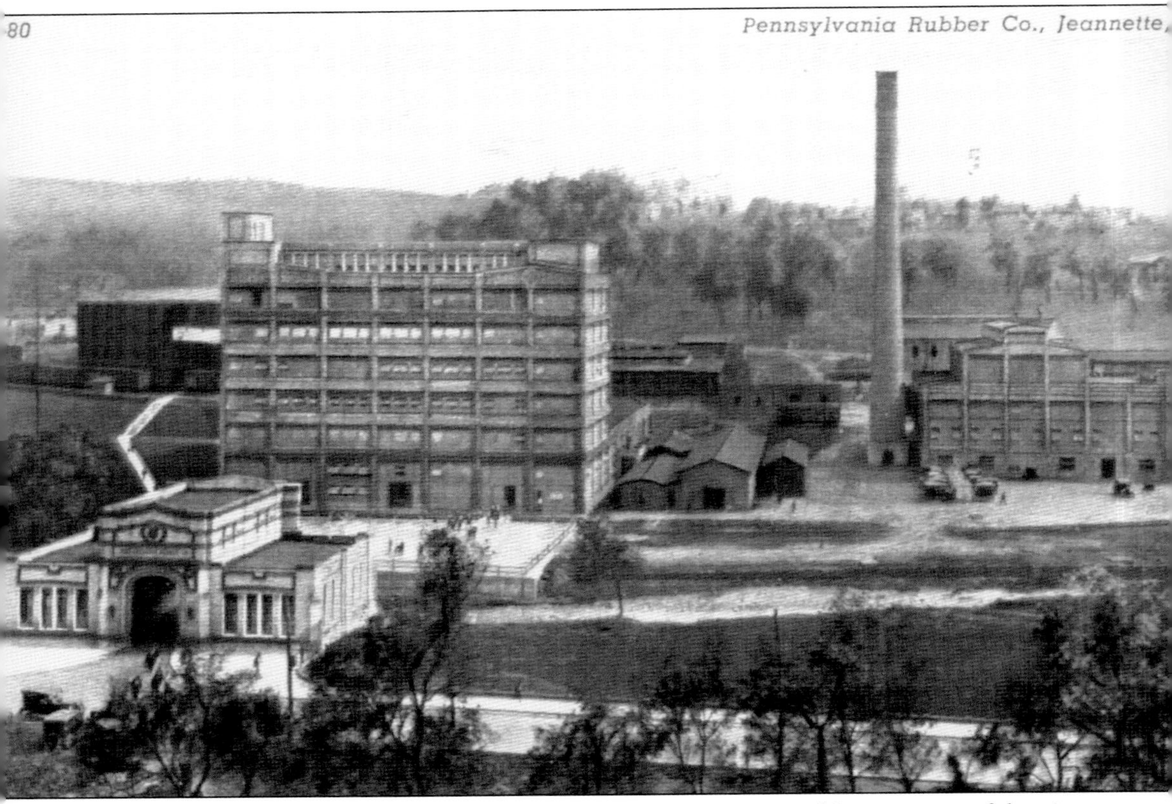

In 1910, the Pennsylvania Rubber Company came to Jeannette and became one of the pioneer companies manufacturing tennis balls. That year, the factory produced more than 13,000. The balls were constructed of four pieces of rubber fitted together and inflated using an ammonia pill and water to form the right amount of gas pressure.

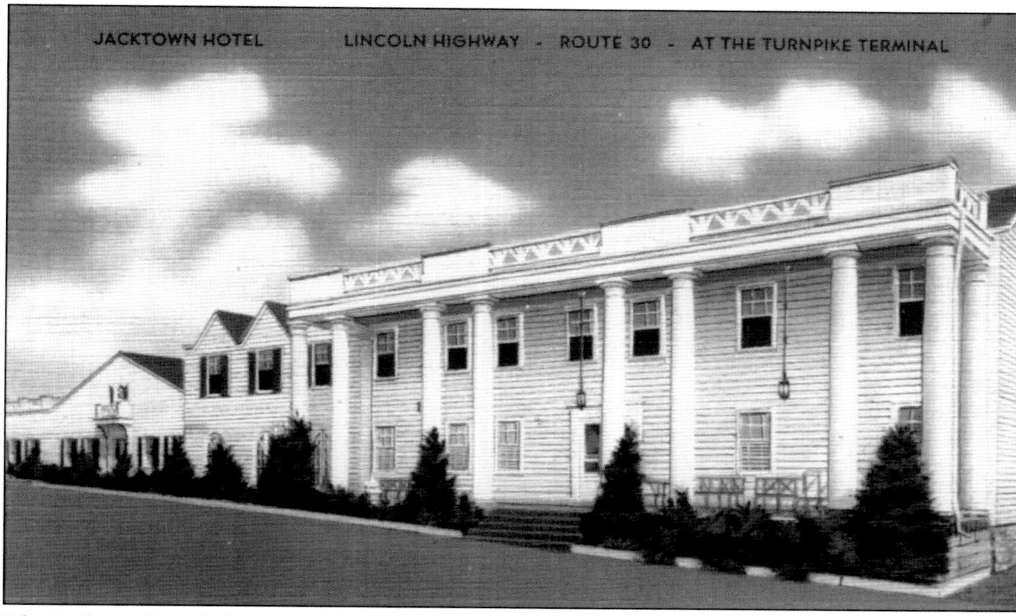

The Jackson Hotel, located along the Lincoln Highway in Irwin, was originally a stagecoach stop. In its over 100 years of existence, it served Irwin and the surrounding towns as a hotel and restaurant before being destroyed by fire in 1966.

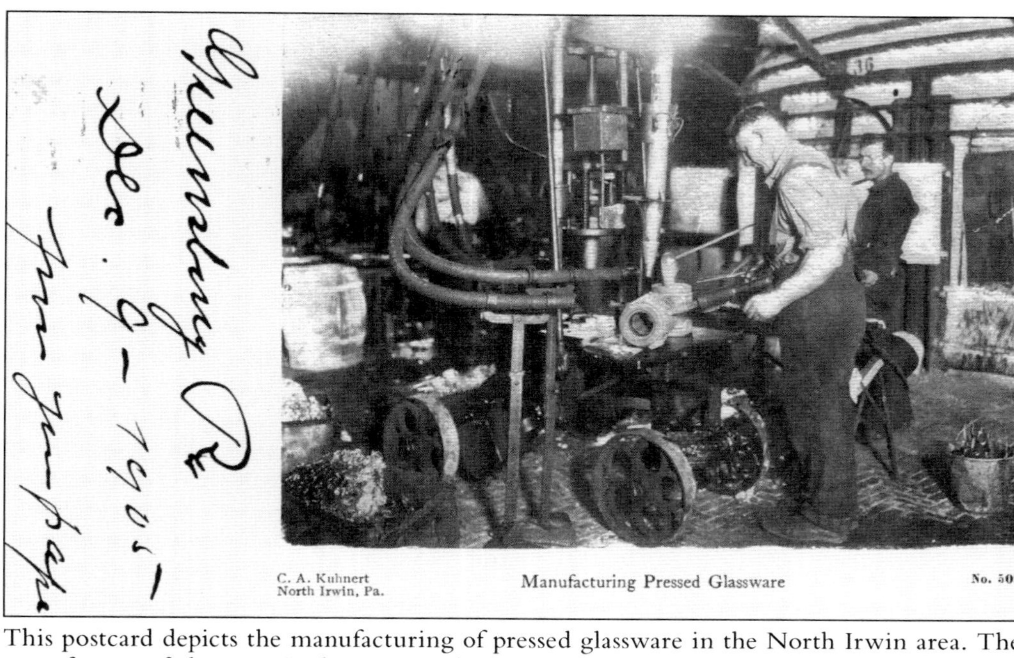

This postcard depicts the manufacturing of pressed glassware in the North Irwin area. The manufacture of glassware in the Irwin and Jeannette areas was very popular around the 1900s. Skilled journeymen from Pittsburgh and immigrants from Europe came to the Brush Creek Valley to work in the area's factories and manufacture the glassware.